THE
BABY CRAFT
BOOK

BABY CRAFT

CONTRIBUTING EDITOR **PENELOPE CREAM**

SMITHMARK

This edition published in 1994 by
SMITHMARK Publishers Inc.
16 East 32nd Street
New York
NY 10016

SMITHMARK books are available for bulk purchase for sales promotion and premium use. For details write or call the manager of special sales, SMITHMARK Publishers Inc., 16 East 32nd Street, New York, NY 10016: (212) 532-6600.

Produced by Anness Publishing Ltd
1 Boundary Row
London SE1 8HP

ISBN 0-8317-0650-3

Printed in Hong Kong

10 9 8 7 6 5 4 3 2 1

Threadbear, the little teddy bear featured in some of the pictures, appears by kind permission of his owner Mick Inkpen and his publishers Hodder & Stoughton, Euston Road, London NW1 3BH

HOW TO USE THE MEASUREMENTS

All craftspeople have their own way of working and feel most comfortable calculating in their preferred measurements. So, where applicable, the option of metric, imperial and cup measures are given. The golden rule is to choose only one set of measurements and to stick with it consistently throughout each project to ensure accurate results.

PUBLISHER'S NOTE

Crafts and hobbies are great fun to learn and can fill many hours of rewarding leisure time, but some special points should be remembered for safety, particularly when making gifts for babies and young children.

■ Always be aware of the materials you are using; use natural fabrics such as cotton and felt wherever possible, and make sure all sewing is strong and firm: double seam or stitch if in any doubt.

■ Always choose non-toxic materials, especially paints, glue and varnishes. Wood must always be smooth and free from splinters and sharp corners. Only use non-toxic flame retardant polyester stuffing or batting to fill soft toys.

■ Any gift with small pieces should not be given to young babies: they are experts at fitting even the most unlikely things into their mouths. Always pull with all your strength on buttons, safety eyes and other parts attached to a project: if an adult cannot remove them, a baby will not be able to either.

■ Secure small items such as bells or squeakers within soft toys inside a little fabric bag for extra safety.

■ Finally, make sure you do not leave your craft materials – such as craft knives, small saws, knitting needles, crochet hooks or adhesives – within the reach of young children.

SOME USEFUL TERMS

UK	US
Calico	Cotton fabric
Cast off	Bind off
Chipboard	Particle board
Cotton wool	Absorbent cotton
Double knitting yarn	Sport yarn
Drawing pins	Thumb tacks
Fretsaw	Scroll saw
Icing sugar	Confectioner's sugar
Lawn	Fine cotton
Matt emulsion paint	Flat latex paint
Muslin	Cheesecloth
Palette knife	Spatula
Panel pins	Finishing nails
Plain flour	All-purpose flour
Polystyrene	Styrofoam
PVC plastic	Vinyl plastic
Towelling	Terrycloth
Zip	Zipper

Contents

NEW
ARRIVALS

An array of clothes, bright toys and eye-catching nursery items – everything you need to welcome home the new parents and to entertain tiny babies

Appliquéd Sleepsuit

LIVEN UP A PLAIN SLEEPSUIT BY ADDING A FRIENDLY ANIMAL MOTIF

YOU WILL NEED ■ Fabric with pretty motif ■ Scissors ■ Fusible iron-on bonding paper
■ Iron ■ Plain sleepsuit ■ Needle and embroidery thread

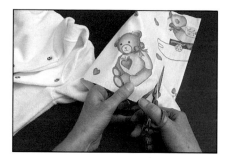

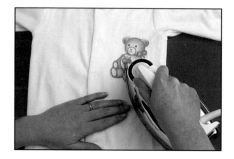

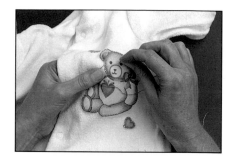

1 Decide on the motif to be used and cut out of the fabric, leaving a wide margin all around the motif.

2 Cut a piece of fusible bonding paper to the same size and iron on according to the manufacturer's instructions. Cut out the paper-backed motif and iron into place on the sleepsuit.

3 Using two strands of embroidery thread, neatly blanket stitch around the motif. Press well with the iron.

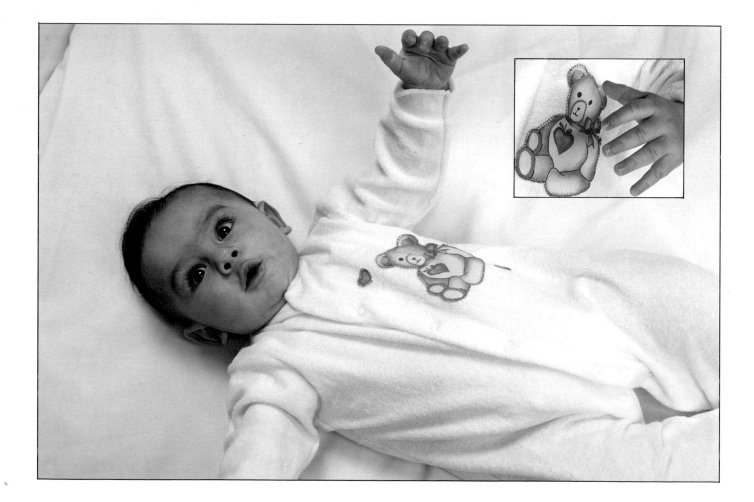

Quilted Card

THE TECHNIQUE USED FOR THIS CARD IS CALLED SHADOW QUILTING

YOU WILL NEED ■ *Tracing paper* ■ *Pencil* ■ *Scissors* ■ *Pins* ■ *13 × 13 cm*
(5¼ × 5¼ in) square of blue felt ■ *Needle and embroidery thread* ■ *Cotton voile* ■ *Blue stranded*
cotton ■ *Blank pre-cut window card* ■ *Blue wax crayon* ■ *Rubber-based glue*

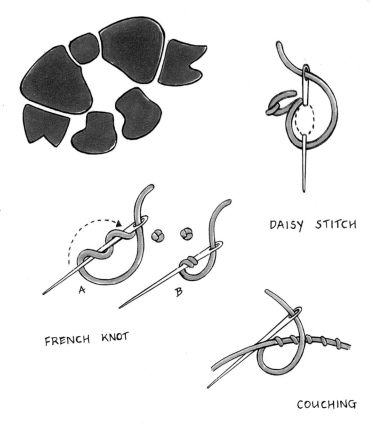

DAISY STITCH

FRENCH KNOT

COUCHING

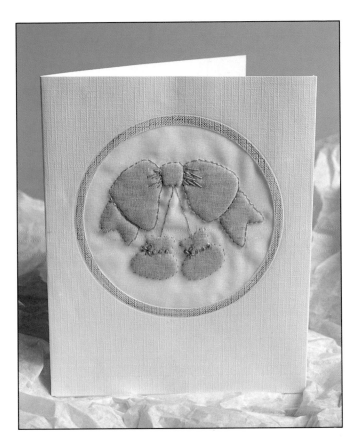

1 Trace around the template and cut out each section separately before pinning it onto the square of felt. Cut out all the pieces and pin then tack (baste) in position between 2 layers of voile.

2 Using 2 strands of embroidery thread in the needle, back stitch round the edge of the bow pieces and prick stitch round the bootees.

3 Decorate the bootees with lazy daisy stitch bows and French knots. Couch 2 lines from the bootees to the bows. Colour the edge of the card window with blue wax crayon before gluing the voile embroidery into place inside the front of the card.

Tie-dye Stretchsuit

A STRETCHSUIT IS ONE OF THE MOST USEFUL AND POPULAR BABYWEAR ITEMS

YOU WILL NEED ■ *Scissors* ■ *Ball of string* ■ *Tape measure* ■ *Plain white stretchsuit* ■ *Dye*
■ *Large saucepan or bucket* ■ *Rubber gloves* ■ *Iron*

1 Cut several pieces of string about 18 cm (7 in) long. Pinch an area of the stretchsuit and tie string tightly around it, making a 'peak'. Repeat at intervals all over the front and back of the stretchsuit until all the spaces are used up.

2 Prepare the dye in a large saucepan or bucket, according to the manufacturer's instructions. Wearing rubber gloves if you wish, immerse the stretchsuit in the dye, making sure that it is completely covered, then leave for the recommended time.

3 Still wearing gloves (if used), rinse out the stretchsuit under cold running water until the colour stops running. Cut the strings, open out the stretchsuit and leave it to dry naturally. Wash the suit and press it with a cool iron before use.

Stripy Toy Sack

RECYCLE AN OLD PILLOW CASE TO MAKE THIS BRIGHT TOY SACK

YOU WILL NEED ■ *White cotton pillow case* ■ *Yellow, red and blue dyes* ■ *Dye fix* ■ *Plastic bowl or bucket* ■ *Iron* ■ *Drawing pins (thumb tacks)* ■ *Newspaper* ■ *Large paintbrush* ■ *Short length of rope*

1 Wash the pillow case and allow to dry naturally. Mix the yellow dye following the manufacturer's instructions and add the dye fix. Pour the dye into a plastic bowl or bucket. Place the pillow case into the dye and leave for the recommended time. Rinse under running water and allow to dry naturally. Iron the pillow case, and pin it onto a clean even surface that has first been covered with a layer of newspaper to absorb any excess dye.

2 Using a large brush, paint bold stripes of red and blue dye onto the pillow case, leaving a gap of yellow between each stripe. Leave for at least 30 minutes to allow the dye to soak into the fabric. Remove, and hang up to dry naturally.

3 Use the leftover dyes to paint the rope in stripes. Pin the rope to the edges of the pillow case and stitch firmly. Do not leave excessive lengths of loose rope near a small baby.

Bathtime Apron

A PRACTICAL APRON TO KEEP PARENTS DRY AT BATHTIME

YOU WILL NEED ■ *Scissors* ■ *Bright cotton fabric* ■ *Tape measure* ■ *Pins* ■ *Needle and thread*
■ *Safety pin* ■ *Pencil* ■ *White paper* ■ *Towelling (terrycloth) fabric* ■ *Iron*

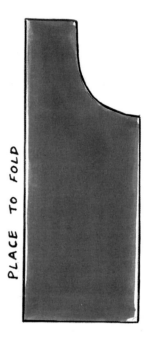

PLACE TO FOLD

1 Cut 3 strips of cotton fabric about 6 cm (2¼ in) wide and of sufficient length to make into the 2 apron ties and a neck loop. Make up the strips by folding each one in half along its length, with the right sides together. Pin and sew up each strip. Carefully turn each tube through to the right side using a safety pin.

2 Scale up the template onto white paper and cut out. Fold the fabric in half and pin the template along the fold. Cut out one shape from cotton fabric and one from towelling (terrycloth). Pin the neck-loop ends to the fabric 15 cm (6 in) in from the top edge and at right angles to it. Tack (baste) into place.

3 Position the apron ties at the top of the apron sides. Place the patterned cotton and the towelling (terrycloth) right sides together, and pin and tack (baste) all round the edge, enclosing the ends of the ties and rounding off the bottom corners as you stitch.
   Leave an open length on one straight edge. Trim the excess fabric on the rounded corners and turn the apron to the right side through the opening. Oversew the opening to close. Press and topstitch all round about 1 cm (⅜ in) from the edge.

Hooded Towel

THIS COSY HOODED TOWEL USES BRIGHT COTTON AND ABSORBENT FABRICS

YOU WILL NEED ■ *Scissors* ■ *Towelling (terrycloth) fabric* ■ *Bright cotton fabric*
■ *Tape measure* ■ *Pins* ■ *Needle and thread* ■ *Iron*

1 Cut 2 triangles, one each of towelling (terrycloth) and cotton. The edges on the right angle should be 27 cm (10½ in) long. Pin, tack (baste) and stitch right sides together on the diagonal to make a 27 cm (10½ in) square. Press the seam to one side and trim the excess fabric on the seam edges at the corners.

2 Press the square back into a triangle along the seam, with right sides out. Cut a piece of towelling (terrycloth) 80 cm (32 in) square. Pin and tack (baste) the hood to the right side of the towelling at one corner matching the raw edges, with the cotton side of the hood uppermost.

3 Cut a strip of cotton fabric about 4 cm (1½ in) wide to go around the whole towel. Turn back the raw edge of one binding end diagonally along the grain and pin and tack (baste) the right sides of the binding to the towel, stitching the hood to the towel on the corner. Round off all 4 corners.

Overlap the binding ends and turn back the second raw edge. Stitch the binding to the towel. Trim the excess fabric at all corners where the edges are rounded. Press, turn the binding to the wrong side and hem to enclose the raw edges. Press.

Folded Hold-all

THIS HOLD-ALL IS PERFECT FOR CARRYING BABY-CHANGING ITEMS

YOU WILL NEED ■ *Tape measure* ■ *Pre-washed strong cotton ticking* ■ *Scissors*
■ *Assorted plain and patterned cotton fabrics* ■ *Pair of compasses* ■ *Pencil* ■ *Iron-on interfacing*
■ *Iron* ■ *Pins* ■ *Needle and thread* ■ *Gingham fabric* ■ *Narrow ribbon*

1 Cut a piece of ticking 66 × 37 cm (26½ × 14½ in) with stripes running lengthwise. From the assorted fabrics, use a pair of compasses to cut a circle about 18 cm (7 in) across. Also cut 8 triangles about 6 cm (2¼ in) high.

Use iron-on interfacing on all appliquéd pieces. Position the circle and triangles onto the ticking to make a sun shape. Pin and tack (baste) each shape. The triangles should not cross the seam allowance at the top and sides. Appliqué the shapes into place and press.

2 Cut a 40 × 36 cm (16 × 14 in) shape from the ticking for the pocket, with the stripes running down the longer side. Turn under 1 short raw edge and stitch a hem. Turn the hemmed edge to the front of the pocket, folding it about 8 cm (3¼ in) from the top, and stitch the 2 layers together at the sides to form the facing. Carefully snip into the pocket seam allowance where the facing hem meets the pocket side just as far as the stitching line. Then tack (baste) a hem on the pocket bottom with the facing/pocket stitch line and the fold of the pocket hem on the sides forming a continuous line. Turn the facing to the inside and press. Fold a box pleat in the pocket so that it will fit snugly within the width of the bag and tack (baste) it in place. Press well. Choosing another plain fabric, make up the second pocket in the same way.

3 Cut a piece of gingham 66 × 37 cm (26½ × 14½ in) for the bag lining. With right sides together, pin, tack (baste) and stitch the lining to the bag leaving an opening at the side for turning. Turn right side out, oversew the opening to close and press.

4 From the ticking, make 2 straps, each about 64 cm (25½ in) long and 5 cm (2 in) wide. Turn under the raw edges and pin both straps to the inside of the bag at both ends. Test and adjust their lengths and positions before stitching, noting that the stitched strap ends should eventually be concealed under the top edge of the pockets.

Pin, tack (baste) and stitch the pockets through all layers of the bag, stitching the pleat down at the same time. Cut and sew lengths of narrow ribbon to the pleat tops as ties. Sew more ribbon to the top sides of the bag so it can be tied closed when carried to keep the contents safe.

Ric-rac Mitts

THESE SNUG MITTS WILL PREVENT A YOUNG BABY FROM SCRATCHING ITSELF

YOU WILL NEED ■ *Marker pen* ■ *White paper* ■ *Piece of cotton jersey fabric* ■ *Pinking shears*
■ *Needle and thread* ■ *Elastic* ■ *Scissors* ■ *32 cm (12 in) ric-rac braid*

1 Using the template as a guide, cut out the mitt shape from a piece of white paper. Draw around this 4 times on the cotton jersey fabric and cut out the pieces with pinking shears.

2 Fold over the straight edge of each mitt piece and sew it down. Sew the pieces together in pairs, right sides together, leaving the straight edges open.

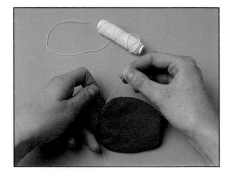

3 Turn the mitts right side out and sew a line of elastic about 2.5 cm (1 in) from each of the mitt openings.

4 Cut the ric-rac in 2 and sew a length around the opening edge of each mitt.

Geometric Mobile

THIS BRIGHT MOBILE WILL FASCINATE ANY CHILD

YOU WILL NEED ■ *Pair of compasses* ■ *Ruler* ■ *Pencil* ■ *White card* ■ *Scissors* ■ *Paintbrushes*
■ *Non-toxic acrylic paints* ■ *Gummed paper in several bright colours* ■ *Needle* ■ *Gold thread*

1 Using a pair of compasses, ruler and pencil, draw onto card all the shapes needed for this mobile. You will need a long narrow strip 8 × 40 cm (3¼ × 16 in) to form the coronet and 2 circles, a square, a diamond and a triangle, each 7 cm (2¾ in) across. Also draw 2 smaller circles. Cut out all of the shapes with a sharp pair of scissors.

2 Paint all the shapes different colours using the acrylic paints. Paint the long narrow strip, 1 large circle and the 2 small circles black. Cut out a range of smaller shapes from the coloured gummed paper.

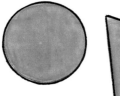 

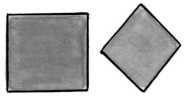

3 When the paint is dry, stick the gummed coloured shapes onto both sides of the black painted shapes. Glue the long narrow strip together at the ends to form a coronet. With a needle, pierce 4 pairs of holes into the top and bottom edges of the coronet. Also pierce a hole at the top of each shape.

Thread 10 cm (4 in) of gold thread through each of the 4 coloured shapes and secure them with a knot. Suspend each shape from the bottom of the coronet and secure each with a knot tied on the inside of the coronet.

4 Pierce the 3 black circles top and bottom and connect up with gold thread, spacing them out and securing them at each hole with a knot. Cut four 40 cm (16 in) lengths of gold thread and thread them through the holes at the top of the coronet. Then gather these 4 threads together with the central thread at the top and tie a knot. The mobile will now hang in a well-balanced display.

Cutie Bootees

MAKE THESE SOFT BOOTEES FOR AN 8 TO 14-MONTH-OLD BABY

YOU WILL NEED ■ Tracing paper ■ Ruler ■ Pencil ■ White paper ■ 10 x 115 cm (7 × 45 in) main fabric ■ Pins ■ Scissors ■ 10 × 32 cm (4 × 12½ in) velvet fabric ■ 10 × 32 cm (4 × 12½ in) foam, 1 cm (⅜ in) thick ■ Felt-tip pen ■ Needle and thread ■ 2.72 m (3 yd) of 1.5 cm (⅝ in) wide reversible ribbon ■ Tape measure ■ Coloured pencil ■ Iron

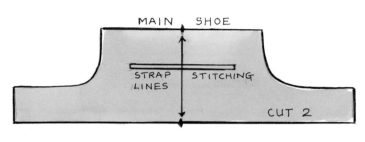

MAIN SHOE

STRAP LINES   STITCHING

CUT 2

1 Scale up the templates using tracing paper. Seam allowances are included. Transfer to white paper, marking the grain lines and notch positions. Fold the main fabric in half by placing selvages together. Lay all pattern pieces on the fabric, making sure grain lines run parallel to the selvages. Pin and cut out pieces.

Mark the notch positions with a snip in the fabric. Fold the velvet fabric in half and pin sole pattern on. Cut out and notch. Place sole pattern on foam. Using a felt-tip pen, draw around pattern twice. Cut out, just inside the pen line.

2 Lay the main fabric sole wrong side up. Place foam sole onto it and top with the velvet fabric sole, right side up. Pin and tack (baste) all 3 pieces together. Sew all the way around, 5 mm (³⁄₁₆ in) from the edge.

FRONT PANEL

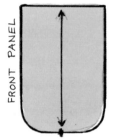

CENTRE FRONT

SOLE

CENTRE BACK

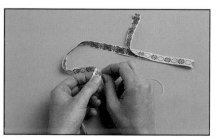

3 For each bootee, cut a piece of ribbon to 112 cm (42 in). Turn each end back 26 cm (10¼ in) (wrong sides together). Tack (baste) and sew along both edges.

4 On main shoe piece mark a line with coloured pencil to indicate where bootee strap is to be stitched (see template). Fold strap in half to find the centre. Match this point with the centre back line of main shoe piece. Pin strap along pencil line, with both pieces having right sides up. Sew strap in place along the top and bottom edges. Remove the pins.

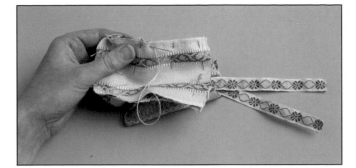

5 On the main shoe piece, neaten the centre front edges with zigzag stitch. Fold the main shoe piece in half, right sides together. Sew the centre front seams together, 1 cm (⅜ in) from the edge. Press the seam open.

Pin the front panel to the main shoe piece. Match the centre front positions. Tack (baste) and sew 6 mm (¼ in) from edge. Neaten the edge with zigzag stitch.

6 Turn the upper shoe's unfinished edge in 1 cm (⅜ in) to wrong side. Tack (baste) into position. Neaten with a length of ribbon measuring 24 cm (9½ in). Tack (baste) ribbon into place. Sew along top and bottom edges of the ribbon. Remove all the tacking (basting) threads.

7 Turn the upper shoe inside out. Place the upper shoe onto the sole, right sides together. Match back and front positions; the wide part of the sole is the front. Pin and tack (baste) pieces together. Sew all the way around the shoe, 6 mm (¼ in) away from edge. Neaten edge with zigzag stitch. Turn shoe right side out.

Practical Apron

AN ESSENTIAL PROTECTIVE LAYER FOR THE BUSY PARENT

YOU WILL NEED ■ *Tracing paper* ■ *Pencil* ■ *Ruler* ■ *White paper* ■ *Scissors*
■ *60 × 75 cm (24 × 30 in) fabric for apron* ■ *Pins* ■ *Needle and thread* ■ *180 cm (72 in) ribbon or
fabric binding* ■ *2 pieces of 48 × 48 cm (19 × 19 in) fabric for pocket* ■ *Felt*

1 Scale up the apron and pocket shapes from the templates and transfer them onto white paper. Cut out the apron in fabric. Fold over and pin a neat edge all the way round the apron and sew down. Cut the ribbon or fabric binding into 3 pieces. Sew to the top and sides to make a neck loop and 2 waist ties.

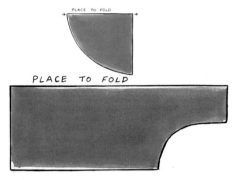

PLACE TO FOLD

PLACE TO FOLD

2 Cut out the fabric pieces for the pocket. Join the 2 pieces together by sewing around the curved edge, and turn right side out. Sew up the gap at the top.

3 Sew the pocket onto the apron. Cut out flower shapes, stalks and leaves from the felt and sew them onto the apron.

Lined Basket

THE LINER IN THE BASKET CAN EASILY BE REMOVED FOR WASHING

YOU WILL NEED ■ *Scissors* ■ *4 m (4½ yd) bias binding* ■ *Needle and thread* ■ *2 pieces of fabric large enough to cover the inside of the basket* ■ *Iron* ■ *Wicker basket with handles*

1 Cut 12 ties from the length of bias binding. Fold each length over and then sew down along the edge.

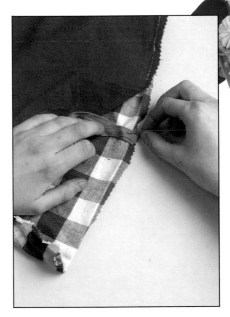

2 Trap one end of each tie between the 2 fabric pieces (right sides together) in convenient places for them to fasten to the basket. Sew round all the edges of the 2 pieces, leaving a gap at one edge.

3 Turn the fabric right side out, using a pin to 'pull out' the corners if necessary to make good right angles. Press the fabric firmly with an iron on a medium to hot setting, depending on the type of fabric you have used. Oversew the gap to complete the stitching. Place the fabric in the basket and fasten the ties to edges.

Play Cube

A BRIGHT, FUN, SQUEEZY PLAY CUBE

*YOU WILL NEED ■ Pinking shears ■ 6 assorted fabric squares 18 × 18 cm
(7 × 7 in) ■ Needle and thread ■ 16 cm (6½ in) cotton fringing in 2 different colours ■ Scissors
■ Non-toxic, flame retardant polyester filling (batting)*

1 Cut around the fabric squares with pinking shears. Sew 2 of the squares together trapping a piece of fringing in between them.

2 Attach a third square to the others and continue attaching the squares as shown, including fringing on 3 sides, until you have joined all the pieces together with the exception of a gap to allow the filling (batting) to be inserted.

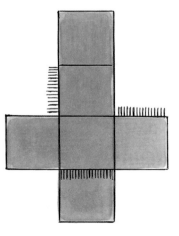

3 Stuff the cube with the polyester filling (batting) until the cube is quite firm and sew up the gap.

Pompon Mobile

THIS EYE-CATCHING MOBILE WILL FASCINATE THE SMALLEST CHILD

YOU WILL NEED ■ *2 green garden stakes, 37 cm (14½ in) long*
■ *Florist's wire* ■ *Scissors* ■ *Lengths of red, blue, yellow and green yarn*
■ *Large darning needle* ■ *4 red pompons; 4 blue pompons; 4 yellow pompons; 4 green pompons;*
all 5 cm (2 in) in diameter ■ *Needle and thread* ■ *Curled ribbon in matching colours*

1 Lay the stakes to form a cross. Secure in the centre using florist's wire. Thread 3 lengths of yarn, approximately 51 cm (20 in) long, onto the darning needle. Sew the yarn through the first pompon, tying a knot at the end to secure.

Continue to thread the yarn through the next pompon. Knot the yarn 8 cm (3¼ in) from the first pompon and slide the pompon down to the knot. Continue until all 4 colours have been used. Tie the end of the yarn to the centre of the stake leaving 12 cm (4¾ in) between the pompon and stake.

2 Next, thread 2 pompons onto the yarn as before. Repeat 4 times, using a different colour combination each time. Tie onto the stake 8 cm (3¼ in) from the centre. Thread each remaining pompon onto the yarn and tie at each end of the stake. Sew the ribbon between each hanging pompon. Tie a length of yarn from the centre to allow the mobile to be hung from the ceiling.

Bedtime Friends

THIS FAMILY OF DELIGHTFUL COMPANIONS WILL ENTRANCE ANY BABY

YOU WILL NEED ■ *1 pair of 3 mm (US 3) knitting needles*
■ *Oddments of double knitting (sport) yarn in 5 different colours: Boy*
Colour A – Shoes; Colour B – Trousers; Colour C – Sweater stripe; Colour D – Skin;
Colour E – Hair; Girl Colour A – Shoes, Body, Hair and Arms; Colour B – Skin; Colour C – Skirt
■ *Stitch holder* ■ *Large darning needle* ■ *Non-toxic, flame retardant polyester*
filling (batting) ■ *Oddments of yarn for facial embroidery* ■ *Length of*
round cord elastic ■ *Wooden beads* ■ *Bells*

BOY DOLL

Legs, body and head
Using yarn A, cast on 4 sts for the shoe.
Inc row: double sts (k twice into each st) 8 sts.
Next row: P to end. Break yarn. Change to yarn B and work 10 rows garter st (every row knit) for leg. Break yarn and leave these sts on a holder. Work other leg as the first, but do not break yarn.
Next row (body): k 8 sts then k 8 sts from holder: 16 sts. Work 3 rows in garter st. Join in yarn C for jumper stripe pattern. Garter st: 2 rows C 2 rows B. Work 12 rows in stripe pattern.
Change to yarn D and work 10 rows st st (k 1 row p 1 row) for the head.
Dec row: (k 2 tog) to end. Break yarn, thread end through remaining sts, pull up and secure.

Arms
(Knit 2 alike)
Using yarn D, cast on 8 sts. Work 2 rows st st. Break yarn, change to

stripe pattern (2 rows C, 2 rows B) and work 7 rows garter st. Cast (bind) off.

TO MAKE UP
Join leg, body and head seams leaving an opening. Stuff and close opening. Fold arms

lengthwise (right sides together) and join seam. Stuff and sew arms to body. Tie a length of yarn tightly around neck. Embroider facial features.*** Using D yarn knot short lengths into top and back of head for hair. Separate lengths of yarn and trim.

GIRL DOLL

Legs, body and head
Using yarn A, cast on 4 sts for shoe.
Inc row: (knot twice into each st) 8 sts.
Next row: p to end. Break yarn. Change to yarn B and work 9 rows st st, change to yarn A and p 1 row (for leg). Break yarn, leave these sts on a holder.
Work other leg as given for first leg, but do not break yarn.
Next row (body): k 8 sts then k 8 sts from holder (16 sts).

Next row: p to end. Work 14 rows st st. Break yarn. Change to yarn B and work 10 rows st st for head.
Dec row: (k 2 tog) to end. Break yarn, thread end through remaining sts, then pull up and secure neatly.

Arms
(Knit 2 alike)
Using yarn B, cast on 8 sts. Work 2 rows st st. Change to yarn A and work 7 rows st st. Cast (bind) off.

Skirt
Using yarn A, cast on 35 sts. Work 2 rows garter st.
Change to yarn C and work 8 rows st st. Break yarn. Thread end through remaining sts.

TO MAKE UP
Make up as instructed for boy doll to ***. Join back seam of skirt, gather up stitches to fit around waist and sew to body.
Hair: cut yarn C into 11 cm (4½ in) lengths. Knot each length into centre of head starting at front and finishing at centre back of head. Separate each length of yarn. Tie into 2 pigtails, secure with an oddment of yarn B and trim if required.

Make 2 boy and 2 girl dolls. Thread elastic carefully through the arms, inserting a large bead between each doll and a large bell in the centre. Make a loop with the elastic threading a bead through the end. Secure firmly with a large knot. Thread the end of the elastic back through the doll.

Hoppy Cushion

HOPS HAVE TRADITIONALLY BEEN USED FOR THEIR SOPORIFIC EFFECT!

YOU WILL NEED ■ *Ruler* ■ *Pencil* ■ *Paper* ■ *Tracing paper* ■ *Pins* ■ *Strong cotton fabric*
■ *Scissors* ■ *Contrasting velvet fabric* ■ *Non-toxic, flame retardant polyester filling (batting)* ■ *Oddments of red, white and black felt* ■ *Needle and thread* ■ *Oddments of yarn* ■ *Bodkin or large needle* ■ *Hops*

1 Scale up the templates to the required size and trace over and mark positions for eyes and mouth. Pin the paper patterns to the cotton fabric and cut out 4 side panels and 2 centre panels. Cut 1 base and 2 arms from the velvet fabric. Cut out matching pieces in filling (batting). Sew each piece of filling (batting) to reverse side of each piece of matching fabric. Cut the mouth and eye pieces from felt. Tack (baste) them to the front section and then zigzag stitch them securely in position.

2 Making a 12 mm (½ in) seam, join all sides right sides together, leaving 1 back seam half open for filling. Fold the arms in half lengthwise with right sides together and sew. Turn right side out. Pin the top section to the base, wrong sides out, and push both arms into position. Double stitch round to join. Turn right side out.

3 To make the hair, push lengths of yarn through a small circle of fabric using a bodkin or large needle to form loops. Leave a 1.5 cm (⅝ in) seam allowance around the edges. When the circle is completely covered with looped lengths of yarn, fold in the seam allowance and sew the circle to the top of the cushion.

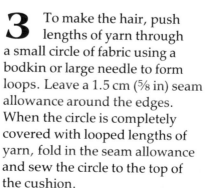

4 Stuff the cushion through the back seam with a mixture of filling (batting) and hops. Finally, sew up the seam to close the gap.

Twirly Fish

HAVE FUN MAKING THIS DECORATIVE FISH TO HANG OVER A BABY'S COT

YOU WILL NEED ■ Pencil ■ 45 × 33 cm (18 × 13 in) card
■ Scissors ■ Drawing pins (thumb tacks) ■ 60 × 60 cm (24 × 24 in)
cotton fabric ■ Wooden frame ■ Wax and wax pot or bain-marie ■ Paintbrushes ■ Fabric dyes
in red, yellow, green and blue ■ Iron ■ Newspaper ■ Paper ■ Pins ■ Needle and thread
■ Non-toxic, flame retardant polyester filling (batting) ■ Cord ■ 2 wooden beads

1 Scale up the template onto the card and cut it out. Pin the fabric onto a wooden frame or board using drawing pins (thumb tacks), ensuring that it is held firmly in place. Place the fish template onto the fabric and draw around it twice to produce 2 fish shapes.

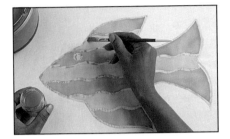

2 Melt the wax in a wax pot or in a bain-marie placed over a low heat. Use a brush to paint the wax around the 2 fish outlines. Then paint wax stripes onto the fish. Make up dyes following the manufacturer's instructions. You will have excess dye to use for another project as you need very little for painting the fish design. Paint both fish using 2 different colours for each. Allow to dry then cut out both fish shapes.

3 Set an iron to its highest setting and place some newspaper on an ironing board. Sandwich each fish between 2 sheets of paper and iron over the top, pressing evenly throughout. The paper will absorb most of the wax. Hand wash the batiked cloth in mildly soapy lukewarm water to remove the excess dye. To remove every trace of wax, dry cleaning is necessary.

4 Place the 2 fish shapes right sides together. Pin, tack (baste) and sew them together, leaving the upper fin open for stuffing and to attach the cord.

5 Turn right side out and stuff the fish from the open upper fin. Knot the length of cord and attach 2 beads in the centre with a knot between and on either side to ensure that they are held firmly in place. Turn in the fin edges and sew, placing one end in the centre of the cord and securing it in the final stitching.

Padders

SOFT AND COMFORTABLE, THESE PADDERS ARE MORE DURABLE THAN BOOTEES

YOU WILL NEED ■ *Pencil* ■ *White paper* ■ *Tape measure* ■ *Scissors*
■ *0.5 m (½ yd) of fabric for the padders* ■ *0.5 m (½ yd) of contrasting fabric for the lining* ■ *Pins*
■ *Needle and thread* ■ *Iron* ■ *Narrow elastic* ■ *1 m (40 in) ribbon, 1 cm (⅜ in) wide*

3 Place the wrong sides of the outer and lining bases together and tack (baste). Find the centre of the padder and base and pin together. Continue to pin around the base. Tack (baste) and sew leaving a 1.5 cm (⅝ in) seam allowance.

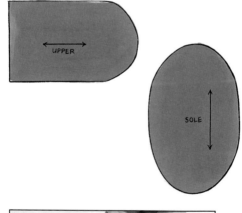

1 Using the templates, cut out a pattern in paper, adjusting the height of the curve and the length of the base to fit the baby's foot. Using this pattern, cut out 2 tops and 2 bases from each of the fabrics (8 pieces).

With right sides together, pin and tack (baste) the lining to the outer fabric along the long edge. Sew leaving a 1.5 cm (⅝ in) seam allowance. Press open. Place the elastic 3.5 cm (1¼ in) from the seam on the wrong side of the outer fabric. Sew the elastic in place, stretching it as it is sewn.

2 Pin and tack (baste) the side seams together. Sew together leaving a 1.5 cm (⅝ in) seam allowance. Fold the padder with wrong sides together and pin the two raw edges together. Tack (baste) the edges.

4 Using zigzag stitch, sew around the base and trim the seam. Turn out. Sew the ribbon at the back of the padder on the elastic line. Bring it to the front and tie into a bow.

Spiky Cushion Cover

A BRIGHT, FUN CUSHION FOR THE BEDROOM AND PLAYROOM

YOU WILL NEED ■ Black pen ■ Paper ■ Tape measure ■ Scissors
■ 2 pieces of 45 × 45 cm (18 × 18 cm) fabric for the main cushion ■ 2 pieces of 16 × 45 cm
(6¼ × 18 in) fabric for the inner flaps ■ 12 pieces of 4.5 × 26 cm (1¾ × 10¼ in) fabric for the ties ■ 6 fabric
triangles ■ Pinking shears ■ Pins ■ Needle and thread ■ 24 cm (9½ in) cotton fringing ■ Cushion pad

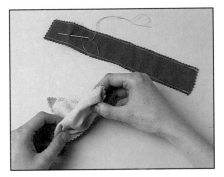

1 Using the templates, cut out paper patterns for all the pieces, and cut them out of contrasting fabrics with a pair of pinking shears.

2 Make 6 ties and 3 spikes by pinning together the fabric pieces in pairs, right sides together. Sew along the edges leaving a gap at one side, and turn right sides out.

3 Place one flap piece along the edge of one main cushion piece of fabric, right sides together. Trap the ends of the 3 ties between the 2 pieces of fabric and sew along the edges. Turn right side out. Repeat with the other flap, cushion piece and ties.

 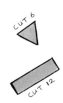

CUT 6

CUT 12

CUT 2

4 Join the 2 main pieces, right sides together, trapping the piece of fringing and the 3 spikes in between the layers and sew around the edge. Turn inside out and place the cushion pad inside.

Decorated Towel

ADD A LIVELY TRIMMING TO A PLAIN TOWEL

YOU WILL NEED ■ *Pins* ■ *Length of blue cording or piping* ■ *Towel* ■ *Embroidery thread* ■ *Needle and thread* ■ *Scissors* ■ *Length of ric-rac braid*

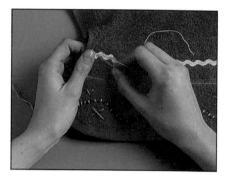

1 Pin blue cording along one end of the towel in a wiggly line. Oversew down its length to secure it, using embroidery thread in a contrasting colour.

2 Using a different colour of embroidery thread, embroider cross-stitches along each side of the blue cording at regular intervals.

3 Cut 2 equal lengths of ric-rac braid in contrasting colours and then sew them neatly in place above the blue cording using a needle and thread.

Smiley Toys

THESE FUNNY LIPS WILL KEEP ANY BABY SMILING

YOU WILL NEED ■ *Fine black felt-tip pen* ■ *Thin card* ■ *Scissors* ■ *Coloured felt*
■ *Black embroidery yarn* ■ *Large darning needle* ■ *Length of narrow ribbon* ■ *Needle and thread*
■ *Non-toxic, flame retardant polyester filling (batting)* ■ *Squeaker or bell (optional)*

1 Using the template as a guide, draw a lip shape onto thin card. Cut it out and place it on the coloured felt. Draw around the shape twice and cut out.

2 Using the embroidery yarn, sew a line of chain stitch through the middle of one of the felt lip shapes.

3 Cut a short length of ribbon, fold in half to make a loop and sew the ends to the top of the other felt lip shape.

4 Put the lips wrong sides together and chain stitch them together using the embroidery yarn and leaving a small gap for stuffing. Stuff gently. If you want to insert a squeaker or bell, be sure to enclose it in a tightly-sewn cotton bag as a safety measure. Chain stitch the gap together.

Bright-finned **F**ish

THIS FISH CAN BE MADE FLAT FOR A CUSHION OR DOUBLE-SIDED FOR A TOY

YOU WILL NEED ■ *Pencil* ■ *Paper* ■ *Scissors* ■ *Striped cotton fabric*
■ *Pins* ■ *Needle and thread* ■ *Tape measure* ■ *Satin fabric in red and green* ■ *Iron*
■ *Iron-on interfacing* ■ *Non-toxic, flame retardant polyester filling (batting)* ■ *2 patterned cotton
fabrics* ■ *Scrap of white fabric* ■ *Embroidery thread* ■ *2 plain cotton fabrics*

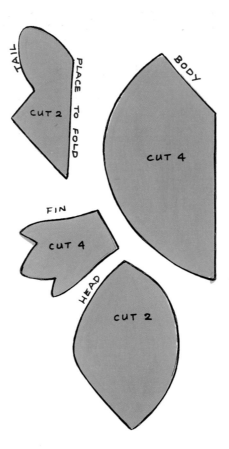

TAIL

PLACE TO FOLD

CUT 2

FIN

CUT 4

BODY

CUT 4

HEAD

CUT 2

1 Make paper patterns for each of the pieces, using the templates as a guide. Cut 2 sets of opposite shapes in striped cotton for the fish body, lining up the fabric stripes with the pattern edge at the tail end of the fish.

Pin, tack (baste) and sew the body sides right sides together along the straight central seam using a 1 cm (⅜ in) seam allowance and stopping 1 cm (⅜ in) short of the tail end. Turn back the raw edges by 1 cm (⅜ in) at the tail ends, press and tack (baste) the hems.

2 Back the red satin fabric with iron-on interfacing using a cool iron. Cut out 4 fin shapes. Pin and tack (baste) two of them with right sides together, and sew 6 mm (¼ in) from the edge. Clip carefully into the inner corners and turn right side out. Repeat for the other pair of fin shapes. Stuff firmly, pushing the filling down into the points with a pencil, but leave them loosely filled at the open end.

3 Cut out 2 pieces of patterned fabric for the head and 2 of green interfaced satin for the tail. Cut 8 small dark patterned circles for spots. (If the fish will be used as a cushion, you only need decorate one side.) Appliqué the spots to the side. Position the patterned cotton for the head and insert 1 of the fins midway round the seam. Tack (baste) then appliqué the seam in place, enclosing the fin.

Cut circles for the eyes, and appliqué them in place. Embroider a smiley mouth. Overlay the wrong side of the V-shaped end of the striped section 1 cm (⅜ in) onto the right side of the green fish tail. Tack (baste) in place and appliqué them together. Repeat for the other side.

4 Cut 10 diamond shapes for back fins from the satins and the plain cottons. The diamonds should fold in half to form triangles with 13 cm (5¼ in) sides. Fold and stitch 1 side seam of each fin and turn the fins right side out to press. Pick the points with a pin to make them sharp.

Tack (baste) a vertical tuck in each fin so they measure about 8 cm (3¼ in) across the open ends. Pin each fin in position within the striped area of the top and bottom of each side, turning in the striped raw edges 1 cm (⅜ in) as you go. The fins must overlap and should fan out around the fish. Tack (baste) and stitch into position.

5 Position both sides together with right sides facing. Pin and tack (baste) tail and head up to the stitching lines with the striped area. Stitch the seam 1 cm (⅜ in) from the edge. Clip the tail curves. Turn right side out and press the seams firmly.

Stuff the tail, pushing the filling well into the ends. Stitch the top and under seams together by turning under the striped raw edges on the sides without fins, and hemming them securely to the backs of the fins on the opposite side. Fill the fish as you sew the last seam.

Reversible **B**umper

ADD TO THE COMFORT OF A BABY'S COT OR CRIB WITH THIS SIMPLY-MADE BUMPER

YOU WILL NEED ■ *Tape measure* ■ *2 pieces contrasting fabric* ■ *Scissors* ■ *Pins*
■ *Needle and thread* ■ *Thick wadding (batting)* ■ *3 m (3 yd) narrow bias binding* ■ *Wide bias binding*

1 Measure the end and halfway along the sides of the cot (crib). Cut 2 side pieces and 1 end piece from the contrasting fabrics. Join the 3 pieces by pinning, tacking (basting) and sewing 2 seams right sides together. Cut 1 backing piece to match the front.

2 Cut wadding (batting) to fit and sandwich between the backing and the main fabric. Where the 3 front pieces of fabric join, sew down those seams to secure all 3 layers. Tack (baste) around the edge of the bumper.

3 Cut 8 × 36 cm (14 in) ties from the narrow bias binding. Fold and stitch. Sew the wide bias binding around the edge of the bumper, trapping the ties in the appropriate places to fit the bars of the cot (crib).

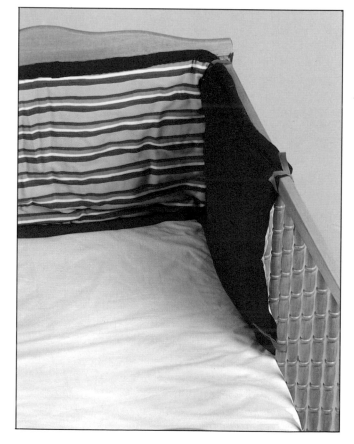

Sun Toy

THIS HAPPY SUN WILL BRIGHTEN UP A BABY'S DAY

YOU WILL NEED ■ *Pinking shears* ■ *2 fabric circles* ■ *Pins*
■ *6 felt triangles* ■ *18 cm (7 in) yellow fringing* ■ *30 cm (12 in) red cord*
■ *Scissors* ■ *Needle and thread* ■ *Oddments of felt* ■ *Rubber-based glue* ■ *Plastic squeaker*
■ *Oddments of fabric* ■ *Non-toxic, flame retardant polyester filling (batting)*

1 Cut out the fabric circles using pinking shears. Pin the triangles on 1 of the round pieces of fabric so that they are pointing towards the centre. Pin the fringing around the top, with the cord ends, to make a loop.

2 Place the other round fabric piece on top, with right sides facing, and sew around the edge leaving a gap at one side. Turn the shape right side out.

3 Remove all the pins. Cut out 2 eyes, a nose and a mouth from oddments of felt and glue them down onto the front to make a face. Add a few stitches to each piece to secure them down.

4 For safety, make a small fabric case for the squeaker from 2 pieces of fabric, place the squeaker inside it and sew up.

5 Wrap the squeaker inside some polyester filling (batting) and stuff the toy lightly. Finish by sewing up the gap.

Baby Announcement Card

YOU WILL NEED ■ *Pieces of black and white card* ■ *White and lead pencils*
■ *Craft knife* ■ *Tracing paper* ■ *Coloured paper* ■ *Length of narrow lace* ■ *Scissors* ■ *Paper glue*
■ *Satin roses* ■ *Non-toxic acrylic paints* ■ *Small paintbrush*

1 Fold the black and white pieces of card in half. Draw the oval shape, crescent moon and the star onto the front of the black card using a white pencil and cut them out with a craft knife.

2 Trace the outlines for the face, hat, hand and cuff onto the coloured paper and cut out using a craft knife. Cut the lace to the correct length to fit around the central frame.

3 Position the head, hands and other coloured cut-outs and glue them down. Glue a rose onto the baby's collar. Glue down the lace and position a rose bud at the base of the oval.

4 Finally, paint in the eyes, nose, ears and mouth.

Washbag

A PRACTICAL BAG FOR STORING AWAY THE BATHROOM ESSENTIALS

YOU WILL NEED ■ *Scissors* ■ *Red PVC (vinyl-coated) fabric*
■ *Needle and thread* ■ *2 pieces of 28 × 30 cm (11 × 12 in) polkadot plastic fabric* ■ *8 metal eyelets* ■ *Hammer* ■ *60 cm (24 in) ribbon or fabric binding*

1 Cut out 2 red hearts from the PVC (vinyl-coated) fabric and sew 1 heart onto each piece of polkadot plastic fabric.

2 Fold over the top edge of both pieces of polkadot plastic fabric and sew.

3 Lay the 2 sides with the right sides together and sew around 3 edges.

4 Attach the metal eyelets evenly along the top edge, using a hammer and working on a firm surface.

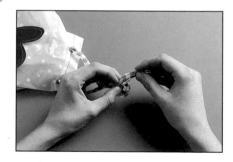

5 Thread the ribbon or fabric binding through the eyelets and tie a knot.

Bathroom **P**ockets

PRACTICAL WALL STORAGE FOR BATHROOM ITEMS

YOU WILL NEED ■ *Scissors* ■ *90 m (1 yd) fabric binding or ribbon*
■ *Needle and thread* ■ *Clear PVC (vinyl) plastic: 1 piece 42 × 55 cm (16½ × 21½ in);*
2 pieces 14 × 14 cm (5½ × 5½ in); 1 piece 13 × 21 cm (5¼ × 8½ in) ■ *Pieces of brightly*
coloured felt ■ *Rubber-based glue* ■ *Fabric for pockets: 2 pieces 14 × 14 cm (5½ × 5½ in); 1 piece*
13 × 21 cm (5¼ × 8½ in) ■ *Coloured PVC (vinyl) plastic for the backing of each pocket: 2 pieces*
14 × 16 cm (5½ × 6½ in); 1 piece 14 × 21 cm (5½ × 8½ in) ■ *Pinking shears*

1 Cut the fabric binding or ribbon into 2 pieces of equal length and sew the centre of each onto the top edge of the largest piece of clear PVC (vinyl) plastic. You may find a thimble helpful for pushing the needle through the plastic more easily.

2 For the pockets, cut out 16 felt spots and glue them to the 3 fabric pieces. Sandwich between clear and coloured PVC (vinyl) plastic with the clear plastic on top. Sew the 3 sides, leaving the extra coloured plastic overlapping at the top.

3 Trim the top coloured edge with pinking shears. Fold it over the front and sew down.

4 Place the pockets on the clear plastic base and sew.

Cylindrical Bag

THE PERFECT CONTAINER FOR ABSORBENT COTTON BALLS

YOU WILL NEED ■ *Tape measure* ■ *Pinking shears* ■ *2 pieces of 15 × 38 cm (6 × 15 in)*
patterned fabric ■ *2 pieces of 15 × 38 cm (6 × 15 in) plain fabric* ■ *Scissors* ■ *2 pieces of 15 × 38 cm (6 × 15 in)*
wadding (batting) ■ *Needle and thread* ■ *6 metal eyelets* ■ *Hammer* ■ *35 cm (13½ in) cord*

1 Cut out the 4 fabric pieces using pinking shears and the 2 wadding (batting) pieces using scissors. For each bag side, trap one piece of wadding (batting) between 2 contrasting pieces of fabric and sew along one edge.

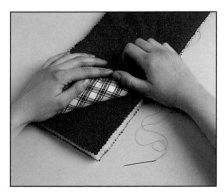

2 Position the 2 sides so that a patterned side is facing a plain one. Sew through all the layers around 3 sides, leaving an opening. Stitch around the open edges to sew down.

3 Turn right side out. Attach the metal eyelets along the open edge of the bag using a hammer and a firm work surface. Thread the cord through the eyelets and tie a knot.

Changing Bag

A HANDY PADDED CHANGING MAT AND BAG WITH LARGE POCKETS

YOU WILL NEED ■ *Plain cotton fabric* ■ *Scissors* ■ *Tape measure* ■ *Pins* ■ *Needle and thread*
■ *Iron* ■ *Towelling (terrycloth)* ■ *Patterned cotton fabric* ■ *Medium-weight wadding (batting)* ■ *Toggle*

1 From the plain cotton cut 2 pocket flaps each 46 × 26 cm (18¼ × 10¼ in). Fold each flap in turn across its longest edge to make a shape 23 × 26 cm (9 × 10¼ in). Stitch along the 2 shorter edges, making a bag. Turn the seams to the inside and press.

2 To make the mat, cut 1 piece each of towelling (terrycloth), patterned cotton fabric and wadding (batting) to 80 × 46 cm (32 × 18¼ in). Place the towelling (terrycloth) right side up on the wadding (batting). Make a narrow loop of patterned fabric for the toggle and tack (baste) it in place at the centre bottom of the mat so that the ends can be stitched into the seam.

Tack (baste) the pocket flaps 6 cm (2¼ in) from the top of the mat. Position the patterned cotton right side down on top. Pin and tack (baste), then stitch, leaving a 20 cm (8 in) gap on a long side for turning. Turn right side out and press lightly. Oversew the opening neatly.

3 Cut 2 facings of patterned fabric 40 × 13 cm (16 × 5¼ in) and 2 pieces of plain fabric 40 × 23 cm (16 × 9 in) for the pockets. Turn under 1 long edge to the wrong side and hem. Place the hemmed facing right side down onto the wrong side of 1 pocket, matching the raw top and side edges of the facing to the pocket. Pin, tack (baste) and stitch the facing to the pocket top on 3 sides. Snip into the pocket seam allowance where the facing hem meets the pocket side.

Tack (baste) a hem on the pocket bottom, with the facing/pocket stitch line and the fold of the pocket hem on the sides forming a continuous line. Trim the facing/pocket seam edges, turn the facing to the right side and press firmly with an iron on a medium setting. Stitch the facing to the pocket front. Fold a box pleat in pocket so that its finished width is about 20 cm (8 in). Tack (baste) the pleat in place, pressing firmly. Repeat the same procedure to make up the second pocket.

4 Make 2 lengths of fabric for the straps about 5 cm (2 in) wide and approximately 70 cm (28 in) long. Fold the pocket flaps in and fold the mat up just below the flaps. Turn the mat over. The bottom of the mat with the loop folds down to overlap the front, becoming the top of the bag. Pin the loop temporarily to the front and also mark the correct position for the toggle with a pin. Pin the straps in position, adjusting until the bag hangs well and the straps are even. Turn under the raw edges at the ends and stitch the straps in place through all thicknesses of the mat.

5 Pin and tack (baste) and hem the pockets to the pocket backs. Oversew at the top pocket corners for strength. Fold the pocket flaps in. Make 2 ties from patterned fabric and stitch 1 to each flap where their edges meet so that when tied the pocket flaps will stay in position. Sew the toggle to the bag front.

Pop-up Card

A DELIGHTFUL SURPRISE CARD TO WELCOME A NEW BABY

YOU WILL NEED ■ *Craft knife* ■ *Thin card* ■ *Ruler* ■ *Pencil* ■ *Wax crayons*
■ *Felt-tip pens* ■ *Scissors* ■ *Strong clear glue*

  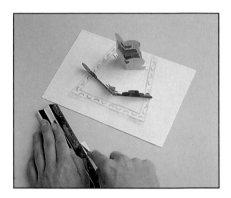

1 Cut a piece of card 22 × 15 cm (8¾ × 6 in), score lightly across the middle and fold in half along the score-line. Draw a rug in pencil and colour it in with wax crayons, picking out the details with pencil.

2 Draw the cradle and toy shapes carefully onto the thin card. Colour the cradle with wax crayons, outlining the detail of the lace pattern with a sharp pencil. Use felt-tip pens and wax crayons for the toy designs.

3 Carefully cut out the designs and score along the tabs on the front. Spread glue on the tabs, and stick into position on the rug.

4 Cut out, score and glue the remaining design in position. Check that the card closes properly.

Scented Sachets

THESE CRIB-SHAPED SACHETS ARE PERFECT FOR FRESHENING DRAWERS

YOU WILL NEED For each sachet: ■ *9 × 7.5 cm (3½ × 3 in) piece of wadding (batting)* ■ *20 × 18 cm (8 × 7 in) white cotton fabric* ■ *Pins* ■ *Needle and thread* ■ *Dried lavender* ■ *Scissors* ■ *36 cm (14 in) broderie anglaise ribbon, 7.5 cm (3 in) wide* ■ *Tape measure* ■ *36 cm (14 in) double-sided satin ribbon, 6 mm (¼ in) wide*

1 Place the wadding (batting) in the centre of the white fabric, pin down the fabric over the wadding (batting) and tack (baste). Fold the ends to form triangles as if wrapping a parcel. Place a spoonful of dried lavender in the centre.

2 Carefully fold in half lengthwise so that the sides meet, and slip stitch together. At end of the seam, fold down the triangle and sew to the centre seam. Oversew back along the seam, and catch in the other triangle to finish the inner bedding of the crib.

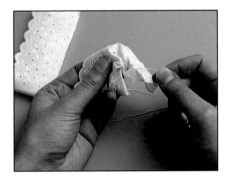

3 Cut a 23 cm (9 in) length of broderie anglaise and fold in half, right sides together. Fold in 2.5 cm (1 in) of the selvage edge, sew the end and then turn right side out. Use the remaining broderie anglaise ribbon to make the crib hood by gather stitching 12 mm (½ in) from the selvage edge. Pull the thread while tucking in the seam, and fasten to form the hood.

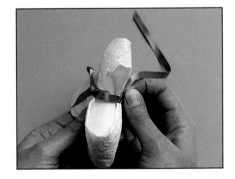

4 Tuck the hood into the crib, pin into position and then oversew to secure. Position the lavender 'bedding' in the crib. Tie a bow in the satin ribbon. Sew the bow onto the crib, passing the needle through to secure the bedding. Pass the ribbon over the crib and sew to the outside. Leave the end of the ribbon hanging if you are going to hang the sachet inside a wardrobe.

Sweetheart Shoes

THESE IRRESISTIBLE SHOES ARE VERY EASY TO MAKE

YOU WILL NEED ■ *2 squares of 23 × 23 cm (9 × 9 in) blue felt* ■ *Pins* ■ *Pencil* ■ *Pinking shears*
■ *Square of 23 × 23 cm (9 × 9 in) lilac felt* ■ *Needle and thread* ■ *Iron* ■ *Red stranded embroidery thread*
■ *Small sharp scissors* ■ *45 cm (18 in) red ribbon, 3 mm (⅛ in) wide* ■ *Scrap of red felt*

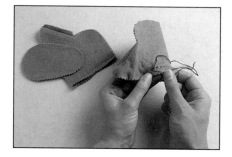

1 Fold the blue felt squares diagonally in half and pin together. Using the template as a guide, draw the shoe upper on 1 half of each piece and cut out with pinking shears. Cut out 2 shoe soles from lilac felt. Pin the uppers together in pairs and then stitch along the centre front and centre back edges, taking a 1 cm (⅜ in) seam allowance.

2 Press the seams open. Turn the shoe uppers right side out. Pin the uppers to the soles matching the seams to the dots. Sew together taking a 1 cm (⅜ in) seam allowance using stranded embroidery thread.

3 Cut the ribbon in half. Cut 4 hearts from red felt and sew each heart securely to the ends using 2 strands of red stranded embroidery thread. Sew the centre of each ribbon to the back seam 3.5 cm (1½ in) below the upper edge. Turn down this edge as a cuff. Tie the ribbon in a bow at the front. Sew the bow to the shoe.

Waist Hold-all

THE IDEAL HOLD-ALL FOR PARENTS ON THE MOVE

YOU WILL NEED ■ *Scissors* ■ *27 × 43 cm (10½ × 17 in) fabric*
■ *20.5 × 43 cm (8¼ × 17 in) fabric in contrasting colour* ■ *Pinking shears* ■ *Needle and thread*
■ *126 cm (50 in) bias binding* ■ *126 cm (50 in) ribbon or fabric binding*

1 Cut out the 2 fabric pieces and trim the edges with pinking shears. On the smaller piece sew a line of bias binding along the longest edge.

2 Sew 2 lines of stitching down the smaller piece to divide it into 3 pockets. Sew the smaller fabric piece onto the large piece, around the 3 unbound edges, and leave the extra fabric at the top edge.

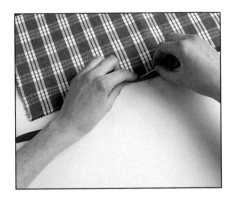

3 Sew a length of bias binding round the bottom and side edges of the hold-all.

4 Sew the length of ribbon or fabric binding just below the top edge of the reverse side of the hold-all, to make the waist ties. Fold over the top edge and sew down over the waist tie.

Busy Bee Slippers

THESE FUN SLIPPERS FIT CHILDREN AGED 18–24 MONTHS

YOU WILL NEED ■ *3.5 mm (E) crochet hook* ■ *40 (1½ oz) black double knitting (sport) cotton* ■ *Scissors* ■ *40 g (1½ oz) yellow double knitting (sport) cotton* ■ *Tape measure* ■ *Large darning needle* ■ *10 g (1½ oz) white double knitting (sport) cotton* ■ *10 g (½ oz) light blue double knitting (sport) cotton*

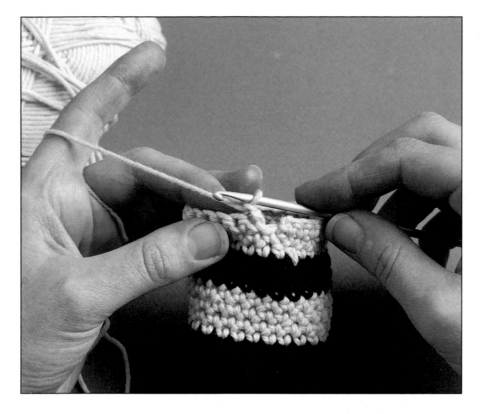

MAIN SLIPPER

Starting at the toe end of the slipper, use black cotton to work the bee's head as follows:

1st row: 3 ch, join into a ring with 1 ss in 1st chain, 1 ch, 6 dc (sc) into ring. Close with 1 ss in first st.

2nd row: 2 ch, 2 dc (sc) in each of next 6 sts, ss in first st.

3rd row: 2 ch, 2 dc (sc) in each of next 12 sts, ss in first st.

4th row: 2 ch, 1 dc (sc) in each of next 24 sts, ss in first st.

Repeat 4th row five more times.

10th row: Cut black cotton and join yellow cotton to work bee's body as follows:

Repeat 4th row four times.

14th row: Cut yellow cotton and join black cotton; using black cotton work as follows:

Repeat 4th row three times.

17th row: Cut black cotton and cast (bind) off last st. Rejoin yellow cotton 12 sts away from last black stitch. This is the centre front of the slipper. Using yellow cotton, work 2 ch, 1 dc (sc) in each of next 24 sts, 1 ch, turn. Now work back along this row as follows:

18th row: 1 dc (sc) in each of next 24 sts, 1 ch, turn. Repeat 18th row twice more.

21st row: Cut yellow cotton and

join black cotton; using black cotton work 1 dc (sc) in each of next 24 sts, 1 ch, turn. Repeat 21st row twice more.

24th row: Cut black cotton and join yellow cotton; using yellow cotton work 1 dc (sc) in each of next 24 sts, 1 ch, turn. Repeat 24th row three more times.

28th row: Cut yellow cotton and join black cotton; using black cotton work 1 dc (sc) in each of next 24 sts, 1 ch, turn.

29th row: 1 dc (sc) in each of next 8 sts, miss 1 st, 1 dc (sc) in each of next 6 sts, miss 1 st, 1 dc (sc) in each of next 8 sts, 1 ch, turn.

30th row: 1 dc (sc) in each of next 7 sts, miss 1 st, 1 dc (sc) in next st, miss 1 st, 1 dc (sc) in next 2 sts, miss 1 st, 1 dc (sc) in next st, miss 1 st, 1 dc (sc) in last 7 sts. Cast (bind) off leaving a 20 cm (8 in) end. Turn slipper inside out and stitch in all ends. Repeat rows 1–30 for 2nd slipper.

EYES

(Make 4 alike)

Using black cotton, work bee's eyes as follows:

1st step: 3 ch, ss in first chain to form ring, 1 ch, 5 dc (sc) into ring, ss in first st.

2nd step: Cut black cotton and join white cotton. Work 1 ss in each of next 6 sts. Cast (bind) off last st leaving a 20 cm (8 in) end of cotton to stitch eye to head.

WINGS

(Make 4 alike)

Using light blue cotton, work bee's wings as follows:

1st step: 3 ch, join into a ring with 1 ss in first ch. 1 ch, 5 dc (sc) into ring, ss in first st.

2nd step: 1 ch, 2 dc (sc) in first st, 1 dtr and 1 tr (dc) in next st, 1 tr (dc), 2 dtrs, 1 tr (dc) in next st, 1 dtr and 1 tr (dc) in next st, 2 dc (sc) in last st, ss in first st, 2 ch, cast (bind) off, leaving a 15 cm (6 in) end.

TO MAKE UP

Stitch eyes to bee's head using the 20 cm (8 in) ends of cotton still attached to each eye. Stitch wings to bee's body using the 15 cm (6 in) ends of cotton still attached to each wing. Position wings at beginning of the first black stripe up from bee's head and about 1.5 cm (⅝ in) either side of the centre front.

Lastly, using the 20 cm (8 in) end of cotton still attached to the back end of the slipper, stitch up the back opening.

Hooded Sweater

THIS COSY SWEATER IS GIVEN IN TWO SIZES, 3 AND 6 MONTHS

YOU WILL NEED ■ *200 g (8-ounce skein) ecru double knitting (sport) yarn* ■ *100 g (4-ounce skein) yellow double knitting (sport) yarn* ■ *1 pair size 3 mm (US 3) knitting needles* ■ *1 pair size 3.5 mm (US 4) knitting needles* ■ *Tape measure* ■ *Scissors* ■ *Iron* ■ *Large darning needle*

Tension (Gauge)
Using 3.5 mm (US 4) needles, 21 sts and 30 rows to 10 cm (4 in) (st st).

BACK AND FRONT
Start at lower front edge. With 3 mm (US 3) needles and yellow yarn cast on 58(62) sts. Work 4 rows in k 1, p 1 rib. Change to 3½ mm (US 4) needles and the ecru yarn. Continue in st st (1 row k, 1 row p) and increase 1 st at both ends of every alternate row 13 times (84(88) sts). Continue in st st until work measures 34(39.5) cm (13¼ (15½) in).

Shape neck
K 37(38), cast (bind) off 10(12) sts, k 37(38) sts. Work each side of neck separately. Cast (bind) off at neck edge on alternate rows, 3 sts once, 2 sts twice and 1 st 3 times. Continue straight until work measures 39(45) cm (15¼(18) in) ending on neck edge, at the centre of the work.

Inc row: cast on 10 sts for back neck, k to end.
Next row: p to end.
Leave remaining 37(38) sts on a spare needle.
Rejoin yarn at neck edge and complete other side of neck to match reversing shaping and ending at straight edge.
Inc row: k 37(38), cast on 10(12) sts, k 37(38) from spare needle (84(88) sts). Continue straight until work measures 69(81) cm (27½(32½) in) ending with a wrong side row.
Dec row: dec 1st each end of next and following alternate row 12 times more (58(62) sts). Change to 3 mm (US 3) needles and yellow yarn. Work 4 rows k 1, p 1 rib. Cast (bind) off.

HOOD
With 3.5 mm (US 4) needles and yellow yarn cast on 42(44) sts. Continue in st st, keeping front edge straight throughout and inc 1 st at beginning of every 10th row 1(2) times, then every following 8th row 5(4) times (48(50) sts). Continue straight until work measures 19(20) cm (7½(8) in) ending with a right side row. Cast (bind) off 1 st at beginning of next and following alternate rows 3 times more. Cast (bind) off 2 sts at beginning of alternate rows twice. Work 1 row ending at back edge (centre of work) (40(42) sts).

Cast on at beginning of next and following alternate rows 2 sts twice and 1 st 4 times (48(50) sts). Dec 1 st at back edge on next and every following 8th row 5(4) times more and then every following 10th row 0(1) time (42(44) sts).

Continue straight until work measures 46(49) cm (18¼(19¼) in ending with a wrong side row. Cast (bind) off.

Hood edging
Using 3 mm (US 3) needles and ecru yarn, pick up 99(103) sts along front edge of hood. Work 4 rows k1, p1 rib. Cast (bind) off.

SLEEVES
(Knit 2 alike)
Using 3 mm (US 3) needles and ecru yarn, cast on 32(34) sts. Work 6 rows k 1, p 1 rib. Change to 3½ mm (US 4) and yellow yarn. Inc 1 st each end of next and every alternate row 13 times (60(62) sts). Then every following 3rd row 5(6) times (70(74) sts). Cast (bind) off.

TO MAKE UP
Press all the pieces. Join back hood seam. Sew hood to neck. Place markers 15(16) cm (6(6¼) in) below shoulder on front and back for sleeve position. Sew sleeve between markers using backstitch. Join sleeve and side seams.

Knitted Cuff Bootees

THESE STRIPY BOOTEES WILL FIT BABIES UP TO 3 MONTHS OLD

YOU WILL NEED ■ *1 pair of 3.5 mm (US 4) knitting needles* ■ *Small quantity of double knitting (sport) yarn in ecru and yellow* ■ *Large darning needle*

Tension (Gauge)
Using 3.5 mm (US 4) needles, 21 sts and 30 rows to 10 cm (4 in) (st st).

Starting at the cuff and using ecru yarn, cast on 29 sts. Work 16 rows garter st (every row knit). Change to yellow yarn and work 10 rows garter st.

Instep
Slip 10 sts from each side of work onto a thread and leave. Continue on 9 sts in the centre. Work 14 rows garter st.
Next row: change to yellow yarn, and with right side facing k 10 sts from thread, pick up and k 12 sts along side of instep, k 9 sts in centre, pick up and k 12 sts along other side of instep, k 10 sts from thread (53 sts).
Work 7 rows garter st. Change to ecru yarn.

Shape sole
Next row: k 30, k 2 tog, turn.
Next row: k 8, k 2 tog, turn.
Next row: k 8, k 2 tog, turn.
Rep last 2 rows until 6 sts remain each side of centre 9 sts.
Next row: turn, k to end. Cast (bind) off.
Work second bootee to match.

TO MAKE UP
Join the heel and back seams, reversing the seam on the last 6 rows to turn over for the cuff.

Knitted Mittens

THESE COSY MITTENS WILL FIT BABIES UP TO 6 MONTHS

YOU WILL NEED ■ *1 pair 3 mm (US 3) knitting needles* ■ *Small amount of yarn and acrylic mix double knitting (sport) yarn in ecru and yellow* ■ *1 pair 3.5 mm (US 4) knitting needles* ■ *Large darning needle* ■ *Scissors*

Tension (Gauge)
Using 3.5 mm (US 4) needles,
21 sts and 30 rows to 10 cm (4 in)
(st st).

CUFF
Using 3 mm (US 3) needles and
ecru yarn cast on 32 sts. Work 10
rows k 1 p 1 rib. Break yarn.
Change to 3½ mm (US 4) needles
and yellow yarn.

To make eyelets:
(k 2 ynfwd, k 2 tog) to end.
Starting with a p row work 18
rows st st.
Dec row: (k 2 tog) to end.
Next row: p to end.
Dec row: (k 2 tog) to end.

Next row: p to end.
Dec row: (k 2 tog) to end.
Break yarn and thread through
remaining sts. Pull up and secure.

To make the braided cords
Cut 6 × 70 cm (28 in) strands of
yarn, 3 of ecru and 3 of yellow.
Knot strands together at one end
leaving 2 cm (¾ in) of yarn at end
for the tassel. Pin the knot to a
fixed object. Braid the yarn then
knot, leaving spare yarn at one
end. Brush and trim the ends.

TO MAKE UP
Join seams lengthwise, right sides
together. Thread cords through
eyelets of mittens.

Tall Bootees

THESE LONG, STRIPED BOOTEES WILL FIT BABIES UP TO 4 MONTHS

YOU WILL NEED ■ *1 pair 3.5 mm (US 4) knitting needles* ■ *Oddments of double knitting (sport) cotton in red, pink, yellow, orange, turquoise and purple* ■ *Large darning needle*

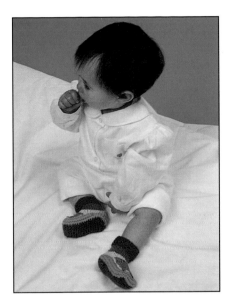

Tension (Gauge)
Using 3.5 mm (US 4) needles, 21 sts and 30 rows to 10 cm (4 in) (st st).

Top
Using red cotton, cast on 27 sts and work 8 rows in garter st (every row knit). Change to pink and work 6 rows in st st. Change to yellow and work a further 4 rows st st.

To shape the instep
Slip 9 sts either side onto a thread and leave. Continue on 9 sts in centre. Using orange work 14 rows garter st.
Next row: with right side facing and yellow yarn k 9 sts from thread, pick up and k 12 sts along side of instep, k 9, pick up and k 12 sts along other side of instep, k 9 st from thread (51 sts).
P 1 row yellow.
Change to turquoise and work 6 rows garter st.

To shape the side
Change to purple and continue in garter st.
Next row: k 29, k 2 tog, turn.
Next row: k 8, k 2 tog, turn.
Next row: k 8, k 2 tog, turn.
Repeat last 2 rows until 6 sts remain each side of centre 9 sts, turn, k to end, cast (bind) off.

TO MAKE UP
Join heel and back seam.

Beetle Drawer Freshener

AN UNUSUAL DESIGN FOR A SCENTED SACHET

YOU WILL NEED ■ *Paper* ■ *Pen* ■ *Pins* ■ *Scissors* ■ *15 × 23 cm (6 × 9 in) black felt*
■ *12.5 × 12.5 cm (5 × 5 in) red felt* ■ *Non-toxic, flame retardant polyester filling (batting)* ■ *Hole punch* ■ *Rubber-based glue* ■ *Needle and thread* ■ *Chamomile and lavender pot pourri*

BODY

PLACE TO FOLD
WING

1 Scale up the templates and make paper patterns. Pin the patterns to the felt and draw round. Cut two body shapes from the black felt, and two wing shapes from the red felt. Cut out a body shape to match from the filling (batting). Remove the paper pattern and mark the arrangement of holes on the wing shapes with a pen. Punch the holes using the hole punch.

3 Stuff the beetle's body with chamomile and lavender pot pourri and then oversew the opening to close.

2 Using rubber-based glue, stick the wing shapes onto one of the body shapes, leaving a small gap in between for a strip of black felt to show through. Leave to dry then turn over and pin the filling (batting) to the upper body piece. Slip stitch the two body pieces together, wrong sides together, leaving the head open for stuffing.

Pop-up Cloud Card

USE A PICTURE OF YOUR CHOICE TO CREATE THIS DELIGHTFUL CARD

YOU WILL NEED ■ *Coloured card* ■ *Craft knife* ■ *Metal ruler* ■ *Scissors*
■ *Rubber-based glue* ■ *Bright picture or motif*

1 Fold a rectangle of coloured card in half by lightly scoring it down the middle using a craft knife and metal ruler. Fold in a triangle from the top about 5 cm (2 in) from the centre.

Cut out the clouds, making sure you leave about 6 mm (¼ in) for the tab along the bottom of the main pop-up cloud for the angles.

2 Glue the flat clouds down and then stick on the tabs of the pop-up cloud, pressing them down firmly.

3 Cut out your chosen motif for the card, and glue it onto the back of the central cloud, folding it in half to fit inside when the card is closed up.

Sarah Sock Doll

A SOFT, SAFE FIRST DOLL USING AN ODD SOCK FROM THE LAUNDRY BASKET!

YOU WILL NEED ■ *Scissors* ■ *A large man's sock, clean and in good condition* ■ *Tape measure* ■ *Needle and strong cotton thread* ■ *Non-toxic, flame retardant polyester filling (batting)* ■ *Patterned cotton fabric* ■ *Pins* ■ *Iron* ■ *Pre-gathered broderie anglaise* ■ *Oddments of felt* ■ *Embroidery thread*

1 Cut the sock into 4 pieces as shown: the leg and heel section will be used for making the doll's body. Allow at least 4 cm (1½ in) beyond the curve of the heel before making the cut to separate the large section. The second cut should be about 8 cm (3¼ in) long. This is cut in half and used for the sleeves and arms. The toe is discarded.

2 Using doubled strong cotton thread, secure a thread about 1 cm (⅜ in) below the cut top of the body section and gather round it, pulling it in tight. Pass the needle back and forth through the gathers to strengthen the closure and secure the thread. Stuff the head firmly and gather round as before to make a head about the size of a tennis ball. Secure the thread. Stuff the body section firmly and oversew the opening to close it.

3 Cut 2 sleeves 8 × 8 cm (3¼ × 3¼ in) from patterned cotton. Open up the remaining sock sections from the centre and select the least worn parts. Cut 2 pieces, 8 × 5 cm (3¼ × 2 in), with the grain of the knitting running along the short length. Pin the fabric to the sock piece right sides together along the long sides. Tack (baste) and stitch, then press the seam flat and oversew the raw edges on both arms. Fold in half lengthwise and press.

Round off the doubled corners of the sock ends. Tack (baste) and stitch, starting at the underarm and leaving a 1 cm (⅜ in) edge. Taper the seam into the folded edge. Turn the sleeves out, stuff firmly and oversew the ends to close. Attach them securely to the body sides.

4 Cut a piece of fabric for the dress about 65 × 20 cm (26 × 8 in). Sew a seam joining along the shorter sides and neaten the raw edges. Make a 1 cm (⅝ in) hem at one end for the neck, and run a doubled gathering thread around the neck just over 1 cm (⅜ in) down from the edge. Turn up the bottom hem of the dress and sew on the broderie anglaise.

Cut a piece of fabric for the bonnet measuring 20 × 10 cm (8 × 4 in). Turn the short sides of the fabric under and stitch down, then sew broderie anglaise to one long edge. Pin the bonnet to the doll with the broderie anglaise running around the front, and arrange the sides and back in even tucks and pleats before hemming the whole bonnet securely to the head.

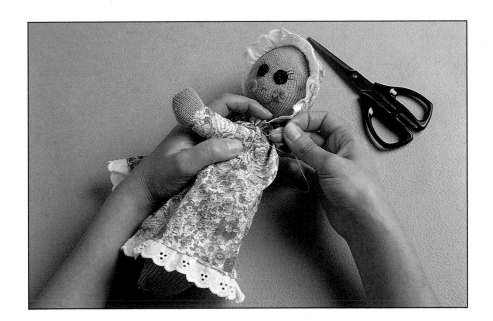

5 Put the dress on the doll with the seam down the back. Gather up the neck and draw it tight. Sew the gathering threads back and forth through the neck to ensure it cannot come undone. Arrange the gathers carefully before making two slits (the width of the arms) in the dress for the arms to emerge.

Turn under the raw edges of the slits as you sew the sleeves and slits together. Cut felt for the eyes and cheeks and embroider them to the head, stitching a star shape on each of the circles. Finally, embroider eyelashes, nostrils and a big smile.

Cuddly Duck

THIS SOFT AND FRIENDLY DUCK CONTAINS A RATTLE

YOU WILL NEED ■ *Pencil* ■ *Paper* ■ *Scissors* ■ *Plain and patterned cotton fabrics in related shades* ■ *Pins* ■ *Needle and thread* ■ *Non-toxic, flame retardant polyester filling (batting)* ■ *Corduroy or needlecord fabric* ■ *Dried peas in a plastic container* ■ *Oddments of felt* ■ *Embroidery thread*

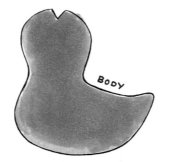

1 Make paper patterns for all pieces using the templates as a guide. Cut out 1 shape from the plain and 1 from the patterned cotton fabric for the feet. Tack (baste) them together and stitch, leaving the flat edge open. Clip into the central corner and turn right side out. Lightly stuff the feet with filling (batting).

3 Starting at the duck's tail, pin the back point of the gusset to the duck, right sides together, and work forward under the duck until you reach the front of the gusset. Tack (baste) and stitch the seam. Repeat with the second body shape. Break off the stitching line and restart it, having first pressed the bodies flat so that the gusset is folded along its centre. Leave the duck's back open to turn but work 2 cm (¾ in) of the seam from the tail to allow you to achieve a neat point.

Turn the body right side out and stuff the duck firmly, enclosing a small pea-filled container. Oversew the opening. Cut 2 sets of wing shapes and stitch in pairs leaving the flat edges open. Turn right side out and stuff lightly, then turn in the flat edges and oversew them. Stitch the wings very firmly to the body.

2 Cut the 2 gusset pieces from corduroy or needlecord. The longer piece will be for the front of the duck. Enclosing the feet within the seam, stitch the gussets right sides together along the flat edge. The patterned side of the feet must face upwards. Cut 2 opposite shapes for the duck's body. Stitch the small darts in the head on both sides.

4 Cut 2 pieces of felt for the beak and stitch them together close to the edge. Fold the beak through the centre and stitch it firmly to the head. Cut 2 white felt circles for eyes and attach them to the head as shown. Cut a triangle of patterned fabric for a headscarf, neaten the edges and sew it to the head, tying in a knot under the chin.

Denim Bear

BABY'S FIRST BEAR: A SIMPLE-TO-MAKE CUDDLY TOY

YOU WILL NEED ■ *Pen* ■ *Paper* ■ *Scissors* ■ *Strong cotton fabric such as denim or broadcloth* ■ *Patterned cotton fabric* ■ *Pins* ■ *Needle and thread* ■ *Safety eyes* ■ *Non-toxic, fire retardant polyester filling (batting)* ■ *Knitting needle or pencil* ■ *Embroidery thread*

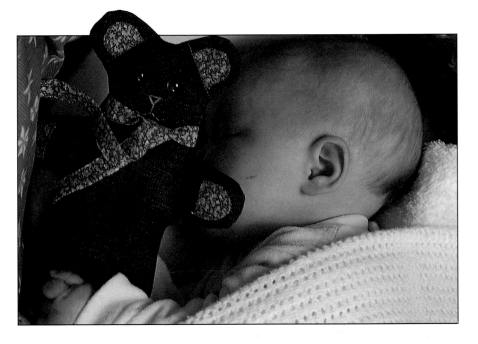

1 Scale up the template to the size required and make a paper pattern for the bear. Cut 2 bear shapes from the strong cotton. Cut 4 shapes for paws and 2 for ears from the patterned cotton and position them 1 cm (⅜ in) in from the raw edges of the bear's body. Pin and then tack (baste) them in place, and sew onto the bear's body front.

Make a vertical slit in the centre of the body back 8 cm (3¼ in) long. Place the right sides of the bodies together and stitch around the outside. Clip the main curves and turn the body to the right side through the slit.

2 Mark the positions for the safety eyes and attach them according to the manufacturer's instructions. Lightly stuff the bear's ears and stitch diagonally across to give them shape. Stuff the head, ensuring there is plenty of filling (batting) behind the eyes.

Make 3 backstitches from the front through to the back across the neck to keep the filling (batting) in place and also to give shape. Stuff the remainder of the body firmly, pushing the filling (batting) down to the ends of the paws with a knitting needle or a pencil. Oversew the opening.

3 Embroider the nose and mouth onto the bear. Sew a 'belly button' by making stitches back and forth through the centre of the bear, pulling the thread tight to give a dimpled shape. Make a narrow tie from the patterned cotton fabric. Trim the ends in a forked shape and then tie the tie round the bear's neck with a proper tie knot. Sew the back tie end firmly to the bear so that it cannot be pulled undone.

Appliquéd Toys

SHAPES AND TEXTURES TO DELIGHT AND AMUSE A BABY

YOU WILL NEED ■ *Pair of compasses* ■ *Ruler* ■ *Pencil* ■ *Scissors* ■ *Pins*
■ *Oddments of fabric in bright colours, patterns and textures* ■ *Needle and thread* ■ *Ribbon in assorted colours*
■ *Non-toxic, flame retardant polyester filling (batting)* ■ *Large wooden beads* ■ *2 wooden rings*

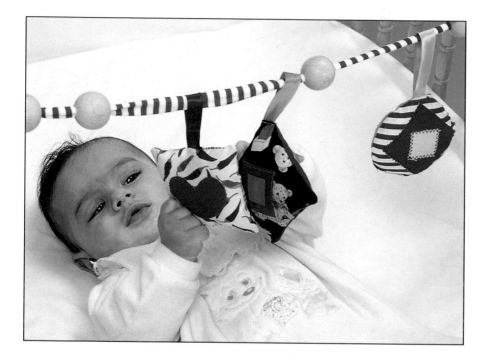

3 Turn the shape right side out and stuff it firmly with polyester filling (batting). Oversew the opening to close. Repeat with the other shapes.

1 Each of the 3 different hanging shapes is made in the same way. The appliqué decorations are simply triangles, squares, hearts and circles which you can arrange as you please. To make the shapes, first draw, cut and assemble your chosen elements and motifs. Use a pair of compasses to draw the circles accurately.

2 Appliqué the decorative elements to the right sides of your hanging shape. Cut a length of ribbon about 7 cm (2¾ in) long, fold it in half and tack (baste) it to the seam edge within the shape so that it will be incorporated into the seam. Leaving an opening to turn, tack (baste) and sew around the shape with right sides together.

4 Make a strong fabric tie of sufficient length to reach across the cot (crib) or pram. Thread on the wooden beads. Sew a wooden ring very securely to each end of the tie. Thread the shapes onto the tie, with a bead between each. Make 2 short ties in contrasting colours and thread one through each ring, sewing firmly across close to the ring to hold them in place. Use these to tie the toy to the cot (crib) edge. Do not leave excessive lengths of loose tie near a small baby.

Fringed Bootees

THESE COSY FRINGED BOOTEES ARE PERFECT FOR COLDER WEATHER

YOU WILL NEED ■ *White paper* ■ *Black felt-tip pen*
■ *Piece of cotton jersey fabric* ■ *Pinking shears* ■ *Pins* ■ *Needle and thread* ■ *Elastic thread*
■ *Scissors* ■ *32 cm (12½ in) cotton fringing*

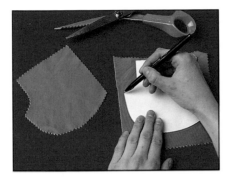

1 Transfer the template onto white paper. Draw around the template and cut out 4 pieces of jersey fabric for the bootees using pinking shears.

2 Fold over and pin the top edge of each piece of fabric and sew down. Sew the 2 sides of each bootee together.

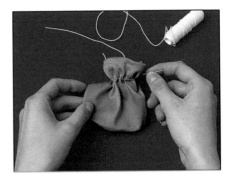

3 Sew a line of narrow elastic thread around the top of the bootee about 2.5 cm (1 in) in from the opening.

4 Cut the fringing in half and sew around the opening edge of the bootee.

Bedroom Tidy

A BRIGHT AND CHEERFUL HOLDER FOR BEDROOM CLUTTER

YOU WILL NEED ■ *Scissors* ■ *1.5 m (1½ yd) of red cotton fabric,*
90 cm (36 in) wide ■ *Tape measure* ■ *Pins* ■ *Needles and thread* ■ *Iron* ■ *20 cm (8 in)*
yellow cotton fabric, 90 cm (36 in) wide ■ *46 cm (18 in) dowelling* ■ *80 cm (32 in) length of red braid*
■ *Pieces of felt in various colours* ■ *Rubber-based glue*

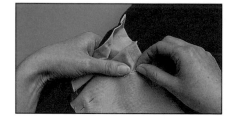

1 Cut a piece of red cotton fabric 1.1 m × 40.5 cm (43 × 16 in). With right sides together, fold in half widthways and pin together. Tack (baste) down each side. Remove the pins and stitch with a 1.5 cm (⅝ in) seam allowance. Trim, turn through the open top seam and press.

Next, cut 2 pieces of red cotton fabric to 39.5 × 18 cm (15½ × 7 in) plus 1 piece of yellow cotton the same size. Turn under 1.5 cm (⅝ in) on 3 edges and fold 1 long length over an extra 1.5 cm (⅝ in). Pin and tack (baste). Remove the pins. Stitch along the long double folded edge.

2 Place the first red pocket at the bottom of the large piece of fabric. Pin in place. Lay the yellow pocket above it, leaving a 5 mm (¼ in) gap between them and pin. Repeat with the next red pocket and pin. Measure 12 cm (4¾ in) in from each side to divide each long pocket into 3, and mark the position with pins along the length. Tack (baste) along all pin lines and remove the pins. Sew and remove tacking (basting).

3 Make a casing at the top of the bedroom tidy by turning down a hem 2 cm (¾ in) wide. Pin, tack (baste) and sew. Slip the piece of dowelling through the casing. Tie one end of the braid to each end of the dowelling.

4 Cut out coloured motifs from the felt. Glue into place, one on each pocket, and leave to dry.

THE NURSERY

*Every child loves a well-equipped
nursery: fill it with pretty furniture, helpful accessories,
and delightful toys and mobiles*

Patchwork Quilt

ESSENTIAL FOR THE NURSERY, THIS TRADITIONAL QUILT IS SIMPLE TO MAKE

YOU WILL NEED ■ *Tape measure* ■ *Pencil* ■ *Graph paper* ■ *Ruler* ■ *Scissors*
■ *Traditional cotton fabrics in 8 different patterns* ■ *Pins* ■ *Needle and thread* ■ *Iron* ■ *Darker*
cotton fabric ■ *Wadding (batting)* ■ *Patterned cotton for quilt back*

1 Measure the cot (crib) to find the overall quilt size required, and then draw up a simple plan on graph paper showing the finished border widths and square sizes. The design shown here uses 28 squares in all.

Start the centre patchwork squares by cutting 8 strips using the 8 different patterned cottons. The strip widths should be cut accurately to the width of your squares *plus* 2 × 6 mm (¼ in) seam allowances. Calculate the length in the same way, adding 2 sets of 6 mm (¼ in) seam allowances for *each square*. Arrange 2 sets of 4 strips keeping adjoining tones varied, and pin, tack (baste) and stitch 1 set of 4 together, following your seam allowance as accurately as possible. Secure all loose threads and press the seams open at the back. Repeat the same procedure to make up the second set of 4 strips.

Next, cut across the strips to make strips of squares. Remember when you cut that you will need to include the seam allowances for each square. You will need 4 strips from 1 set and 3 strips from the other to make a total of 28 squares for the quilt.

2 Arrange the strips side by side taking 1 from each set and reversing the direction each time so that the patterns are varied and no adjoining squares are the same. Pin, tack (baste) and stitch and secure all loose threads. Press all seams open at the back.

Make up the long border strips, using contrasting triangles at the corners to make squares and sewing the squares to the long border ends. Pin, tack (baste) and stitch the short border ends to the squared section and press, and then join the long borders to the quilt edges. Press firmly on the back and front.

3 Cut the wadding (batting) and a piece of fabric for the quilt back to the overall quilt size plus seam allowances. Place the patchwork onto the wadding (batting), right side up. Position the quilt back on top of both layers, right side down. Smooth the layers outwards from the centre and pin and tack (baste) all 3 layers together.

Stitch all round, rounding off the corners and leaving an open length on one edge for turning. Trim the corners and turn the quilt to the outside. Press firmly with a medium iron. Oversew the edge to close. Topstitch the quilt about 1.5 cm (⅝ in) all round the edge.

Patchwork Curtains

A SIMPLE WAY TO CO-ORDINATE NURSERY FURNISHINGS

YOU WILL NEED ■ *Ready-made curtain or a curtain you are making yourself*
■ *Tape measure* ■ *Pencil* ■ *Paper* ■ *Scissors* ■ *Assorted fabrics to match or co-ordinate with the curtain* ■ *Iron-on interfacing (optional)* ■ *Iron* ■ *Needle and thread* ■ *Pins*

1 This design can be adapted to fit across any curtain as the strip is sewn or appliquéd onto it. On a home-made curtain, do the decorative work before making it up. On a bought curtain, unpick the hem and enough of the lining at the side to allow you to sew the appliquéd strip to the front.

2 Calculate the sizes and number of squares and strips you will need, remembering to add in seam allowances. Using the template as a guide, cut out paper patterns for the flower shapes and cut out all the elements for your work using iron-on interfacing on any flowers cut out in delicate or easily frayed fabric. Join the dividers and light squares first to make the basic strip, with right sides together. Press all the seams open.

3 Appliqué the flower shapes onto the dark squares then tack (baste) the dark squares onto alternate light squares and appliqué them in place. Finish by appliquéing the remaining flower shapes onto the remaining light squares. Turn under the raw edges of the completed strip and tack (baste), then use a decorative stitch to stitch the hem down.

4 Take the completed strip and pin and tack (baste) it to the front of your curtain. Sew it to the front either by hemming or using a decorative stitch. Press firmly. Re-sew any unpicked work on an existing curtain, or continue making up your own new curtain.

Batik Quilt

YOU WILL NEED ■ *1.5 m × 60 cm (60 × 24 in) white cotton fabric*
■ *Scissors* ■ *Drawing pins (thumb tacks)* ■ *Wooden frame* ■ *Soft pencil* ■ *Wax pot or bain-marie* ■ *Wax granules/block* ■ *Wax brush* ■ *Blue, yellow, red and green cold water dyes*
■ *Paintbrushes* ■ *Newspaper or plain paper* ■ *Iron* ■ *Medium-weight wadding (batting)*
■ *Pins* ■ *Needle and thread* ■ *Fabric edging*

1 Cut the cotton fabric in 2 and pin half onto the frame, making sure that it is evenly stretched. Using the template as a guide, draw the fish design and border onto the material using a soft pencil.

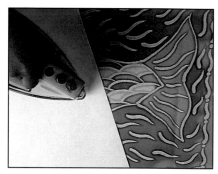

2 Heat the wax, following the manufacturer's instructions if using a wax pot. If heating wax in a bain-marie, check that it is sufficiently hot by testing it on a spare piece of fabric. The wax should soak into the fabric. If the wax seems to lie on the surface, it is not yet hot enough. Paint the wax onto all the areas of the design which are to remain white.

Make up the dyes following the manufacturer's instructions. Paint the dye onto the fabric beginning with the blue border area and using a medium brush. Use a smaller brush to paint the colours of the fish. Some 'bleeding' may occur between colours. Do not worry, as this can add to the attractiveness of the design. Allow to dry naturally.

3 Remove the fabric from the frame. Put some newspaper or plain paper on an ironing board, place the fabric on the paper and place another sheet of paper on top. Iron the fabric with a very hot iron, pressing evenly throughout. The paper will absorb and remove most of the wax. Hand-wash the batiked cloth in lukewarm soapy water to remove any excess dye. Dry clean to remove every trace of wax from the fabric.

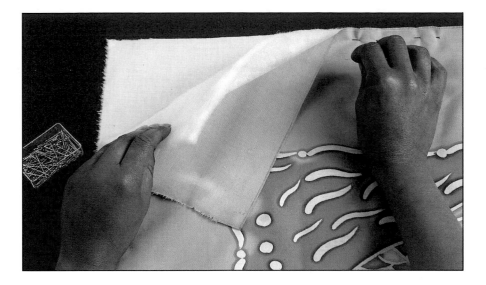

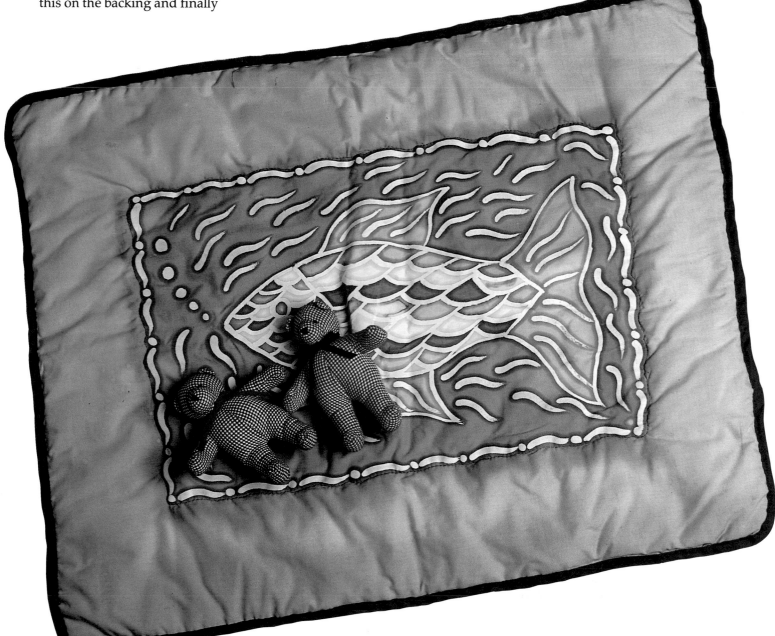

5 Pin around the border design in the centre and tack (baste) again. Pin the edging fabric around the border of the quilt, tack (baste) and sew. Stitch around the centre border design to create the quilted effect.

4 Place the unpainted piece of white fabric onto a clean, even surface. Cut a piece of wadding (batting) to size, position this on the backing and finally place the cover design on top. Carefully pin all the layers together and then tack (baste).

Mosaic Mirror

THIS MOSAIC IDEA IS A MUST FOR A BABY'S BATHROOM

YOU WILL NEED ■ *Saw* ■ *Piece of square plywood 10 mm (3/6 in) thick* ■ *Hand drill* ■ *Picture hanger* ■ *Mirror tile* ■ *Spreader* ■ *Self-adhesive grout* ■ *Mosaic tile strips* ■ *Soft cloth*

1 Use a saw to cut out a square of plywood about 20 × 20 cm (8 × 8 in), or ask your wood dealer for a piece already cut to that size. Drill 2 small holes, slightly higher than the centre, and attach the picture hanger.

2 Place the mirror tile in the centre of the piece of wood to hide the underside of the picture hanger. Secure the mirror tile by its own self-adhesive tabs. With the toothed end of the spreader, spread a 3 mm (⅛ in) layer of self-adhesive grout around the mirror tile. Place cut strips of gummed mosaic tiles onto the grout with the gummed paper showing at the top.

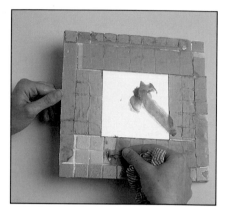

3 Allow the self-adhesive grout to dry thoroughly or as recommended by the manufacturer's instructions. Wet the gummed paper with a damp cloth until it is easy to peel off. Remove all the gummed paper to reveal the mosaic tiles beneath.

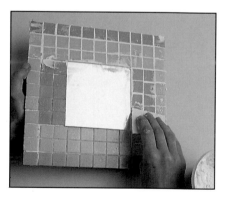

4 Using the smooth end of the spreader, smooth the self-adhesive grout over the tiles and round the edges of the mirror, filling in all the gaps. While the grout is still wet, clean off the excess with a damp cloth until the tiles are clean. You may have to repeat the grouting process when it is dry, as gaps may reappear between the tiles.

Marine Chest of Drawers

TRANSFORM AN OLD CHEST OF DRAWERS WITH SIMPLE SPONGE EFFECTS

YOU WILL NEED ■ *Chest of drawers* ■ *Sandpaper* ■ *Soft cloth* ■ *Matt white emulsion*
(flat latex) paint ■ *Paintbrushes* ■ *Matt peach emulsion (flat latex) paint* ■ *Matt turquoise emulsion*
(flat latex) paint ■ *Scissors* ■ *Sponge scourers* ■ *Dishes* ■ *Non-toxic clear acrylic varnish*

1 Prepare a piece of furniture by sanding it to smooth the surface. Then rub it down with a damp cloth to remove any dirt and dust. Next paint on a coat of white emulsion (flat latex) paint to seal the wood. When this is dry apply 2 coats of peach emulsion (flat latex) paint. Mix a little white with the peach emulsion (flat latex) paint to make the pale peach used on the drawers.

2 While the paint is drying, and using the templates as a guide, cut out the fish and starfish from sponge scourers.

3 Pour some white and turquoise emulsion (flat latex) paint into two dishes. Dip the fish-shaped sponge into the white paint, taking care not to overload it, and lightly sponge on to the piece of furniture. When the white paint is dry, repeat the process with the turquoise emulsion (flat latex) paint and the starfish shape until the design is completed.

4 Finally, when the paint is dry, to protect the piece of furniture varnish it all over with 2 coats of acrylic varnish.

Tie-dye **S**heet

BRIGHTEN UP BEDTIME WITH THIS EYE-CATCHING SHEET

YOU WILL NEED ■ *100 per cent cotton cot (crib) sheet* ■ *String* ■ *Scissors* ■ *Pink and yellow dyes*
■ *2 buckets* ■ *Rubber gloves* ■ *Iron*

1 Lay the sheet onto a flat surface and fold in half and then into quarters. Fold the sheet up, about 2.5 cm (1 in) at a time, like a concertina, alternately once over, once under, until the whole sheet is folded.

2 Tie string tightly at each end and once in the middle to hold the sheet together. Then in a spiral motion firmly wrap the string all the way down to the end and back again. Fasten in a knot and cut the string.

3 Prepare the dyes in separate buckets, following the manufacturer's instructions, and wearing rubber gloves, immerse the sheet first in the pink dye and then in the yellow.

4 Take the sheet out of the dye and rinse under cold water until the dye stops running. Cut the string and open out the sheet. Wash carefully by hand and iron before use. Further dye may come out of the sheet during subsequent laundering, so wash the sheet either by hand, or separately in a warm machine wash.

Laundry Basket

THIS SPRING-FRESH LAUNDRY BASKET IS PERFECT FOR THE NURSERY

YOU WILL NEED ■ *Matt white emulsion (flat latex) paint* ■ *Paintbrushes*
■ *Wicker laundry basket* ■ *Blue and red acrylic paints* ■ *Dishes*

1 Paint the wicker laundry basket with 2 or 3 coats of matt white emulsion (flat latex) paint. Make sure that all the cracks and holes are well covered.

2 Leave until completely dry. Mix on separate dishes a little of the blue and red acrylic paints with white emulsion to make the colours paler. Paint the pale blue and pink onto any details showing on the wicker basket such as the handle on the lid. Remember to make sure that the paints are completely dry before using the basket!

Egg Cosies

KEEP THE BREAKFAST EGGS HOT WITH THESE FUN EGG COSIES

YOU WILL NEED ■ *Scissors* ■ *Plain paper* ■ *Marker pen*
■ *Assorted pieces of coloured felt* ■ *Contrasting coloured felt for the hearts, spots and spikes*
■ *Needle and embroidery thread* ■ *3 flower-shaped sequins* ■ *Thread*

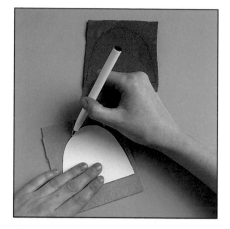

1 Cut out an egg cosy shape from plain paper. Use it as a template and cut 2 shapes from the felt for each cosy.

2 Cut out the hearts, spots and spikes, and then sew the felt spots and sequins neatly onto one of the felt shapes using embroidery thread.

3 Fasten the cut-out hearts onto the other piece with small stitches.

4 Position one edge of each felt spike in between the two sides of the egg cosy and sew the 3 layers together. Turn inside out. If the cosy should become dirty in use, it can be washed in lukewarm water and allowed to dry naturally, but this should be done as infrequently as possible.

Two-height Chair

THIS VERSATILE CHAIR CAN BE USED EITHER WAY UP

YOU WILL NEED ■ *Ruler* ■ *Pencil* ■ *Tracing paper* ■ *Masking tape* ■ *2 pieces of 30 × 30 cm (12 × 12 in) plywood, 8 mm (⁵/₁₆ in) thick* ■ *Clamps* ■ *Hand drill* ■ *Fretsaw (scroll saw)* ■ *Coarse and fine sandpaper* ■ *2 plywood side pieces, each 30 × 30 cm (12 × 12 in), 8 mm (⁵/₁₆ in) thick* ■ *1 plywood seat piece, 30 × 32 cm (12 × 12½ in), 8 mm (⁵/₁₆ in) thick* ■ *2 plywood back pieces, 18 × 32 cm (7 × 12½ in) and 12.5 × 32 cm (5 × 12½ in), both 8 mm (⁵/₁₆ in) thick* ■ *Craft knife* ■ *2 softwood battens, 30 × 4 cm (12 × 1½ in), 2.5 cm (1 in) thick* ■ *4 × 5 cm (2 in) brass screws and cups* ■ *Screwdriver* ■ *Non-toxic clear acrylic varnish* ■ *Paintbrush*

1 Scale up the template onto tracing paper. Attach the paper with masking tape to one of the square pieces of plywood and transfer the design.

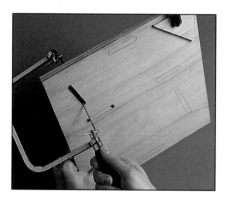

2 Clamp both side pieces together. Drill out the ends of the slots with an 8 mm (⁵/₁₆ in) drill bit and cut out the surplus with a fretsaw (scroll saw). Smooth the edges with sandpaper.

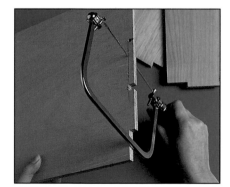

3 In turn, place the seat and the 2 back pieces in position on the slotted sides and mark off the position of the tongues to fit the slots. The tongues should be 1 cm (³/₈ in) deep. Cut away the excess wood. Use a craft knife to round the ends of the tongues so that they fit the slots exactly.

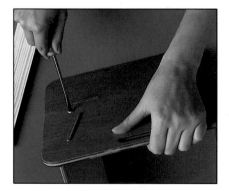

4 To complete the chair, assemble the seat and 2 back pieces and then position the 2 softwood battens beneath the front edges of the seat at both heights. Drill the screw through the ends, protecting the screw heads with the screw cups. Finish with 2 coats of varnish.

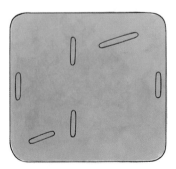

Stencilled Toy Box

THIS JOLLY JUGGLER MOTIF WILL BRIGHTEN UP A PLAIN WOODEN TOY BOX

YOU WILL NEED ■ *Pencil* ■ *White paper* ■ *Masking tape* ■ *Sheets of acetate*
■ *Marker pen* ■ *Cutting board* ■ *Craft knife* ■ *Toy box* ■ *Stencil brush* ■ *Non-toxic acrylic paints*
■ *Non-toxic clear acrylic varnish* ■ *Paintbrush*

1 Scale up the stencil design from the template onto plain white paper and include 4 position marks. Tape down the acetate onto the drawing and, using the permanent marker pen, draw in the position marks and the outlines of the areas to be stencilled with the first colour.

Take off the acetate and, using a cutting board, cut out the first area of colour with a craft knife. Repeat this process, using a new sheet of acetate for each separate colour, including a sheet for all the juggling balls. Remember to include the position marks.

2 Tape the first colour onto the toy box and mark the position marks onto the box making sure that the final stencil will be correctly positioned.

3 Using the stencil brush, apply the first colour. Repeat with each separate piece of acetate, being careful to line up the position marks accurately each time, until you have finished all the colours. Do each juggling ball as you go along. When the paint is completely dry, seal with a coat of non-toxic varnish.

Family of Bears

THESE STURDY BEARS MAKE GOOD DECORATIVE TOYS

YOU WILL NEED ■ *White paper* ■ *Pencil* ■ *Scissors* ■ *40 cm × 20 cm*
(16 × 8 in) piece of wood, 2 cm (¾ in) thick ■ *Fretsaw (scroll saw)* ■ *Matt white emulsion (flat latex)*
paint ■ *Paintbrushes* ■ *Non-toxic acrylic paints* ■ *Non-toxic clear acrylic varnish*

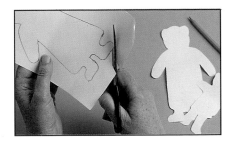

1 Transfer the templates onto white paper and cut them out. Draw around them onto the wood then cut out the bear shapes with a fretsaw (scroll saw).

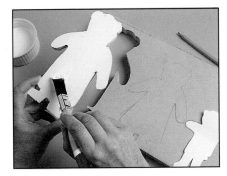

2 Paint the bears with 2 coats of matt white emulsion (flat latex) paint and allow to dry.

3 Paint the bears with bright colours, adding details such as buttons to make the clothes more lifelike. Finish with 2 coats of clear varnish.

Butterfly and Daisy Lampshade

YOU WILL NEED ■ *Paper- or fabric-covered lampshade with wire support rings* ■ *Pressed daisy flowers* ■ *Tweezers* ■ *Rubber-based glue* ■ *Toothpick* ■ *Scissors* ■ *Paper butterflies* ■ *Iron-on protective laminating film* ■ *Soft cloth* ■ *Heat resistant foam* ■ *Iron* ■ *Strong clear glue*

2 Still using the tweezers, turn each one over and press lightly into position.

4 Laminate the finished design with the iron-on protective laminating film. To do this, cut a piece of film to cover the shade generously, and peel back the first 10 cm (4 in) of the backing paper. Overlap one end by 12 mm (½ in), and gently smooth down the film, peeling off the back paper as you unroll. Make sure that no air bubbles are formed. Use a soft cloth to rub down the film evenly as you work.

1 Carefully peel apart the seam of the lampshade covering and remove from the metal rings. Lay it out and leave under a weight to flatten. Starting at the edges, hold each flower using the tweezers and apply a dot of rubber-based glue to the centre back of each one with a toothpick.

3 Carefully cut out the paper butterflies and stick several of these among the daisies.

5 Cover with a sheet of heat resistant foam, and fix down the protective film by pressing down in sections with an iron at wool heat setting. Trim any excess film, but leave the 12 mm (½ in) overlap at one end, and turn the covering over. Apply a thin line of strong clear glue to the bottom and top edges of the inside of the covering, and glue to the wire rings. Seal the 12 mm (½ in) overlap to finish.

Three Little Pigs

SMALL CHILDREN WILL BE CAPTIVATED BY THIS TRIO OF SALT-DOUGH PIGS

YOU WILL NEED ■ *For the dough: 225 g/8 oz/2 cups plain (all-purpose) flour;
225 g/8 oz/2 cups salt; 1 tbsp wallpaper paste; 1 tbsp cooking oil; water to mix* ■ *Polythene
bag* ■ *Coloured paper clips* ■ *Scissors* ■ *Table knife* ■ *Bamboo skewer* ■ *Rolling pin* ■ *Palette knife (spatula)*
■ *Garlic press* ■ *Non-toxic acrylic paints* ■ *Paintbrushes* ■ *Non-toxic clear acrylic varnish*

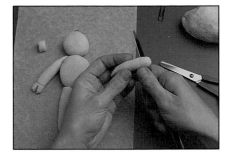

1 Mix all the salt dough
ingredients together with a
little water to make a stiff mixture.
Knead well and leave in a
polythene bag to rest, overnight if
possible. Make the head and body
from balls of dough and press a
paper clip into the head as a
hanger. Roll sausage shapes and
cut into lengths for the snout,
arms and legs. Snip the ends of
the arms and legs to make the
trotters and mark the 'ankles'
with a knife.

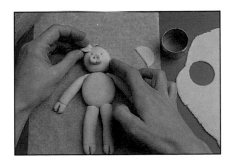

2 Make creases on the snout
and stick in position with
water. Use the skewer to make
holes for the eyes and nostrils.
Thinly roll out the remainder of
the dough. Make ears from semi-
circles and stick in position with
water. A palette knife (spatula)
will help to pick up the shapes.

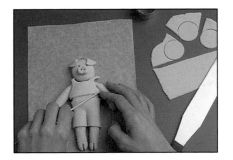

3 Cut out a wide vest shape
and trousers and position
over the the front of the pig,
turning the edges under.

4 Squeeze some dough
through a garlic press for
the bundle of sticks and add the
remaining details such as buttons
and belt. The outfits for the other 2
pigs can be made in the same way.

5 Bake on baking parchment
for 4–8 hours in a very low
oven before painting with acrylic
paints. When dry apply 2 coats of
clear varnish.

Tissue Box Cover

YOU WILL NEED ■ *Scissors* ■ *0.5 m (20 in) pretty cotton fabric*
■ *Tape measure* ■ *Medium-weight wadding (batting)* ■ *Pink bias binding* ■ *Needle and thread*
■ *Pins* ■ *1 m (40 in) pink ribbon, 1 cm (³⁄₈ in) wide* ■ *1 m (40 in) pink ric-rac braid*

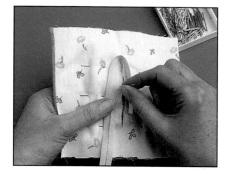

1 Cut out 2 pieces of fabric, one 15 × 15 cm (6 × 6 in) and the other 16 × 46 cm (6¼ × 18¼ in). Cut 2 pieces of wadding (batting) to the same size as each piece. Pin together the squares of fabric and wadding (batting). Cut through the centre of both layers to make a 7 cm (2¾ in) opening. Lay a small piece of bias binding along the cut edge. Stitch along the fold line around the opening. Trim off any excess and fold through to the wrong side. Slip stitch into place.

2 Lay the remaining piece of fabric on top of the wadding (batting) and pin together. Sew the ribbon along the centre line, catching the wadding (batting) at the same time. Pin a length of ric-rac braid on each side and sew into place. Remove the pins.

3 With right sides together, sew the material down the side seam with a 1.5 cm (⁵⁄₈ in) seam allowance. Trim. Carefully pin the sides to the top and tack (baste). Remove pins and stitch together. Trim the seams and clip the corners. Turn through. Hem the bottom. Make two small bows with the remaining ribbon and sew at the top opening.

Scented Coat Hanger

THIS HANGER WILL LEND ITS SUBTLE FRAGRANCE TO A SPECIAL OUTFIT

YOU WILL NEED ■ *30 cm (12 in) wooden coat hanger* ■ *2.5 × 60 cm (1 × 24 in) strip of fabric, cut on the bias* ■ *Needle and thread* ■ *1 m × 10 cm (40 × 4 in) strip of non-toxic, flame retardant polyester filling (batting)* ■ *56 × 18 cm (22 × 7 in) fabric for hanger* ■ *Scissors* ■ *Iron* ■ *Tape measure* ■ *Pins* ■ *12.5 × 18 cm (5 × 7 in) fabric for bow* ■ *Pot pourri*

1 Fold the long strip of fabric in half lengthwise, fold the end over the top of the hook and sew to secure. Bind the fabric to cover the hook, then wrap around the hanger and knot.

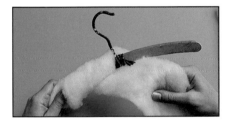

2 Sew the filling (batting) to one end of the hanger and wrap it loosely around the wood. Sew at the other end.

3 Fold the larger piece of fabric in half lengthwise and trim to round the ends. Press in a 1.5 cm (⅝ in) seam and cut small notches at the rounded ends. Sew a gather stitch along the central

fold line then pull the thread to ruche up the fabric until the centre fold measures 36 cm (14 in).

4 Mark the centre, then fold the fabric around the hanger to meet at the top. Pin on either side of the hook. Using a double thread and starting at one end, join the open edges over the hanger with a running stitch to the centre. Pull the thread to adjust the gathers. Fasten off then repeat with other side.

5 Fold the fabric for the bow in half, right sides together, and stitch along the long edge and down one side. Turn right side out and trim 2.5 cm (1 in) from the open end. Lightly fill with pot pourri and slip stitch the open end together. Shake to distribute the pot pourri down the bow. Gather the centre and fold over the trimmed fabric. Slip stitch to secure. Sew the bow neatly to the hanger at the base of the hook to add the final touch.

Découpage Clock

MAKE LEARNING TO TELL THE TIME MORE FUN WITH THIS DECORATED CLOCK

YOU WILL NEED ■ Hand drill ■ Circular piece of thin plywood ■ Clock mechanism and battery ■ Matt blue emulsion (flat latex) paint ■ Paintbrush ■ Rubber-based glue ■ Clock face and hands ■ Scissors ■ Victorian scraps or pictures cut from old magazines ■ Non-toxic acrylic varnish

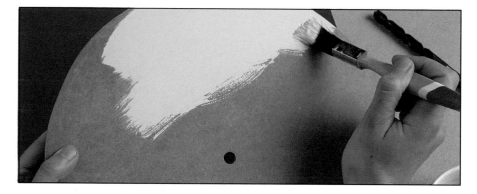

1 Drill a hole in the exact centre of the plywood circle to the same diameter as the clock mechanism. Paint the wood with an even coat of light blue emulsion (flat latex) paint.

2 Glue down the clock face so that the hole in the centre is in line with the hole in the piece of plywood. Next cut out all the Victorian pictures and arrange them around the clock face until you are happy with the design. Stick them in place with glue and wipe off any excess.

3 Leave the glue to dry for at least 2 hours; then attach the clock mechanism to the back and put the clock hands in place on the front. Paint on a protective coating or two of acrylic varnish and leave to dry. Finally, place a battery in the back of the clock and set to the correct time.

Bird on a Stick

THIS BIRD MAKES AN ATTRACTIVE ORNAMENT FOR THE NURSERY

YOU WILL NEED ■ *White paper* ■ *Pencil* ■ *Piece of plywood,*
10 mm (3/8 in) thick ■ *Fretsaw (scroll saw)* ■ *Piece of thicker plywood* ■ *Ruler*
■ *Sandpaper* ■ *Drill* ■ *Wood glue* ■ *15 cm (6 in) length of dowelling* ■ *Paintbrushes*
■ *Non-toxic acrylic paints* ■ *Non-toxic clear acrylic varnish*

1 Scale up the template and transfer onto a piece of white paper, then transfer the outline onto a piece of thin plywood. Cut out the bird shape with a fretsaw (scroll saw). Cut out a square for the base from the thicker piece of plywood. Draw from corner to corner on the square base piece to find the centre. Sand the edges until they are smooth.

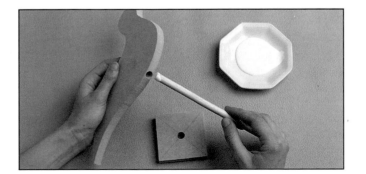

2 Drill a hole to the same diameter as your dowelling through the centre of the base. Drill a hole into the bottom of the bird shape, about 2 cm (3/4 in) deep. Paint a little wood glue onto both ends of dowelling and glue the 3 pieces together, the bird at one end and the base at the other.

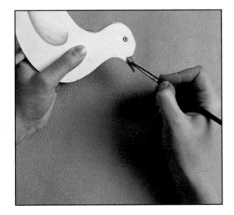

3 With a small paintbrush, paint the dowelling and base sky blue, and add the bird's features. Finish off the piece with a protective coat of acrylic varnish.

Kite Box

YOU WILL NEED ■ *Hat box* ■ *Large paintbrush* ■ *Matt emulsion (flat latex) paint*
■ *Yellow paper* ■ *Non-toxic acrylic paints* ■ *Small paintbrush* ■ *Pencil* ■ *Ruler* ■ *Scissors*
■ *Paper glue* ■ *Natural sponge* ■ *Non-toxic clear acrylic varnish*

1 Paint the box with the matt emulsion (flat latex) paint and, while this is drying, paint some yellow paper with red paint allowing streaks of background colour to come through giving an orange glow.

2 Using the templates as a guide, draw equal numbers of triangular and ribbon shapes onto the orange paper and the yellow paper. Cut out all the shapes and glue onto the box to make the kite pattern.

3 Using white paint, carefully sponge on the cloud shapes with a natural sponge, making sure as you work that the sponge is not overloaded with paint.

4 Paint in a fine dark line between the ribbons to make the kite string. Allow everything to dry, and finish with a protective coat of clear varnish.

Ribbon Box

THE PERFECT BOX FOR ALL THOSE DISAPPEARING LITTLE SOCKS

YOU WILL NEED ■ *Hat box* ■ *Yellow matt emulsion (flat latex) paint* ■ *Paintbrushes* ■ *Chalk*
■ *Non-toxic acrylic paints* ■ *Non-toxic clear acrylic varnish*

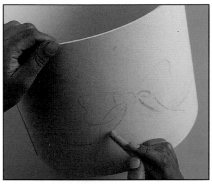

1 Paint the box with yellow matt emulsion (flat latex) and leave to dry. Chalk in the outline of the ribbon pattern.

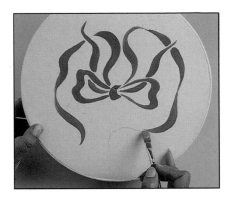

2 Using a small brush, follow the line of chalk with a dark coloured paint.

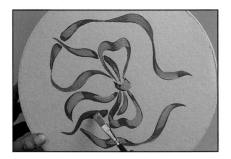

3 Allow to dry, then paint in the highlights of the ribbons with a lighter hue of the same colour. Leave to dry.

4 Finally, paint on a protective coat of clear acrylic varnish.

Beaker Mat

THIS WIPE-CLEAN MAT CAN BE USED ON A HIGH CHAIR

YOU WILL NEED ■ *Pencil* ■ *Scissors* ■ *Paper* ■ *Ruler* ■ *Pinking shears* ■ *10 × 10 cm (4 × 4 in)*
felt ■ *Clear PVC (vinyl) plastic* ■ *Oddments of felt* ■ *Rubber-based glue* ■ *Needle and thread*

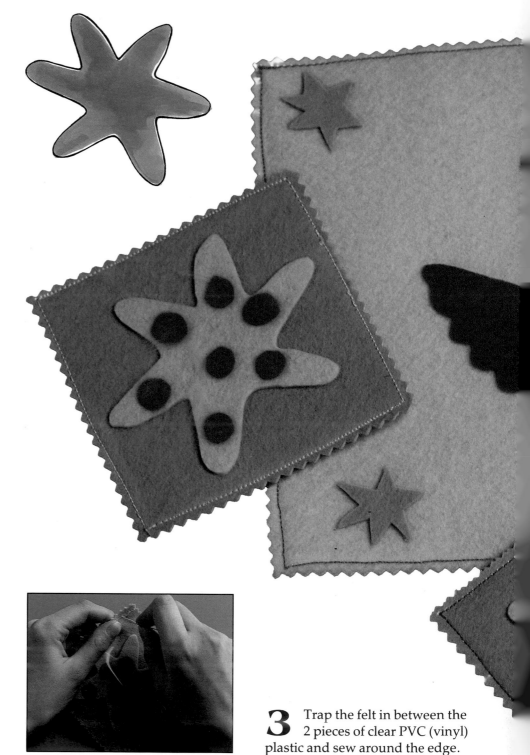

1 Using the template as a guide, draw and cut out a starfish shape from white paper. Draw around the templates onto the materials and cut out 1 square in felt and 2 in PVC (vinyl) plastic using pinking shears, and cut 1 starfish in felt using scissors. Cut out some felt spots.

2 Glue the starfish onto the felt mat and then glue the felt spots onto its body. Press the spots down firmly to secure, as these small shapes can fall off during use if they are not well attached at the start.

3 Trap the felt in between the 2 pieces of clear PVC (vinyl) plastic and sew around the edge.

Place Mat

THIS PRACTICAL MAT WILL MAKE MEALTIMES SIMPLE

YOU WILL NEED ■ *Pencil* ■ *Paper* ■ *Scissors* ■ *Oddments of felt*
■ *Rubber-based glue* ■ *Large sequin* ■ *26 × 20 cm (10¼ × 8 in) felt* ■ *2 pieces of 26 × 20 cm*
(10¼ × 8 in) clear PVC (vinyl) plastic ■ *Pinking shears* ■ *Needle and thread*

1 Using the templates as a guide, cut out the fish shapes in felt, and then cut out the spots and stars in contrasting colours. Assemble the fish using rubber-based glue, and add the large sequin for the eye.

2 Cut out the mat pieces using pinking shears and glue the fish and stars onto the felt piece.

3 Trap the felt between 2 pieces of clear PVC (vinyl) plastic and sew around the edge through all 3 layers.

Pretty Screen

THIS PRETTY SCREEN IS INVALUABLE FOR CONCEALING UNTIDY CORNERS

YOU WILL NEED ■ *Screen (you can pick one up second-hand)* ■ *Sandpaper* ■ *Paintbrushes*
■ *Matt white emulsion (flat latex) paint* ■ *Non-toxic acrylic paints* ■ *Natural sponge* ■ *Scissors*
■ *Wrapping paper with angel motifs* ■ *Rubber-based glue* ■ *Non-toxic clear acrylic varnish*

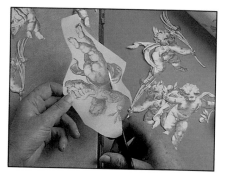

2 Carefully cut out the angels and arrange them on the screen. Stick them into position, wiping away any excess glue.

3 Paint all round the edges of the screen in a dark colour.

1 Smooth down the screen with sandpaper, paint on a coat of matt white emulsion (flat latex) paint and allow to dry. Paint on the base colour, making sure that it is a slightly darker hue than the one to be sponged on top to achieve the two-tone effect. Leave to dry then sponge on the lighter pink with the natural sponge, being careful not to overload it with paint.

4 Finally, paint on a clear protective layer of varnish.

High Chair Mat

THIS PRACTICAL MAT WILL SAVE THE FLOOR FROM UNWANTED SPILLS

YOU WILL NEED ■ *Pinking shears* ■ *100 × 75 cm (40 × 30 in) fabric* ■ *100 × 75 cm (40 × 30 in) coloured PVC (vinyl-coated) fabric* ■ *100 × 75 cm (40 × 30 in) clear PVC (vinyl) plastic* ■ *Scissors* ■ *Oddments of fabric and felt* ■ *Rubber-based glue* ■ *Needle and thread*

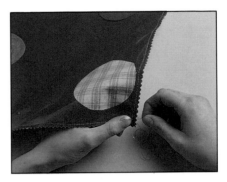

1 Cut out all the fabric pieces, cutting the larger pieces out with pinking shears. Cut fabric for as many spots as you like. Glue the small felt spots onto the larger spots and glue the spots onto the large piece of fabric.

2 Sandwich this fabric between a piece of coloured PVC (vinyl-coated) fabric and clear PVC (vinyl) plastic.

3 Sew all around the edges to attach all 3 layers, either by hand or using a machine set on a fairly loose tension.

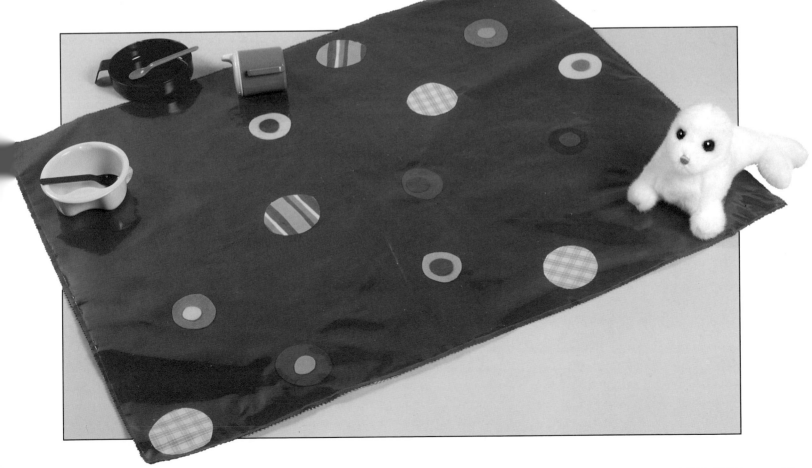

Nursery Frieze

MAKE THIS POTATO PRINT FRIEZE AS LONG AS YOU LIKE TO COVER THE WALLS

YOU WILL NEED ■ *Wallpaper lining paper* ■ *Large paintbrush*
■ *Non-toxic acrylic paints* ■ *Kitchen knife* ■ *Large potatoes*

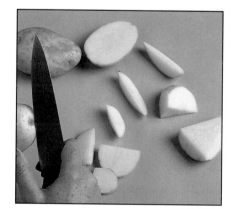

1 Lay out the lining paper and lightly paint in rows of wavy lines in 2 different shades of blue to represent the waves.

2 Using a knife, cut from the potatoes 3 slightly different triangular sail shapes and the 3 hulls for the boats, one for each different colour.

3 Dip the potato shapes into coloured paint and print firmly onto the surface of the paper, positioning them at slightly different angles and spacing them evenly. Leave to dry.

Painted Chair

DECORATE A PLAIN NURSERY CHAIR WITH THIS WOODLAND DESIGN

YOU WILL NEED ■ *Nursery chair* ■ *Sandpaper* ■ *Chalk* ■ *Non-toxic acrylic paints*
■ *Small paintbrush* ■ *Medium paintbrush* ■ *Non-toxic clear acrylic varnish*

1 Lightly rub down the chair with sandpaper. Chalk in the outlines of your design.

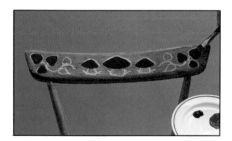

2 Paint in all the base colours with a small paintbrush, red for the strawberries and toadstools, and green for the leaves. Allow the paint to dry.

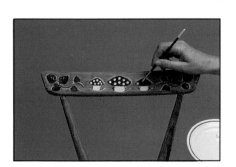

3 Add final details such as the white spots and stalks on the toadstools and the brown flecks on the strawberries.

4 Finally seal the whole chair with a coat of varnish.

Hobby Horse

THIS TRADITIONAL HORSE MAKES A FRIENDLY TOY FOR AN OLDER CHILD

YOU WILL NEED ■ *Pencil* ■ *Paper* ■ *Scissors* ■ *Corduroy or strong cotton fabric*
■ *Patterned cotton fabric* ■ *Pins* ■ *Needle and strong thread* ■ *Iron* ■ *Card* ■ *Tape measure*
■ *Yarn* ■ *Non-toxic, flame retardant polyester filling (batting)* ■ *Safety eyes with moving centres*
■ *Embroidery thread* ■ *Plain fabric for reins and bridle* ■ *2 toy quality wooden rings*
■ *Sandpaper* ■ *Wooden broom-handle* ■ *Fretsaw (scroll saw)* ■ *2 toy bells*

1 Use the template as a guide and draw the head and ear pieces onto white paper and cut them out. Cut 2 shapes for the outer ears from the corduroy and 2 inner ears from the cotton fabric. Pin the right sides of each inner and outer ear piece together and tack (baste) then stitch them, leaving the bottom ends open. Turn out to the right side and press firmly.

Cut a strip of card about 9 cm (3½ in) wide and wind the yarn round it, cutting through the yarn at one side to form 18 cm (7 in) lengths for the mane.

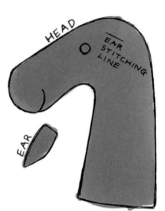

2 Cut out the 2 head pieces from the corduroy or strong cotton fabric. Leaving the neck end open, pin and tack (baste) them, right sides together, around the front of the head and stop short just past the eye position. Enclose the centre of each strand of yarn into the seam as you tack (baste) down the back of the neck.

The mane must stop about 8 cm (3¼ in) short of the neck bottom. Do this firmly, strand by strand, so that it cannot be pulled out. Small children can be surprisingly forceful with their toys, so it is important to ensure that all the components are as securely attached as possible. Sew around the edges and remove the tacking (basting) threads. Stuff the 2 ears firmly with polyester filling (batting), and stitch the bottom ends to close.

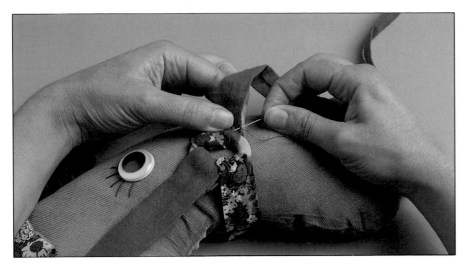

3 Clip the seam at the sharp inner neck curve and turn the head to the right side. Mark the positions for the eyes and attach them according to the manufacturer's instructions. Embroider the eyelashes. Sew a 1 cm (⅜ in) hem around the neck base. Attach the ears to the side of the head by stitching them firmly along the ear bottoms.

4 Stuff the head firmly at the top and down the neck but leave the bottom end of the neck loosely filled. Stitch the top backs of the ears to the head near the top so that they cannot flop. Make hemmed lengths of patterned and plain fabric for the bridle and reins and attach them securely using the wooden rings. Embroider the horse's mouth.

5 Sand down the broom-handle to remove any splinters. With a fretsaw (scroll saw), make a groove all round the handle, about 12 cm (4¾ in) from the end. Thread a needle with a long, double, strong cotton thread and wind the thread a few times around the groove. Push the grooved end of the handle into the neck and arrange the filling so the handle sits centrally inside the neck, stuffing it firmly. Ensure that you don't stuff the needle and thread in with it!

6 Gather the neck evenly round with one hand, about 6 cm (2¼ in) from the hem, and sew through to the outside. Wind the thread tightly round the gathers to catch them tightly, then pass the needle back and forth several times from one side of the neck to the other. Secure the thread firmly.

Make a further length of fabric to wind around the gathers of the neck. Make a bow to hide the threads and the stitching and stitch it down so it cannot be pulled off or be undone. Attach the 2 bells securely on either side of the bridle.

USE THIS BAG TO STORE NAPPIES OR DIAPERS

YOU WILL NEED ■ *Scissors* ■ *Tape measure* ■ *Stiff board* ■ *1 m × 115 cm (1¼ yd × 45 in) fabric* ■ *Rubber-based glue* ■ *Pins* ■ *Needle and thread* ■ *2.5 m (2½ yd) ribbon, 6 mm (¼ in) wide* ■ *2.5 m (2½ yd) ribbon, 2.5 cm (1 in) wide*

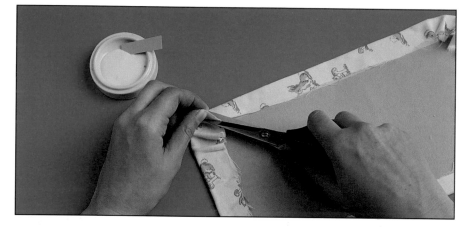

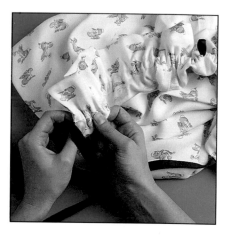

1 Cut out a piece of board 32 × 18 cm (12½ × 7 in) and round the corners. Cut out 2 pieces of fabric 35 × 20 cm (13½ × 8 in). Lay the board on the wrong side of one

piece of fabric then spread glue 2.5 cm (1 in) around the edge of the board. Pull the fabric over the edges and press down. Trim the spare fabric at the corners.

3 Fold the top edge over 7.5 cm (3 in); pin. Stitch close to the edge and again 2 cm (¾ in) above to make a ribbon casing. Cut a slit in the back centre of the basing and buttonhole stitch all the way round. Cut the narrow ribbon in half. Thread one piece through the casing and sew the ends together where they meet at the back. Repeat with the second piece of ribbon, this time joining the ends at the front.

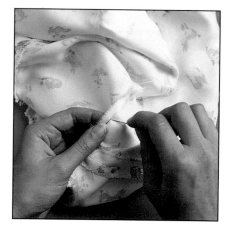

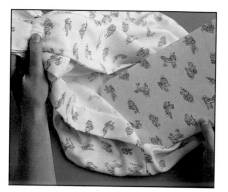

2 Cut a piece of fabric 77 × 115 cm (31 × 45 in) and fold in a 2.5 cm (1 in) seam along each short edge. Join the sides along this fold to a depth of 10 cm (4 in). Now pin this end to the second piece of base material right sides together, and double stitch together allowing a 12 mm (½ in) seam allowance. Trim the seam and turn right side out.

4 Fit the firm base inside the bag, material side up. Pull up the drawstrings and tie the wide ribbon around the top to form a bow.

Nursery Basket

AN ATTRACTIVE CONTAINER FOR A BABY'S TOILETRIES

YOU WILL NEED ■ *Wicker basket with handle* ■ *Tape measure*
■ *Cotton gingham* ■ *Scissors* ■ *Needle and thread* ■ *Elastic* ■ *Pre-gathered lace with ribbon eyelets*
■ *Length of narrow ribbon* ■ *Ribbon for handle* ■ *Sticky tape*

1 Measure the basket from rim to rim, taking the tape measure under the basket, and add on 5 cm (2 in). Using this measurement as the diameter, cut out a circle of gingham. Turn the edge under by 1.5 cm (⅝ in) and tack (baste). To gather the edge, sew the elastic along the hem, hiding the raw edge, stretching it as it is being stitched. Remove the tacking (basting).

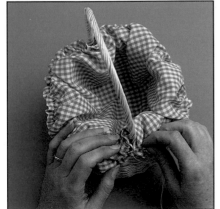

2 Tuck the gingham into the basket and stitch the fabric around each side of the handle to keep it in place.

3 Cut a length of pre-gathered lace to the measurement of the basket rim plus half again. Thread the ribbon through the lace and gather. Position the gathered ribbon around the basket rim to cover the elastic stitching and adjust the gathering to fit. Tie the ribbon securely and knot. Cut off ends. Wind the remaining ribbon around the handle. Secure at each end with sticky tape and tie a bow at each side to cover the tape.

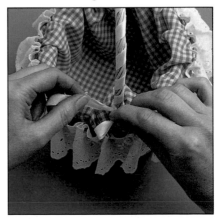

Gift Box

THIS DELIGHTFUL GIFT BOX SHOULD BE KEPT OUT OF THE REACH OF YOUNG CHILDREN

YOU WILL NEED ■ *Length of blue braid, 1.5 cm (⅝ in) wide*
■ *Small wicker box* ■ *Scissors* ■ *Pins* ■ *Needle and thread* ■ *Red yarn* ■ *Tape measure*
■ *Large darning needle* ■ *Strong clear glue* ■ *Blue, red, yellow and green pipe cleaners (2 of each)*
■ *Pencil* ■ *Teddy bear ornament* ■ *Blue shredded paper*

1 Wrap a length of blue braid around the sides of the box. Pin the ends together at the back. Sew in place, attaching the braid to the box at the same time. Measure around the box from front to back, including the inside of the lid down to the base, and cut 2 lengths of blue braid to fit.

Place the braids in position and secure by pinning at each point where they cross. Using the red yarn, sew a cross at each of these positions, pushing the needle through the box and the braid inside the lid. For added strength, use glue to stick the braid on the inside of the box.

2 To make the pipe cleaner curls, wrap each one around a pencil leaving a straight end of 4 cm (1½ in) at one end. Slide out the pencil.

3 Attach the pipe cleaner curls at the centre of the lid of the box, pushing the straight ends right through the lid. Leave a space in the very centre for the teddy bear. Open up the lid and twist the ends together until they are secure. Glue the bear in place and fill the box with the shredded paper, ready for your gift.

Balloons Toy Bag

A USEFUL BAG TO KEEP SMALL TOYS TIDY

YOU WILL NEED ■ Pinking shears ■ 50 × 90 cm (½ yd × 36 in) striped cotton fabric ■ Iron-on double-sided interfacing ■ Oddments of 3 plain coloured fabrics ■ Iron ■ Pair of compasses ■ Pencil ■ Scissors ■ Needle and thread ■ Pins ■ 40 cm (16 in) each of ribbon in 3 colours, 3 mm (⅛ in) wide ■ 2 m (80 in) of ribbon, 1.5 cm (⅝ in) wide ■ Safety pin

1 Cut out two 43 × 34 cm (17 × 13½ in) rectangles of striped fabric with pinking shears. Apply iron-on interfacing to each oddment of plain fabric following the manufacturer's instructions. Use a pair of compasses to draw 6 cm (2½ in) circles on the backing paper. Cut out the 3 balloons.

Peel off the backing paper and arrange the balloons centrally on the right side of 1 of the striped rectangles. Press the balloons to bond them in position. Stitch the balloons to the bag around the circumference.

2 With right sides facing, stitch the rectangles together leaving the upper short edge open and a 2 cm (¾ in) gap 3 cm (1¼ in) below the upper edge on the long sides. Press the seams open. Fold down the upper edge to the wrong side by 3 cm (1¼ in) and pin in place to make a channel for the drawstring. Stitch the channel 2 cm (¾ in) below the folded edge.

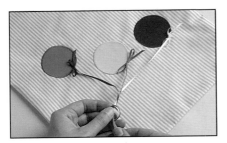

3 Turn the bag right side out. Tie one end of each of the narrow ribbons into a bow. Sew each bow to a balloon. Arrange the ribbons on the bag and knot the extending ends together. Sew the knot to the bag. Cut off the surplus ribbon.

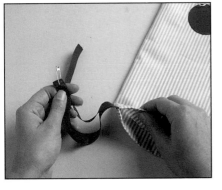

4 Cut the length of wide ribbon in half. Fix a safety pin to the end of one ribbon and thread through an opening in the channel, take all around the channel and bring the pin out through the same hole. Knot the ribbon ends together. Thread the remaining ribbon through the other hole in the same way; knot the ribbon ends together. Pull the ribbons to hide the knots in the channel.

Papier Mâché Bowl

THIS STENCILLED BOWL IS DECORATIVE AND SURPRISINGLY STRONG

YOU WILL NEED ■ *Bowl* ■ *Petroleum jelly* ■ *Newspaper* ■ *Wallpaper paste*
■ *Craft knife* ■ *Matt white emulsion (flat latex) paint* ■ *Paintbrushes* ■ *Gouache paints* ■ *Scissors*
■ *Masking tape* ■ *Stencil paper* ■ *Stencil brush* ■ *Non-toxic clear acrylic varnish*

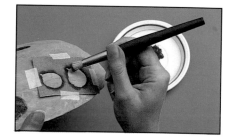

1 Coat the inside of the bowl with a layer of petroleum jelly. Cover this with at least 6 layers of newspaper strips soaked in wallpaper paste. When completely dry, trim the edges with a craft knife. Bind the edges with 2 layers of papier mâché to give a neat finish. Leave to dry out thoroughly.

2 Prime the bowl with 2 coats of white matt emulsion (flat latex) paint. When dry, cover with a wash of blue gouache.

3 Cut out balloon stencils in 2 sizes and hold in place with masking tape. Stencil the design using bright paints and a stencil brush. Paint in the balloon strings. Seal with 2 coats of clear acrylic varnish to finish.

Surprise Play Cube

A RATTLY ROLL-AROUND CUBE WITH A SURPRISE BEHIND THE DOOR

YOU WILL NEED ■ *Assorted fabrics in bright colours, textures and patterns*
■ *Scissors* ■ *Tape measure* ■ *Pencil* ■ *Card* ■ *Iron-on (fusible) interfacing* ■ *Needle*
and thread ■ *Pins* ■ *Wadding (batting)* ■ *Embroidery thread* ■ *Non-toxic, flame retardant polyester*
filling (batting) ■ *Dried peas in a plastic container* ■ *Iron* ■ *Velcro*

1 Cut out sufficient fabric in assorted textures, patterns and colours to make up 6 sides of the cube. Some of the sides can be pieced from a patchwork of 4 smaller squares or from 2 triangles joined diagonally. Each square should be 14 × 14 cm (5½ × 5½ in) to include a 1 cm (⅜ in) seam allowance all round.

2 Make a template for a simple bird shape from a piece of card. Trace around it onto a piece of interfaced cotton and cut it out. Appliqué it to your chosen top 'surprise' square and embroider an eye and feet onto the bird. Join 4 squares edge to edge, right sides together, and join the fourth side to the first to make an open box shape.

3 Arrange the open box with wrong sides outwards. Pin and tack (baste) a fifth square to make the base of the box, sewing the right sides together. Stitch the base, easing gently as you turn the corners to avoid puckers. Still with wrong sides out, sew 3 sides of the top square and just turn the corner on the fourth. Leave the remainder of this side open .

4 To make the 'door', prepare 2 further squares and place them right sides together with a piece of wadding (batting) on the top. Insert a small flat fabric loop into the centre of one edge which should be the centre of the 3 sides you will stitch. Stitch around the 3 sides, turn out and press firmly. Stitch the open edge, which will be the door 'hinge', closed along the seam allowance.

5 Turn the cube right side out and stuff firmly, especially into the corners. A small pea-filled container can be buried in the cube centre to make it rattle. After stuffing the cube oversew the opening securely to close it. Oversew the door to the cube top along the hinge edge. Attach a piece of Velcro to the underside of the flat loop and another to the cube side so it can be fastened.

Nursery Curtains

THESE BRIGHT AND CHEERFUL CURTAINS ARE EASY TO MAKE

YOU WILL NEED ■ *Tape measure* ■ *Fabric for curtains* ■ *Scissors*
■ *32 × 90 cm (12½ × 36 in) contrasting fabric for loops* ■ *Pins* ■ *Needle and thread* ■ *46 × 90 cm*
(18¼ × 36 in) contrasting fabric for spikes ■ *Pinking shears* ■ *Curtain pole*

1 Measure your window and cut 2 pieces of fabric for each curtain to fit, allowing for a 2.5 cm (1 in) seam allowance. Cut 6 pieces 32 × 12 cm (12½ × 4¾ in) for the loops. You will need 3 loops for each curtain. To make the loops, fold over each fabric piece lengthwise, pin and sew along the edge, then turn right side out. Cut 6 large triangles for the spikes. Pin and sew them together in pairs, right sides facing. Trim the edges and turn right side out. You will need 3 spikes for each curtain.

2 Trap the loops and spikes inside each front and back piece of curtain, pin, tack (baste) and sew around the edges leaving a gap to turn inside out. Trim edges with pinking shears, turn right side out and sew up the gap.

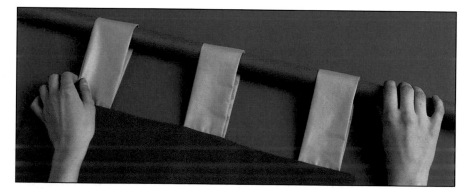

3 Fit the curtains onto the pole before attaching it securely to the wall.

Nursery Pelmet

THIS STRIKING PELMET CO-ORDINATES WELL WITH THE NURSERY CURTAINS

YOU WILL NEED ■ *Tape measure* ■ *Pinking shears* ■ *2 pieces of fabric to match the length and sides of your pelmet board* ■ *Pen* ■ *Paper* ■ *Scissors* ■ *Pins* ■ *Contrasting fabric for the scalloped trim* ■ *Needle and thread* ■ *Velcro* ■ *Large buttons*

1 Measure and cut out 2 fabric pieces to fit the front and sides of the pelmet board. Draw a scallop shape on paper and use it as a template to cut 12 shapes for the 6 scallops. Sew right sides together in pairs leaving the straight side open. Trim and turn right side out.

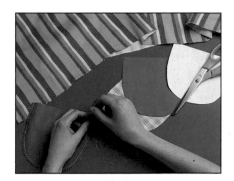

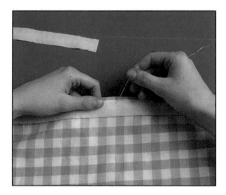

2 Sew a strip of Velcro along the top edge of the back pelmet piece, right side out.

3 Trap the scallop shapes in between the 2 pelmet pieces and sew down both long edges, leaving the ends open to turn right side out.

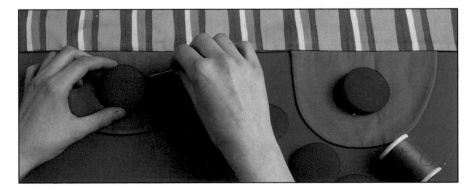

4 Sew the buttons onto the front of the scallop shapes. Sew another strip of Velcro onto the top front edge of the pelmet board and attach the pelmet to the pelmet board.

Seaside Mirror

THIS BEAUTIFUL, RICH-LOOKING MIRROR IS SIMPLE TO MAKE

YOU WILL NEED ■ *Shells* ■ *Rubber-based glue* ■ *Paintbrush* ■ *Mirror with a wooden frame*
■ *Scrap paper* ■ *Masking tape* ■ *Gold spray paint*

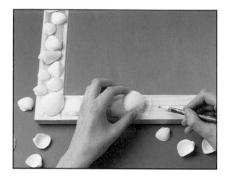
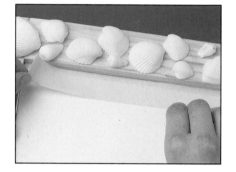

1 Wash the shells and allow to dry completely before using. Glue the shells onto the mirror frame, distributing them evenly.

2 Before painting the shells, protect the mirror glass by covering it up with scrap paper taped down with masking tape.

3 When the glue on the shells is dry, spray the frame with gold paint, working outdoors or in a well-ventilated room.

Tiger Stripes

THIS CRAZY TIGER IS IDEAL FOR A BEGINNER TO KNIT

YOU WILL NEED ■ *Oddments of brightly-coloured double knitting (sport) yarn* ■ *1 pair of 4 mm (US 5) knitting needles* ■ *Scissors* ■ *Darning needle* ■ *Fine black felt-tip pen* ■ *Thin card* ■ *White felt* ■ *Needle and thread* ■ *2 buttons or safety eyes* ■ *Non-toxic, flame retardant polyester filling (batting)*

Tension (Gauge)
This will differ according to the yarn used.

BODY
(*Knit 2 alike*)
Cast on 30 sts. Work in garter stitch (every row knit) throughout, changing yarn frequently for stripes. K 8 rows. Cast (bind) off 9 sts at the beg of the next row, k to end.
Cast (bind) off 7 sts at the beg of the next row, k to end. K 9 rows.
Cast on 7 sts at the beg of the next row, k across these 7 sts and the rest of row (21 sts). K 9 rows.
Cast (bind) off 7 sts at the beg of the next row, k to end (14 sts). K 15 rows.
Cast on 7 sts at the beg of the next row, k across these 7 sts and the rest of row (21 sts).
Cast on 7 sts at the beg of the next row, k across these 7 sts and the rest of row (28 sts). K 5 rows.
Cast (bind) off 4 sts at the beg of the next row, k to end (24 sts). K 2 rows.
Cast (bind) off 7 sts at the beg of the next row, k to end (17 sts). K 6 rows.
Cast on 4 sts at the beg of the next row, k across these 4 sts and the rest of row (21 sts).
Cast on 7 sts at the beg of the next row, k across these 7 sts and the rest of row (28 sts). K 4 rows.
Cast (bind) off 4 sts at the beg of the next row, k to end (24 sts). K 4 rows.
Cast (bind) off 7 sts at the beg of the next row, k to end (17 sts). K 2 rows.
Cast (bind) off the remaining 17 sts. Sew in ends.

TO MAKE UP
Oversew the 2 body pieces together leaving an opening at the cast-off (bound-off) edges (the tiger's mouth). Using the template as a guide, cut out the shape for the tiger's teeth from the white felt. Finally sew 2 buttons on for eyes (if the tiger is intended for a very young child, use safety eyes instead of buttons). Stuff the tiger through the mouth opening. Place the felt teeth inside the mouth and sew up the gap using sewing cotton to complete.

Geese Photo Frame

THIS CHARMING FRAME WILL ENHANCE ANY BABY'S PHOTOGRAPH

YOU WILL NEED ■ *Craft knife* ■ *Pencil* ■ *Mounting board* ■ *Ruler*
■ *Brown parcel tape* ■ *Newspaper, torn into short strips* ■ *Thin wallpaper paste*
■ *Thin card* ■ *Rubber-based glue* ■ *Acrylic gesso* ■ *Non-toxic acrylic paints* ■ *Paintbrushes*
■ *Natural sponge* ■ *Non-toxic clear acrylic varnish*

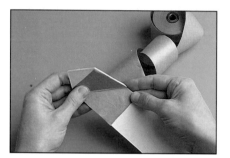

1 Use a craft knife to cut out the frame from mounting board, using the templates as a guide. Make a hinge on the stand using brown parcel tape.

2 Make a ridge of newspaper on the back piece, 4 cm (1½ in) from the edge (this will support the photograph). Cover all the pieces with two layers of newspaper strips dipped in thin wallpaper paste. Assemble the frame pieces with strips of pasted newspaper and allow to dry overnight away from direct heat. Glue the frame stand to the back piece and strengthen it with more papier mâché.

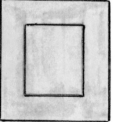

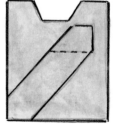

3 Cut the border and geese from thin card, glue in place and cover with a layer of papier mâché. Allow to dry and paint with acrylic gesso.

4 Apply green and yellow paint to the frame using a sponge. Paint the white border and the geese, and allow to dry. Finish with 2 coats of varnish.

Fabric Book

TEXTURES, SOUNDS AND SHAPES ARE ALL STITCHED TOGETHER IN THIS BABY BOOK

YOU WILL NEED ■ *Tape measure* ■ *Ruler* ■ *Pencil* ■ *Scissors*
■ *Assorted washable fabrics such as fur fabric, vinyl, satin and bright plain and patterned*
cottons ■ *Pins* ■ *Needle and thread* ■ *Iron* ■ *Embroidery threads* ■ *Washable satin ribbon in*
assorted colours ■ *Toy bell* ■ *3 large buttons* ■ *Strong cotton thread*

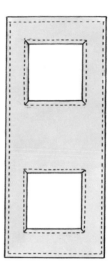

2 Cut some plain cotton slightly larger than the square hole and stitch the ribbons diagonally across it. Trim the ribbon edges and tack (baste) the square behind the hole. Prepare a design for the other side and stitch the two 'pictures' to the cover. Prepare an inside cover with different designs on each side. Remember that the spine section will require a strip 6 cm (2¼ in) wide that is free of design work.

1 The book is made from a folded 'cover' which fastens along the spine to enclose a centre double-sided fabric page. The final arrangement of colours, patterns and textures on each page is up to you, but you could use different combinations of squares, circles, triangles and joined strips.

To assemble, cut pieces of fabric to the pattern dimensions given in the template. Cut out the central squares, clip into the corners and then turn 1 cm (⅜ in) under around the edges, tacking (basting) the hems in place.

3 Sew the inside cover to the cover with right sides together, leaving an opening to turn it. Turn the cover out to the right side, press the seam and stitch the opening to close.

Prepare the central page with a separate design each side leaving a 3 cm (1¼ in) strip on the spine side free of design work. Sew it together like a bag with the open end at the spine. A toy bell in a small cotton bag can be enclosed within the 2 layers of the page if you wish; this should be stitched through all the layers.

4 Fold the cover in half and insert the centre page. With doubled strong cotton thread, sew a button through from the front to the back so that all the layers are joined, and continue sewing the button until there is no possibility of its being pulled off. Sew on 2 more buttons and oversew the top edges of all the pages together at the spine, top and bottom, with the strong thread.

Pecking Woodpecker

PULL THE WOODPECKER TO THE TOP OF THE POLE, AND WATCH AS IT HOPS DOWN!

YOU WILL NEED ■ *Ruler* ■ *Pencil* ■ *Tracing paper* ■ *4 × 2.5 cm (1½ × 1 in)*
softwood, 1 cm (⅜ in) thick ■ *Fretsaw (scroll saw)* ■ *Hand drill* ■ *Coarse and fine sandpaper*
■ *35 cm (13½ in) dowelling, 8 mm (5⁄16 in) in diameter* ■ *10 × 10 cm (4 × 4 in) softwood, 3 cm (1¼ in) thick*
■ *3 × 2.5 cm (1¼ × 1 in) softwood, 2 cm (¾ in) thick* ■ *Medium-tension spring, 5 mm (3⁄16 in)*
in diameter ■ *Pliers* ■ *Non-toxic acrylic paints* ■ *Fine paintbrushes* ■ *Wood glue*

DRILL LINE
FOR SPRING

WOOD
GRAIN

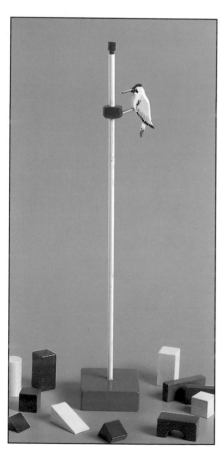

1 Scale up the template and trace onto the 1 cm (⅜ in) thick piece of softwood with the grain horizontal to the woodpecker. Cut out accurately with a fretsaw (scroll saw). Drill a 5 mm (3⁄16 in) hole 1 cm (2.5 cm) deep in the centre front of the woodpecker and sand to shape.

2 Sand the dowelling. Drill an 8 mm (5⁄16 in) hole, 2 cm (¾ in) deep in the centre of the square block and push in the dowelling. Take the softwood block and drill a 6 mm (¼ in) hole through the centre and a 5 mm (3⁄16 in) hole at right-angles to the large hole, to take one end of the spring. Sand the 6 mm (¼ in) hole until the block slides easily up and down the dowelling. If the spring is too long, trim it using pliers.

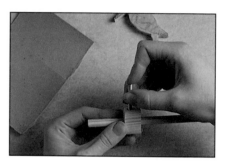

3 Slide the block onto the dowelling. Push one end of the spring into the small block and the other in the woodpecker. Rock the woodpecker, checking that it will cause the block to slide down the rod in a series of small jerks. If the steps are too big, slightly reduce the height of the block.

4 Take all the pieces apart and paint the components, but leave the dowelling and the inside of the sliding block unpainted. (The sanded hole will allow the woodpecker to slide up and down easily, but any paint in the hole will hinder this movement.) When the paint is dry, re-join the base and spring parts with a dab of glue, and fix a small block, cut from the woodpecker scrap, to the top of the dowelling.

Holding Ring

A VERY BASIC FIRST TOY FOR A YOUNG BABY TO HOLD

YOU WILL NEED ■ *Pencil* ■ *Card* ■ *Ruler* ■ *Pair of compasses* ■ *Scissors*
■ *Gingham or similar cotton fabric* ■ *Needle and thread* ■ *2 patterned cotton fabrics* ■ *Iron*
■ *Non-toxic, flame retardant polyester filling (batting)* ■ *2 plain cotton fabrics*

1 Draw 2 circles on card about 10 cm (4 in) in diameter and cut them out. Cut slits from the circle edges to the centre. Cut a circle of gingham about 12 cm (4¾ in) in diameter and place the card centrally over the gingham. Overlap the fabric edge and tack (baste) round the circle, drawing up the fabric to make a neat hem. Press firmly. Repeat with one of the patterned fabrics.

2 Using the slit, carefully remove the cards. Cut circular holes in the centre of both fabrics about 2 cm (¾ in) in diameter. Place the circles right sides together and stitch around the centre hole, about 6 mm (¼ in) from the edge. Clip the seam carefully and pull one of the circles through the centre hole, easing out the seam with your fingers. Press flat.

3 Oversew the 2 tacked (basted) circular hems together and stuff the doughnut-shaped ring firmly as you go.

4 Cut 2 × 7 cm (2¾ in) diameter circles from the 2 plain fabrics and a small flower shape about 5 cm (2 in) across. Cut a gingham centre to the flower. Appliqué the flower and its centre to 1 circle. Make a narrow tie from the second patterned fabric and stitch it firmly to the right side centre of the other small circle. Place the circles right sides together and tack (baste) them, leaving the ties protruding from a small opening on one side.

5 Stitch the circles together, following the outline of the flower which you can gauge from the appliqué stitch line, and leaving the end where the ties are open. Clip excess fabric from the flower corners and turn it to the outside. Stuff the flower shape and oversew the opening closed.

6 Wrap the tie around the stuffed ring, cutting away any excess and tucking the raw edges under to neaten, and stitch very firmly to the ring, leaving the flower facing outwards.

Goldilocks Play Panel

THIS WALL HANGING CAN BE USED TO TELL THE TRADITIONAL FAIRY TALE

YOU WILL NEED ■ *Tape measure* ■ *4 plain cotton fabrics for strips*
■ *Pen* ■ *Paper* ■ *Scissors* ■ *Assorted fabrics for appliqué designs and Goldilocks*
■ *Iron-on interfacing* ■ *Iron* ■ *Pins* ■ *Needle and thread* ■ *Velcro* ■ *Plain fabric for loops* ■ *Plain
fabric for back* ■ *Fur fabric for bears* ■ *Non-toxic, fire retardant polyester filling
(batting)* ■ *Yellow embroidery thread* ■ *Dark embroidery thread* ■ *2 poles*

1 The panel is made from 4 appliquéd strips joined together. The top strip should measure 26 × 48 cm (10¼ × 19 in). The 3 others should measure 17 × 48 cm (6¾ × 19 in). Cut templates for all the appliqué design shapes, scaling up 3 sizes of chairs, porridge bowls, spoons and beds. Choose fabrics carefully to show up the design, and cut them out using iron-on interfacing on easily frayed fabrics. Assemble the cut shapes on each strip, then pin and appliqué each one. Press all the appliqué work.

2 Pin the right sides of the strips together and stitch them in the correct order for the story. Sew small Velcro squares (using the hooked surface) to the path by the house, and on the cushions and beds.

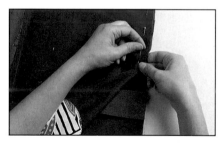

3 Make 6 fabric loops each about 5 × 18 cm (2 × 7 in) in size. Fold in half and pin to the top and bottom of the hanging so that they are spaced evenly and can be incorporated into the final seam.

Cut a back piece the same size as the front, pin to the front with right sides together and then tack (baste) it in place. Stitch all round the hanging, sewing in the loops at top and bottom, and leaving a short length open on 1 side. Trim the seam edges. Turn right side out and press the seam, picking out the corners with a pin.

4 Make patterns for Goldilocks and the 3 bears, scaling the bears in size so they will fit their own chairs and beds. Cut Goldilocks from cotton fabric and the bears from fur fabric. Cut 2 shapes for each, sew them right sides together and cut a small slit in the back of each figure. Turn right side out, stuff and oversew the openings.

Sew yellow embroidery thread to Goldilocks for her hair and embroider dark eyes on the bears. Sew a square of Velcro to the back of each figure.

5 Cut coverlets for each bed and neaten the edges; they should be cut wide enough to go over their own bear. Stitch in a 'hinge' to the left side of each bed, and fix to the right with Velcro. Suspend the hanging from a pole threaded through the top loops, and add a bottom pole.

Picture Bricks

THIS ATTRACTIVE PUZZLE SETS A CHALLENGE FOR 1½ TO 3-YEAR-OLDS

YOU WILL NEED ■ *Sand paper* ■ *Length of pine, 5 × 5 cm (2 × 2 in),
cut into squares* ■ *Masking tape* ■ *Matt white emulsion (flat latex) paint* ■ *Paintbrushes* ■ *Pencil*
■ *Paper* ■ *Chalk* ■ *Non-toxic acrylic paints* ■ *Non-toxic clear acrylic varnish*

1 Rub down the blocks with sandpaper to remove any rough edges. Tape all the bricks together with masking tape.

2 Prime the front with a coat of matt white emulsion (flat latex) paint. Draw out the picture of the duck onto a sheet of paper using the template as a guide, and then carefully transfer the picture, using a piece of chalk, onto the bricks.

3 Paint in the design. Leave the paint to dry and remove the masking tape. Cover with a coat of clear acrylic varnish.

Bright Hangers

HAVE FUN HANGING UP YOUR BABY'S CLOTHES!

YOU WILL NEED ■ *Small paintbrush* ■ *Non-toxic acrylic paints* ■ *2 plain wooden coathangers*
■ *Plastic gems and sequins* ■ *Rubber-based glue*

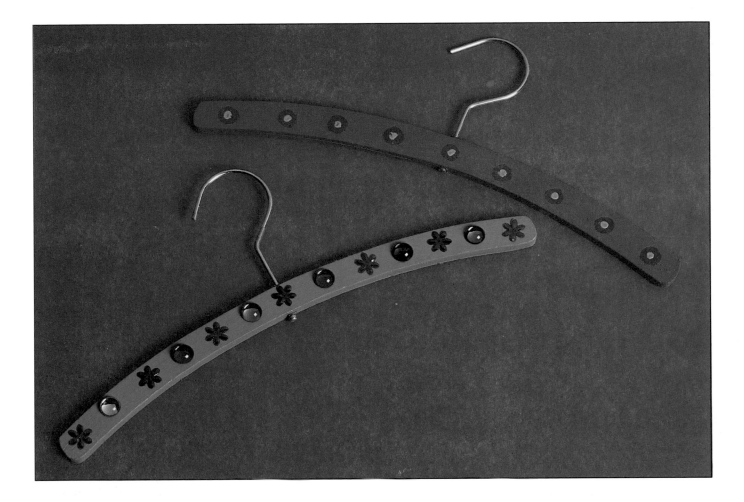

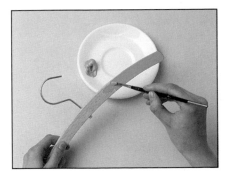

1 For the gem and sequin hanger, first paint your chosen colour onto the hanger and allow it to dry.

2 Stick on the gems and sequins alternately using rubber-based glue applied with a small brush, and allow to dry.

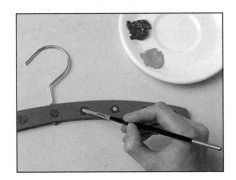

3 For the painted hanger, simply paint on a background coat of paint and allow it to dry. Finish by painting on a pattern of dots in 2 bright contrasting colours.

Ribbon **B**oard

A PRETTY WAY TO DISPLAY ANYTHING FROM PHOTOS TO PICTURES

YOU WILL NEED ■ *75 × 75 cm (30 × 30 in) chipboard (particle board), 1.3 cm (½ in) thick* ■ *100 × 100 cm (40 × 40 in) yellow felt* ■ *Staple gun* ■ *Scissors* ■ *1.8 m (2 yd) green ribbon, 1.8 m (2 yd) pink ribbon, 1.8 m (2 yd) red ribbon, 4.8 m (5 yd) blue ribbon, all 1.3 cm (½ in) wide* ■ *Tape measure* ■ *Pins* ■ *50 cm (19½ in) white cord*

1 Lay the board in the exact centre of the felt. Pull the felt over each side and staple flat along the back of the board, folding each corner in an envelope style and stapling into place. Make sure that you pull the felt tightly in each direction as you work.

Next, cut 2 × 85 cm (34 in) lengths of ribbon in each of the four colours and pin them across the board at 15 cm (6 in) intervals, leaving 5 cm (2 in) free at each end to staple each ribbon to the back. Repeat the same process, this time working crossways to the first ribbons. Take the remaining blue ribbon and run it around the edges of the whole board, stapling at each corner until the ribbon meets. Staple the end securely and trim off the excess ribbon.

2 To make the loop so the board can hang on the wall, knot the cord at each end. Lay on the back of the board, 30 cm (12 in) from the top. Staple at least 3 times on each side near the knot to hold the cord firmly.

Twirling Parrots Mobile

THE MOVEMENT OF THESE TWIRLING PARROTS WILL FASCINATE YOUNG CHILDREN

YOU WILL NEED ■ *Pencil* ■ *Tracing paper* ■ *Thick card* ■ *Scissors* ■ *Poster paints* ■ *Paintbrush*
■ *Coloured ribbon in 3 colours* ■ *Dowelling*

1 Scale up the parrot template to the size required and trace onto thick card. Cut out carefully using scissors. Trace and cut out a total of 3 parrots.

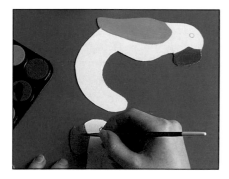

2 Paint the parrots in a variety of bright colours and leave to dry thoroughly.

3 Pierce a small hole in the back of each parrot's neck and thread through a piece of coloured ribbon. Knot the end to secure and tie the other end to the dowelling. Space the parrots evenly along the dowelling, varying the lengths of ribbon to create a balanced effect. Suspend the mobile by tying a length of ribbon around the centre of the dowelling.

Clutch **B**all

A SOFT AND SAFE JINGLY BALL FOR A BABY TO HOLD OR THROW

YOU WILL NEED ■ *Pencil* ■ *Paper* ■ *Scissors* ■ *Plain cotton*
fabrics in several colours ■ *4 contrasting patterned cotton fabrics* ■ *Pins* ■ *Needle and thread*
■ *Non-toxic, flame retardant polyester filling (batting)* ■ *2 toy bells*

1 Using the templates as a guide, cut paper patterns for the outer and inner segments. Cut 8 fabric shapes from the inner segment pattern in plain colours. Cut 4 fabric shapes from the outer segment pattern in the patterned fabrics. With right sides together, pin 1 outer segment to 1 inner, easing the curve as you go. Tack (baste) and stitch together 10 mm (⅜ in) from the edge.

Repeat for the second side of the outer segment, using a second inner segment to form a boat shape. Stop the second stitch line where it meets the first at the pointed ends, and secure all thread ends. Make up the 3 other segments in the same way.

2 Turn each segment right side out. Folding in the straight segment sides about 10 mm (⅜ in) as you sew, oversew each segment closed. Stuff the segments with filling (batting) as you go but don't fill the pointed ends too tight. Enclose each bell in a small cotton bag and insert them in 2 of the segments.

3 Pinch the tops of 2 separate segments together and oversew them together about 4 cm (1½ in) down the straight edges at the top and bottom. Repeat for the second pair of segments.

4 Make a narrow tie from plain fabric about 30 cm (12 in) long. Cut a length of 20 cm (8 in). Hold the 2 pairs of joined segments together and pass the tie between them, threading the 2 sets together. Sew the loop closed by overlapping its ends and conceal the sewn end neatly within the ball.

Pinch the segment tops, draw the loop tight and sew to itself just above the ball, securing all the segments and leaving a looped end. Using the remaining tie, thread the bottom of the ball but sew the tie without leaving a loop. Conceal the sewn ends in the ball.

OUTER SEGMENT

INNER SEGMENT

Apple Tree Hooks

THESE CHARMING COAT HOOKS ENCOURAGE TODDLERS TO BE TIDY

YOU WILL NEED ■ *Pencil* ■ *Paper* ■ *Scissors* ■ *Plyboard, 6 mm (¼ in) thick*
■ *Sticky putty* ■ *Fretsaw (scroll saw)* ■ *Sandpaper* ■ *Matt white emulsion (flat latex) paint*
■ *Paintbrush* ■ *Non-toxic acrylic paints* ■ *3 red wooden doorknobs (or red-painted plain doorknobs)*
■ *Hand drill* ■ *Non-toxic acrylic varnish* ■ *Picture hook*

3 Once the primer is dry, paint the top of the tree green and the trunk an ochre colour. Leave to dry.

1 Draw the shape of a tree onto the paper, using the template as a guide. Cut it out and stick it on to the plyboard with sticky putty. Draw around the template with a pencil.

4 Mark in the positions for the 3 doorknobs and drill a small hole for each with the hand drill. Screw in the knobs from the back and varnish with a coat of non-toxic varnish. Attach to the wall using a picture hook.

2 Cut out the shape with a fretsaw (scroll saw) and rub down the edges with sandpaper wrapped around a block of wood. Prime with a coat of matt white emulsion (flat latex) paint.

Feely **Play Mat**

A LARGE MAT TO PROVIDE BRIGHT COLOURS, TEXTURES AND SOUNDS

YOU WILL NEED ■ *Paper* ■ *Pencil* ■ *Tape measure* ■ *Selection of washable fabrics in different patterns, colours and textures, e.g. towelling (terrycloth), fur fabric, satin, velvet, corduroy and vinyl* ■ *Scissors* ■ *Scraps of yarn* ■ *Card* ■ *Pins* ■ *Needle and thread* ■ *Narrow ribbons in different colours* ■ *Iron-on interfacing* ■ *Non-toxic, flame retardant polyester filling (batting)* ■ *Toy bells* ■ *Dried peas in a secure plastic container* ■ *Old blanket (optional)*

1 The mat is constructed in 3 strips joined together by 2 seams. The final arrangement of colours, patterns and textures is limited only by your imagination! Draw a rough plan on paper to help you keep track of your design and cut the shapes correctly. Remember to calculate with a generous seam allowance.

To insert yarn into a seam, first wind some yarn around a card about 8 cm (3¼ in) wide. Cut along the fold and feed the cut yarn through a sewing machine, sewing a line through the centre of the strips. Fold the yarn along the stitch line and pin and tack (baste) it to one of the fabric pieces so that it can be incorporated into a seam with cut ends outwards. If you do not have a sewing machine, the yarn must be stitched firmly in with the seam.

To make a knotted ribbon strip, cut several 24 cm (9½ in) lengths of satin ribbon, fold in half and tack (baste) to the edge of the fabric, so that they can be incorporated into the required seam in the form of loops. Once the seam is made the ribbons can be knotted in order to make them stand upright.

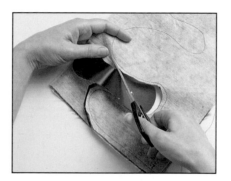

2 Make the satin flaps with a different colour on each side. Use a cool iron and iron-on interfacing to back 2 satin rectangles, slightly shorter than your final strip. Place right sides together and stitch wavy freehand shapes in and out of the satin, starting at one end of the rectangle and ending at the other. Trim, and clip major curves. Turn right side out and press. The finished flap can be incorporated into your chosen seam.

3 Make a 'rattly bag' from 2 contrasting squares, appliquéd with shapes on the outside if you wish, sewn right sides together and with one side left open. Stuff with polyester filling (batting) and incorporate the open end into your chosen seam. Bells can be added in with the filling but should first be enclosed in a small cotton bag. A small pea-filled container will make a good rattle but the container must be secure.

4 Additional play elements can be incorporated into the 2 final seams. Small loops sewn into the mat seam can be used to attach a favourite rattle or teddy when the baby is playing. When all elements are ready, pin, tack (baste) and sew the mat together. Turn under the outer edges and hem. The mat can be used as it is, or it can be backed with an old cut-down blanket.

Braided Mat

A SIMPLE BUT EFFECTIVE MAT USING ODDMENTS OF FABRIC

YOU WILL NEED ■ *Scissors* ■ *Assorted oddments of fabric, torn or cut into long strips about 2 cm (¾ in) wide* ■ *Needle and thread* ■ *Iron*

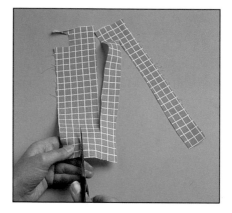

1 Tie 3 strips together, anchor them to a chair or table and braid them fairly tightly. When an individual strip is almost down to its end, add a new one in with it and work the 2 together.

2 Short but wide oddments of fabric can be cut in a zigzag to form a longer piece.

3 Once you have a few metres (yards) of braid, start to make up the mat. Begin by sewing the braid to itself and start to form a spiral, taking the needle over the free end of the braid and catching it to the sewn line. Always work from the same side, which should remain the mat front. Tuck any odd protruding shapes in the strip edges to the back of the mat.

4 When you are happy with the size of your mat, secure the last braid end to the spiral edge. Press the whole mat very firmly to help the shape set in. A very large mat, or one that feels loose, can be backed by sewing it to a heavy cotton fabric.

Flower Pot Tidy

STORE SMALL TOYS IN THESE HANDY FLOWER POT POCKETS

YOU WILL NEED ■ *Scissors* ■ *45 × 90 cm (½ yd × 36 in) contrasting fabric* ■ *Tape measure*
■ *Pins* ■ *Needle and thread* ■ *60 cm (24 in) ric-rac braid* ■ *2 pieces 45 × 90 cm (½ yd × 36 in) fabric*
■ *Oddments of brightly coloured felt* ■ *Embroidery thread* ■ *36 cm (14 in) ribbon or fabric binding*

1 Use the template to cut out 8 flower pot shapes from the contrasting fabric. Each pot should be 21 cm (8½ in) high and 12 cm (4¾ in) wide at the top. Sew in pairs, leaving a gap at the top for turning right side out.

2 Cut the ric-rac braid into 4, and sew a length along the top edge of each flower pot.

3 Sew the flower pots onto one of the large pieces of background fabric. Cut flower shapes from the oddments of felt, using the templates as a guide. Pin the shapes into position and then sew on using embroidery thread in contrasting colours.

4 Cut 3 loops from the ribbon or fabric binding. Pin both sides of the background pieces right sides together, and sandwich the ends of the 3 loops along the top edge. Sew the 2 pieces together leaving a gap and then turn right side out. Sew up the gap.

Asleep/Awake Bear

A DELIGHTFUL, TRADITIONAL CUDDLY TOY TO ENCOURAGE FIRST SPEECH

YOU WILL NEED ■ Pen ■ Paper ■ Scissors ■ Corduroy or strong fabric ■ Tape measure ■ Needle and thread ■ 2 safety eyes ■ Non-toxic, flame retardant polyester filling (batting) ■ Scraps of striped and patterned cotton fabric ■ Plain white cotton fabric ■ Iron ■ Pins ■ Embroidery thread

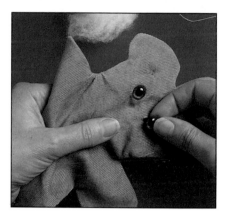

1 Make a paper pattern for the bear using the template as a guide. Cut 2 bear shapes from the corduroy fabric and make a 10 cm (4 in) vertical slit in the centre back of one of the shapes. Place the right sides together and tack (baste) in place before stitching all round, 6 mm (¼ in) from the edge. Carefully clip the main curves to give a smooth finish. Turn to the right side through the slit.

2 Mark positions for the eyes and attach them according to the manufacturer's instructions. Begin stuffing the bear, lightly filling both sets of ears and stitching diagonally across to give them shape. Ensure there is plenty of padding behind the eyes. After stuffing, oversew the back slit to close. Embroider the facial features and details onto the bears' heads and paws.

3 Cut a piece of patterned cotton for Awake Bear's dress 37 × 17 cm (14½ × 6¾ in) and a striped piece for the sleeping bag 37 × 13 cm (14½ × 5¼ in) with stripes running down the shorter side. Stitch the 2 pieces together along the longer edge with right sides facing and press. Cut a heart shape with the stripes running across and appliqué it to the centre of one side of the sleeping bag. Cut a strip of white cotton 37 × 10 cm (14½ × 4 in). Stitch this to the long side of the striped cotton. Press the seam away from the striped cotton and fold the white fabric to the wrong side leaving a 4 cm (1½ in) strip showing for Asleep Bear's sheet. Turn under the raw edge of the fabric and stitch it to the inside.

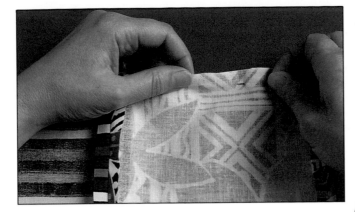

4 Stitch a 1 cm (⅜ in) hem on the long raw edge of the dress section. Press. Make the piece into a tube by stitching the raw side edges together, matching hems and the ends of the seam. Half turn the tube along the centre seam with the wrong sides facing and press firmly.

5 Attach the sleeping bag to Asleep Bear by stitching the sheet section closed close to each side of the head and out to the sheet ends, ensuring that the heart shows on the centre front. Attach the dress top to Awake Bear by centring the dress and firmly stitching the dress back to the dress front, close to each side of the head. Also stitch the front to the back under the arms close to the body. By pulling the central hem up and down, the bears can be asleep or awake!

Cat Book-ends

THE PURRFECT WAY TO ORGANIZE FAVOURITE STORY BOOKS

YOU WILL NEED ■ *Tracing paper* ■ *Pencil* ■ *Thin plywood*
■ *Ruler* ■ *Fretsaw (scroll saw)* ■ *Sandpaper* ■ *Wood glue* ■ *Hammer* ■ *Small tacks* ■ *Non-toxic*
acrylic paint ■ *Paintbrushes* ■ *Non-toxic clear acrylic varnish*

 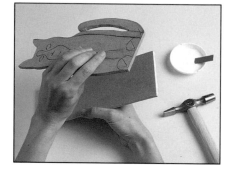 

1 Scale up the cat design from the template onto tracing paper. Trace 2 cat shapes onto the plywood and mark an extra rectangular piece 10 × 26 cm (4 × 10¼ in). Cut out the 3 shapes using a fretsaw (scroll saw) and sand down any rough edges.

2 Spread wood glue onto both ends of the rectangular piece of wood, then using a hammer and three small tacks for each end, nail the cat ends securely to the rectangular base. Allow to dry for at least 2 hours.

3 Paint the whole piece black and allow to dry before adding the cat's features in different colours. Finally, paint on a protective coat of clear acrylic varnish and leave to dry.

Memento Holder

A DELIGHTFUL HOLDER FOR SPECIAL TREASURES

YOU WILL NEED ■ *Craft knife* ■ *Metal ruler* ■ *Decorative paper* ■ *Concertina (accordion)*
file ■ *Pencil* ■ *Tweezers* ■ *Pressed rosebuds and one open rose* ■ *Rubber-based glue* ■ *Toothpick*
■ *Protective laminating film* ■ *Heat resistant foam* ■ *Iron* ■ *Paper glue* ■ *Soft cloth*

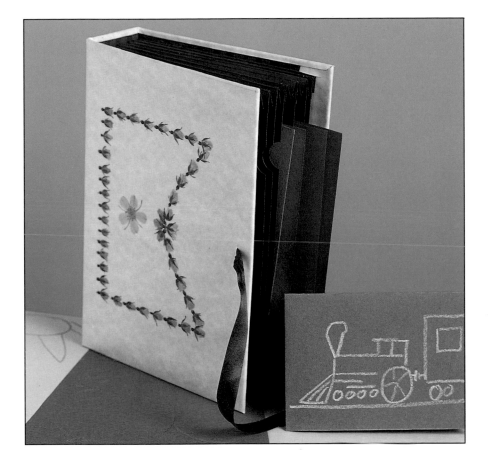

3 Continue to fill in the design positioning the open rose in the centre. Place on a smooth clean surface and cut a piece of protective film slightly larger than the paper. Peel back about 10 cm (4 in) of the backing from the film, and overlapping the first edge of the design paper, smooth the film gently over, unrolling and peeling the backing as you go. Make certain that no air bubbles have formed during the process, as this will spoil the neat finished effect.

1 Cut the paper to cover the whole file, front, base and back. Leave a small overlap and rule these lines in very faintly with a pencil.

2 Mark out your design on the centre front of the ruled-up paper, using a very faint pencil line. Using the tweezers, arrange a line of rosebuds to cover the pencilled outline in a regimented fashion. Fix them in position by applying a dot of rubber-based glue with a toothpick to the centre back of each flower bud.

4 Cover with heat resistant foam, and press down in sections with an iron heated to wool setting. When cool, trim off excess film. Apply paper glue to the file and, following the pencil marks, position the paper over the file and stick down by rubbing with a soft cloth. Turn over the edges and glue down.

Hanging Shoe Tidy

AN ATTRACTIVE WAY TO KEEP TINY SHOES IN ORDER

YOU WILL NEED ■ *Tape measure* ■ *75 × 90 cm (30 × 36 in) fabric* ■ *Scissors*
■ *Pins* ■ *Needle and thread* ■ *75 cm (30 in) elastic* ■ *Safety pins* ■ *43 × 65 cm (17 × 26 in) stiff card*
■ *Rubber-based glue* ■ *Hole punch* ■ *45 cm (18 in) ribbon, 2.5 cm (1 in) wide*

2 Run a line of gathering stitches along the bottom edge of each pocket strip. Adjust the gathering until each strip measures 43 cm (17 in).

3 With right sides together, sew a strip 2.5 cm (1 in) from the bottom of the back piece. Pull the strip up, fold down the edges and sew to the back piece with 15 mm (⅝ in) side seams. Sew the 6 marked positions to form the pockets. Make the second pocket in the same way.

Cut the top 25 cm (10 in) of the cardboard into a triangle and spread with glue. Stretch the back piece of fabric over the cardboard and allow to dry. Trim the fabric corners, then spread glue around the board edges and glue down the edges of the fabric. Punch a hole 5 cm (2 in) from the top and thread a ribbon through.

1 Cut the fabric into 2 strips for the pockets, 18 × 75 cm (7 × 30 in) and 1 main piece, 45 × 65 cm (18 × 26 in), cutting the top 20 cm (8 in) of the main piece into a triangle. Sew a 2.5 cm (1 in) hem along the top of both pocket strips.

Mark the 6 positions for the pocket seams with pins so that you will end up with 8 pockets. Cut the elastic in half and thread a length through each hem, securing it 15 mm (⅝ in) short of the sides with a safety pin.

Hand Painted Stretchsuit

PUT A LITTLE LIFE AND COLOUR INTO YOUR NEWBORN CHILD'S STRETCHSUIT

YOU WILL NEED ■ *Paper* ■ *Plain stretchsuit* ■ *Paintbrushes*
■ *Fabric paints in several colours* ■ *Iron*

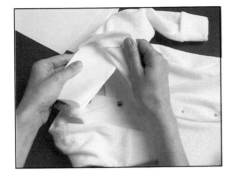

2 Paint on a simple flower design using slightly watered-down fabric paint. Use as many different colours and shapes as you like.

1 Place some paper on the inside of the stretchsuit to prevent the paint from leaking through to the other side.

3 When the fabric paint is completely dry, place a thin sheet of paper on top of it to protect the paint. With a medium to hot iron, iron over the paper following the manufacturer's instructions on the paints. This process will fix the fabric paint.

SPECIAL OCCASIONS

A delightful collection of mementoes, gifts and
keepsakes to commemorate the birth of a new baby and celebrate
the special events of the first few years

Tussie Mussie

THIS ATTRACTIVE BOUQUET IS JUST RIGHT FOR A SPECIAL OCCASION

YOU WILL NEED ■ *18 × 53 cm (7 × 21 in) lace* ■ *Pins* ■ *Needle and thread* ■ *Scissors* ■ *White dressmaking net* ■ *Tape measure* ■ *Small bunch of fresh or artificial flowers* ■ *Florist's wire*

1 Place one edge of the lace over the other to overlap by 2 cm (¾ in). Pin together and stitch to form a tube. Sew running stitches around the lace 12 cm (4¾ in) from the top. Pull up the stitches to gather the lace but leave an opening for the flowers. Cut a circle from the net, 25 cm (10 in) in diameter. Make a small hole in the centre.

2 Arrange the flowers in a small bunch. Trim the ends of the flower stems and bind together with the wire from the bottom to almost under the flower heads. Push the wired bunch through the hole in the netting and finally put flowers and net into the lace tube. Finish by tying a ribbon round the tussie mussie.

Ribbons and **B**ells

YOU WILL NEED ■ *Lengths of different coloured ribbon* ■ *Scissors* ■ *Bells* ■ *20 cm (8 in)*
length of dowelling, 5 mm (³⁄₁₆ in) thick ■ *Rubber-based glue*

1 Taking 3 different coloured lengths of ribbon at a time, attach them to a bell using a strong double knot.

2 Braid the lengths together, leaving enough ribbon free to knot around the dowelling. Finish off the braiding by tying a strong double knot.

3 Tie each braid securely onto the dowelling using another double knot and a dab of glue to stop the bells slipping along the dowelling. Tie a length of ribbon on to either end of the dowelling and suspend from a high point. The decoration can then be spun around and the ribbons will wind around each other.

Sugared Almond Clusters

A TRADITIONAL CELEBRATORY GIFT FOR GUESTS

YOU WILL NEED ■ *Pencil* ■ *Pair of compasses* ■ *Ruler*
■ *30 × 90 cm (12 × 36 in) dress net for each cluster* ■ *Scissors* ■ *Rubber-based glue*
■ *Glitter* ■ *Sugared almonds* ■ *Ribbon* ■ *Artificial flowers*

 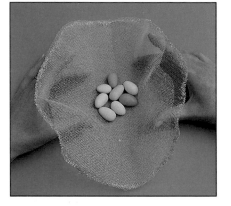 

1 Draw and cut out 2 net circles, 25 cm (10 in) in diameter. Lay one on a board. Spread glue around the edge and sprinkle with glitter. Allow to dry, lifting occasionally to prevent it from sticking to the board.

2 Lay the second piece of netting on top of the first, and place 8 sugared almonds in the centre of the circle.

3 Gather the netting up around the almonds, knot a length of ribbon around the top and tie into a bow. Slip the artificial flowers under the ribbon.

Christening Shoes

THESE PRETTY SHOES COMPLETE THE CHRISTENING OUTFIT

YOU WILL NEED ■ *50 g (2-ounce skein) white double knitting (sport) cotton* ■ *1 pair size 3 mm (US 3) knitting needles* ■ *Scissors* ■ *Large darning needle* ■ *2 small buttons or beads*

Tension (Gauge)
To knit this pattern, use 3 mm (US 3) needles, 21 sts and 30 rows to 10 cm (4 in) (st st).

MAIN SHOE
Beginning at the sole of the shoe, cast on 25 sts.

1st row: k 1, inc 1 (k into front and back of next st), k 9, inc 1, k 1, inc 1, k 9, inc 1, k 1.

2nd row and every alternate even numbered row: k to end.

3rd row: k 1, inc 1, k 11, inc 1, k 1, k 11, inc 1, k 1.

5th row: k 1, inc 1, k 13, inc 1, k 1, inc 1, k 13, inc 1, k 1.

7th row: k1, inc 1, k 15, inc 1, k 1, inc 1, k 15, inc 1, k 1.

9th row: k 1, inc 1, k 17, inc 1, k 1, inc 1, k17, inc 1, k 1.

11th row: k 1, inc 1, k 19, inc 1, k 1, inc 1, k 19, inc 1, k 1.

12th row: k to end (49 sts).

Start the lace pattern
13th row: k 17, sl 1, k 1, psso, k 3, k 2 tog, ynfwd, k 1, ynfwd, sl 1, k 1, psso, k 3, k 2 tog, k 17.

14th row and every alternate even numbered row: p to end.

15th row: k 17, sl 1, k 1, psso, k 2, ynfwd, sl 1, k 1, psso, k 1, k 2 tog, ynfwd, k 2, k 2 tog, k 17.

17th row: k 17, sl 1, k 1, psso, k 1, k 2 tog, ynfwd, k 1, ynfwd, sl 1, k 1, psso, k 1, k 2 tog, k 17.

19th row: k 17, sl 1, k 1, psso, ynfwd, sl 1, k 1, psso, k 1, k 2 tog, ynfwd, k 2 tog, k 17.

21st row: k 9, cast (bind) off 9, k 5, cast (bind) off 9, k 9.

Continue on these last 9 sts. Work 4 rows st st. Cast (bind) off. Return to 5 sts in centre for the front strap. Beginning with a p row and with wrong side facing, work 15 rows st st. Cast (bind) off.

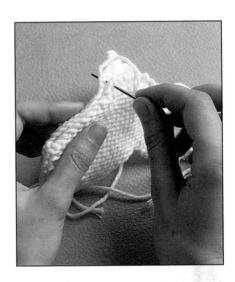

Ankle strap
Cast on 14 sts on same needle as remaining 9 sts (23 sts). Work 4 rows st st. Cast (bind) off.

Work the second shoe to match, this time reversing the position of the strap.

TO MAKE UP
Join the sole and heel seams. Fold the front strap under, making a loop wide enough to thread the ankle strap through. Hem the cast-off (bound-off) edge of the front strap to the inside of the work. Thread the ankle strap through the loop. Make a small buttonhole loop at the end of the ankle strap. Blanket stitch around the loop. Sew the buttons or beads firmly onto the shoes.

Christening Robe

THIS DELICATELY WORKED ROBE IS VERY SIMPLE TO MAKE

YOU WILL NEED ■ *Tracing paper* ■ *Pencil* ■ *Scissors* ■ *2.7 m (3 yd) white lawn*
(fine cotton) ■ *Pins* ■ *Iron* ■ *Needle and fine medium white silk embroidery thread* ■ *Length of bias*
binding, 2 cm (¾ in) wide ■ *4 × 7 mm (¼ in) buttons* ■ *2 m (80 in) narrow ribbon*

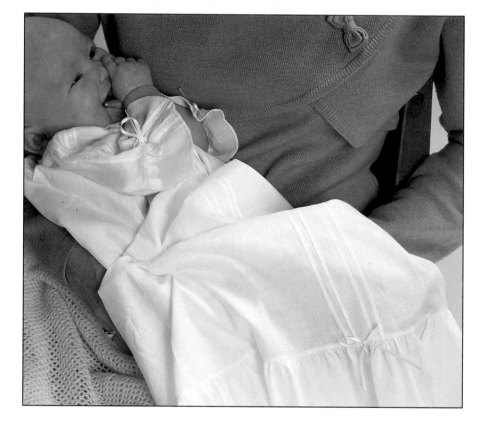

1 Scale up the pattern pieces onto tracing paper and cut them out, marking dots and fold lines for tucks onto the lawn (fine cotton). Press tucks on yoke and sleeve along fold lines and sew 3 mm (⅛ in) tucks. Press yoke tucks down and sleeve tucks outwards. Draw 17 threads from centre of pressed tucks.

2 Hemstitch with fine white silk embroidery thread along both edges of the area with drawn threads.

3 Embroider wheatsheafs in medium silk thread, spacing them at 10 mm (⅜ in) intervals between the tucks.

4 Stay-stitch along the neck edge and join yoke shoulder seams. Neaten all seams with zigzag stitch and trim to 10 mm (⅜ in). Gather the front and back skirts between the notches. Pin to yoke with right sides together. Adjust the gathers and stitch the skirts to the yoke.

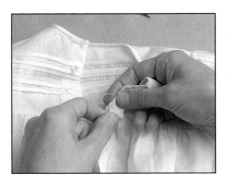

5 To make the sleeves, sew bias binding along the casing line close to the edge. Gather the head of each sleeve between the notches. Pin to armhole edges, adjust the gathers and stitch. Sew the side and back seams and finish the sleeves with a narrow hem.

6 Finish the neck edge neatly with a 2 cm (¾ in) bias strip. Add the buttons and sew thread hoops to fasten.

7 Sew the frill sections together. Sew tucks as before and press downwards. Gather the top edge before attaching it to the skirt, matching up the dots and seams. Narrow hem the frill or draw out several threads and hemstitch into position. Thread ribbon through the casing on the sleeves and secure at the seams. Sew a small bow in the centre of the yoke.

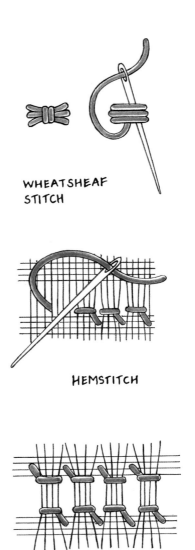

WHEATSHEAF STITCH

HEMSTITCH

LADDER HEMSTITCH

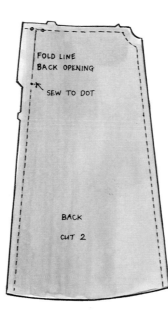

FOLD LINE
BACK OPENING

SEW TO DOT

BACK
CUT 2

SLEEVE – CUT 2

FOLD LINES FOR TUCKS

CASING LINE

FOLD

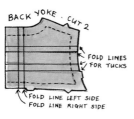

BACK YOKE – CUT 2

FOLD LINES
FOR TUCKS

FOLD LINE LEFT SIDE
FOLD LINE RIGHT SIDE

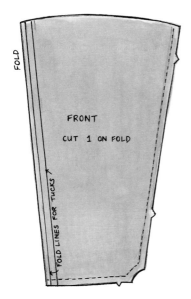

FOLD

FRONT
CUT 1 ON FOLD

FOLD LINES FOR TUCKS

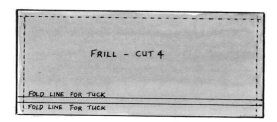

FRILL – CUT 4

FOLD LINE FOR TUCK
FOLD LINE FOR TUCK

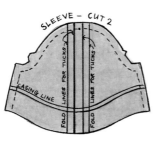

FRONT YOKE – CUT 1

FOLD LINES FOR TUCKS

FOLD LINES FOR TUCKS

Knitted **C**ollar

THIS DELICATE COLLAR IS EASY TO KNIT

YOU WILL NEED ■ *50 g (2-ounce skein) white double knitting (sport) cotton* ■ *1 pair size 4 mm (US 5) knitting needles* ■ *Iron* ■ *Length of narrow white ribbon*

Tension (Gauge)
One repeat (8 rows of pattern) measures 3.75 cm (1½ in) long by 3.75 cm (1½ in) wide.

Cast on 5 sts.
1st row: k 1, ynfwd, k 2 tog, ynfwd, k 2 (6 sts).
2nd row: k 2, (ynfwd, k 1) twice, ynfwd, k 2 tog (8 sts).
3rd row: sl 1, ynfwd, k 2 tog, ynfwd, k 3, ynfwd, k 2 (10 sts).
4th row: k 2, ynfwd, k 5, ynfwd, k 1, ynfwd, k 2 tog (12 sts).
5th row: sl 1, ynfwd, k 5, ynfwd, k 1, ynfwd, sl 1, k 1, psso, k 3 tog, ynfwd, k 2 (12 sts).
6th row: k 3, ynfwd, sl 1, k 1, psso, k 1, k 2 tog, ynfwd, k 2, ynfwd, k 2 tog (12 sts).
7th row: sl 1, ynfwd, k 2 tog, k 2, ynfwd, sl 1, k 2 tog, psso, ynfwd, k 4 (12 sts).
8th row: Cast (bind) off 7 sts, k 2, ynfwd, k 2 tog (5 sts).

Repeat 8 rows 10 times more, ending on 7th row. Cast (bind) off.

TO MAKE UP
Attach ribbon to inside corners.

Knitted Bonnet

THIS COSY BONNET WILL FIT BABIES UP TO 6 MONTHS

YOU WILL NEED ■ 1 pair size 3 mm (US 3) knitting needles ■ 100 g (4-ounce skein) white double knitting (sport) cotton ■ Iron ■ Length of narrow white ribbon ■ Length of wider white ribbon

Tension (Gauge)
Using a pair of 3 mm (US 3) needles, 21 sts and 30 rows to 10 cm (4 in) (st st).

Beginning at the front row edge, cast on 76 sts.
1st row: k to end.
2nd row and every even numbered row from this point: k 6, p 64, k 6.
3rd row: k to end.
5th row: picot edge k 6 (ynfwd, k 2 tog) to last 6 sts, k6.
7th row: k to end.
9th row: k to end.
11th row: eyelets for ribbon k 6 *k 2, ynfwd, k 2 tog. Repeat from * to last 6 sts, k 6 sts.
13th row: k to end.

Begin lace pattern as follows
15th row: k 9, *ynfwd, sl 1, k 1, psso, k 6. Repeat from * to last 9 sts, k 9.
16th row and every even numbered row: k 6, p 64, k 6.
17th row: k 7, *k 2 tog, ynfwd, k 1, ynfwd, sl 1, k 1, psso, k 3. Repeat from * to last 8 sts, k 8.
19th row: as row 15.
21st row: k to end.
23rd row: k 13, *ynfwd, sl 1, k 1, psso, k 6. Repeat from * to last 13 sts, k 13.
25th row: k 11, *k 2 tog, ynfwd, k 1, ynfwd, sl 1, k 1, psso, k 3. Repeat from * to last 9 sts, k 9.
27th row: as row 23.
29th row: k to end.
31st row: k 9, *ynfwd, sl 1, k 1, psso, k 6. Repeat from * to last 9 sts, k 9.
33rd row: k 7, *k 2 tog, ynfwd, k 1 ynfwd, sl 1, k 1, psso, k 3. Repeat from * to last 8 sts, k 8.
35th row: as row 31.

Shape head as follows
Rows 37 and 38: cast (bind) off 27 sts at beginning of next 2 rows. Continue shaping for back of head on remaining 22 sts working in garter stitch (knit every row) for 24 rows then dec 1 st at each end of every 4th row a total of 4 times, 14 sts. Cast (bind) off.

TO MAKE UP
Press bonnet well from wrong side. Fold under front edge of bonnet on picot and hem cast-on edge to wrong side of work. Join back of head seams. Thread narrow ribbon through eyelets and sew ends to inside of work. Cut 2 lengths of wide ribbon. Make 2 loops, 2.5 cm (1 in) long, at one end of ribbon and sew to each corner of bonnet.

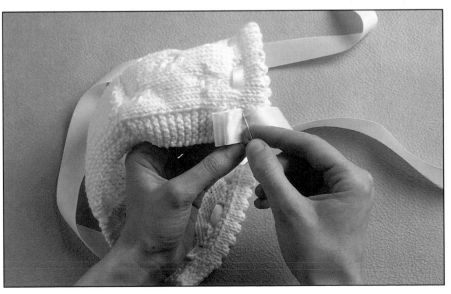

Cherub Place Cards

THE PERFECT FINISHING TOUCH FOR A CELEBRATION MEAL

YOU WILL NEED For each place card: ■ *Scissors* ■ *White card, 8 × 10 cm (3¼ × 4 in)* ■ *Craft knife*
■ *Ruler* ■ *Cherub motif* ■ *Rubber-based glue* ■ *Gold pen*

1 Mark the card halfway down each short side and lightly score across lengthwise using the craft knife and ruler. Place the cherub in the centre of the score line and glue it down firmly.

2 When the glue is dry, use a craft knife to cut around the top half of the cherub, from the score line upwards.

3 Fold the card in half, gently easing the cherub from the top half as you work. Open out the card again and decorate the front using a gold pen. Finally, add the name of your guest.

Cherubic Tablepiece

CROWN YOUR TABLE WITH THIS CHARMING FLORAL DECORATION

YOU WILL NEED ■ *Ring of florist's foam, same diameter as stand* ■ *Scissors* ■ *Flowers and foliage*
■ *Florist's wire* ■ *Glass cake stand* ■ *5 gold cherubs*

1 Soak the ring of florist's foam in water overnight, or for at least 8 hours. Snip the stems of your chosen flowers into short lengths, and twist florist's wire around any softer stems to support them as they are pushed into the foam.

2 Lay the foam on top of the glass cake stand, and push the flower stems in firmly, gradually working your way around the ring. Use the foliage to fill in the gaps and let the leaves hang over the side. Try to keep the overall shape well balanced.

3 To attach the cherubs, twist the wire around each one and push the ends into the florist's foam. Continue decorating around the ring, adding the cherubs at equal intervals.

Child's Jacket

ANY 1 OR 2-YEAR-OLD WOULD LOOK GREAT IN THIS CHINESE-STYLE JACKET

YOU WILL NEED ■ *Tracing paper* ■ *Tape measure* ■ *Pencil* ■ *Scissors*
■ *75 × 115 cm (30 × 45 in) fabric* ■ *Pins* ■ *Needle and thread* ■ *Iron* ■ *2.37 m (2⅔ yd) of 2 cm*
(¾ in) wide satin bias binding ■ *3 × 22 mm (⅞ in) button moulds (optional)*

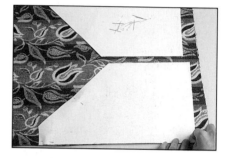

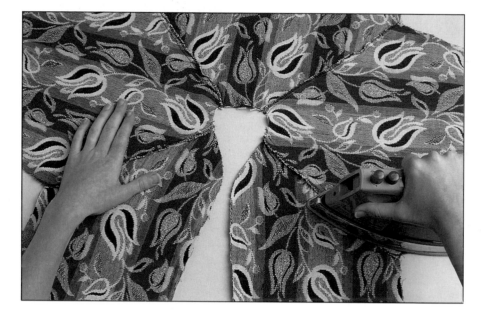

1 Trace the templates and scale them up to the size required. To find this, measure your baby from the back of the neck to the waist and scale up the template accordingly. A 1 cm (⅜ in) seam allowance is included on all template edges.

Fold the fabric in half with the selvages together. Place the centre back edge of the back jacket pattern piece onto the fold. Place the sleeve and front jacket pattern pieces on the fabric, ensuring that grain lines (the double arrowed lines marked on templates) run parallel to the selvages. Pin and cut out all the pieces. Snip the fabric to mark notch positions.

2 Pin sleeve to back, right sides together, along raglan style line, matching notches. Sew along this line. Neaten edge with zigzag stitch. Press seam towards back jacket. Repeat for the other

sleeve. Pin front to sleeve, right sides together, along raglan style line. Sew along this line. Neaten edge with zigzag stitch. Press seam towards front jacket. Repeat with remaining front piece.

3 Pin front and back jacket pieces, right sides together, along sleeve and side seams. Starting at end of sleeve and working towards the underarm seam, sew together. Continue down side seam to end of jacket. Snip at underarm point. Neaten edge with zigzag stitch. Repeat with other side of jacket.

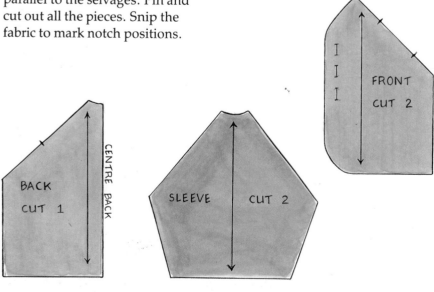

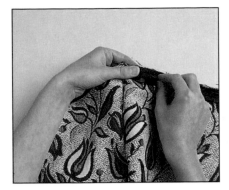

4 To finish the jacket edges, cut a length of satin bias binding measuring 185 cm (74 in). Open out one of the folded edges of the binding. Starting at the centre back of jacket hem, pin and tack (baste) binding to jacket, right sides together, all the way around the edge until you reach where you started. Take care not to stretch the fabric, especially around the corners. Sew in place 1 cm (³⁄₈ in) from the edge.

5 Turn the bias binding over to the wrong side of the work. Pin and tack (baste) binding down, all the way around the jacket. Top stitch into place. Remove all tacking (basting) threads. To finish the sleeve edges, cut a length of satin bias binding measuring 26 cm (10½ in). Work as for the jacket edges and repeat for remaining sleeve.

6 Cover the 3 button moulds with matching fabric, following the manufacturer's instructions. Make 3 buttonholes (on the right side for girls or the left side for boys), each measuring 2.5 cm (1 in). Sew on the buttons.

Rocking Cradle Card

THIS IS A SIMPLE YET EFFECTIVE SPECIAL OCCASION CARD

YOU WILL NEED ■ *45 × 60 cm (18 × 24 in) pink card* ■ *Pencil*
■ *Paper* ■ *Metal ruler* ■ *Scissors* ■ *30 cm (12 in) lace, 12 mm (½ in) wide* ■ *Rubber-based glue* ■ *30 cm (12 in) white satin ribbon, 12 mm (½ in) wide*

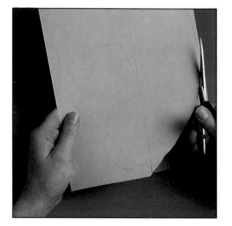

1 Fold the card in half. Scale up the template onto paper and transfer it to the card. Cut out the shape through both layers. Return the template to the back of the card and mark the fold line. Carefully fold the card outwards along this line.

2 Ease the lace strip around the front edge of the card and glue it down. Fold over 6 mm (¼ in) of the lace and stick this to the back of the card.

3 Stick the top halves of card together down to the fold line. Make a ribbon bow and stick it to the front of the card.

Baby's Gift Box

THE PERFECT PRESENT FOR A NEW MOTHER

YOU WILL NEED ■ *Scissors* ■ *Piece of striped fabric to cover base* ■ *Square wooden box with clear lid* ■ *Tape measure* ■ *Sticky tape* ■ *Rubber-based glue* ■ *Length of pre-gathered lace* ■ *White yarn* ■ *Large darning needle* ■ *2 small white pompons* ■ *About 30 cotton buds (swabs)* ■ *Rubber band* ■ *3 pieces of ribbon* ■ *Needle and thread* ■ *3 satin roses* ■ *1 face cloth* ■ *Small bunch artificial flowers* ■ *Piece of lace fabric* ■ *Small round soap* ■ *Duck motif or any other motif* ■ *1 natural sponge* ■ *Baby brush* ■ *Baby bear or other small ornament* ■ *4–6 absorbent cotton balls*

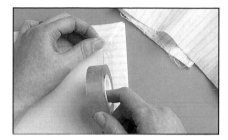

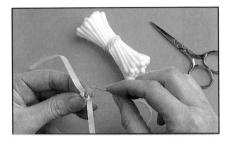

1 Cut the fabric to the size of the box base, plus 6 cm (2⅜ in) all round. Place the base on the wrong side of the fabric and fold the edges over, securing them with pieces of sticky tape.

2 Glue the lace around the box. To make the corner bow, take 3 lengths of yarn and, using a darning needle, pass each strand through a pompon. Tie the strands at one end and trim. Braid the yarn until you reach 5 cm (2 in) from the end. Pass the yarn through the other pompon and pull until the braid meets the pompon. Finish off in the same way. Sew a bow to one corner.

3 Take the cotton buds (swabs) and secure together with a rubber band. Fold a 3 cm (1¼ in) length of ribbon in half to find the centre, and sew a small satin rose in place. Sew the other roses on either side. Wrap the ribbon around the bunch of cotton buds (swabs), ensuring that the rubber band is completely covered and the roses centred. Tie at the back and trim the ends.

4 Fold the face cloth to fit the box and tie a ribbon into a bow around it. Tuck a small bunch of artificial flowers under the bow. Wrap the lace fabric around the soap and gather the edges at one side. Tie a ribbon to hold in place. Trim the top and glue the motif to the front. Arrange the decorated objects attractively in the box together with the sponge, baby brush and the ornament, filling in any gaps with absorbent cotton balls. Replace the lid.

Crocheted Blanket

THIS DELICATE BLANKET HAS AN ATTRACTIVE SHAPED BORDER

YOU WILL NEED ■ *150 g (6 oz) 2-ply yarn* ■ *2 mm (B) crochet hook* ■ *Large darning needle*

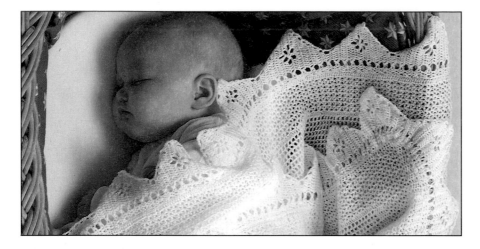

MEASUREMENTS
85 cm (34 in) square.

Make 198 ch.
1st row: tr (dc) into 4th ch from hook, tr (dc) into each ch to end, turn with 3 ch.
2nd row: 3 tr (dc), miss 1 tr (dc), (1 tr (dc), 1 ch, 1 tr (dc)) into next st (1 V st made). Repeat 96 times, 4 tr (dc), turn with 3 ch.
3rd row: 3 tr (dc). V st in each ch 1, space 96 times, 4 tr (dc), turn with 3 ch.
Repeat 3rd row 7 times.
9th row: 4 tr (dc), 7 V st, 3 tr (dc) into each V st until 7 V st remain, 7 V st, 4 tr (dc), turn with 3 ch.
10th row: 7 V st, 4 tr (dc), 1 ch, (miss 1 tr (dc), 1 ch, 1 tr (dc) in next tr (dc)) repeat to last 4 tr (dc), 4 tr (dc), 7 V st, 4 tr (dc). Turn with 3 ch.
11th row: 4 tr (dc), 7 V st, 4 tr (dc), 1 ch, (1 tr (dc) over tr (dc), 1 ch, miss 1 ch) repeat to last 4 tr (dc), 4 tr (dc), 7 V st, 4 tr (dc), turn with 3 ch.
Continue keeping pattern until work measures 60 cm (24 in).
Next row: 4 tr (dc), 7 V st, 4 tr (dc) (1 tr (dc) in ch space, 1 tr (dc) over tr (dc)) to last 4 tr (dc), 4 tr (dc)

over tr (dc), 7 V st, 4 tr (dc). Turn with 3 ch.
Next row: 4 tr (dc), V st to last 4 tr (dc), 4 tr (dc) over tr (dc).
Repeat last row 7 times.
Next row: 4 tr (dc) over 4 tr (dc), 3 tr (dc) into each V st to end of row. Fasten off.

Border
Make 10 ch.
1st row: 1 tr (dc) into 3rd ch from hook. 1 tr (dc), 2 ch, miss 1 ch, 1 dc (sc) into next ch, 2 ch, miss 1 ch (one lacet). 3 tr (dc), 2 ch, 1 dtr into base of last tr (dc), 5 ch. Turn.
2nd row: 2 tr (dc) into ch sp, 3 tr (dc), 3 ch, 2 tr (dc) into next 2 tr (dc), 1 tr (dc) into turning ch, 3 ch, turn.
3rd row: 2 tr (dc), 1 lc, 5 tr (dc), 2 tr (dc) into dtr sp, 2 ch, 1 dtr into sp, 5 ch, turn.
4th row: 2 tr (dc) into ch sp, 7 tr (dc), 3 ch, 2 tr (dc) into next 2 tr (dc), 1 tr (dc) into ch, 3 ch, turn.
5th row: 2 tr (dc), 1 lc, 9 tr (dc), 2 tr (dc) into dtr (dc) sp, 2 ch, 1 dtr into dtr sp, 5 ch, turn.
6th row: 2 tr (dc) into dtr sp, 11 tr (dc), 3 ch, 2 tr (dc) into next 2 tr (dc), 1 tr (dc) into turning ch, 3 ch, turn.

7th row: 2 tr (dc), 1 lc, 7 tr (dc), 3 ch, miss 1 tr (dc), 5 tr (dc), 2 tr (dc) into dtr, sp 2 ch, 1 dtr (dc), into dtr sp, 5 ch, turn.
8th row: 2 tr (dc) into ch sp, 5 tr (dc), 3 ch, miss 2 tr (dc), 5 tr (dc), 3 ch, miss 2 tr (dc), 1 dc (sc) into ch sp, 3 ch, miss 2 tr (dc), 5 tr (dc), 3 ch, 2 tr (dc) into next 2 tr (dc), 1 tr (dc) into turning ch, 3 ch, turn.
9th row: 2 tr (dc), 1 ch, 1 lc, 3 tr (dc), miss 2 tr (dc), 3 ch, 1 dc into ch sp, 1 dc (sc) into dc (sc) of previous row, 1 dc (sc) into ch sp, 3 ch, miss 2 tr (dc), 5 tr (dc), 2 tr (dc) into ch sp, 1 quad tr (dc) into sp, 3 ch, turn.
10th row: miss 2 tr (dc), 5 tr (dc), 2 tr (dc) into ch sp, 3 ch, miss 1 dc (sc), dc (sc) into next dc (sc), 3 ch, 2 tr (dc) into ch sp, 3 tr (dc), 3 ch, 2 tr (dc) into next 2 tr (dc), 1 tr (dc) into turning ch, 3 ch, turn.
11th row: 2 tr (dc), 1 lc, 5 tr (dc), 2 tr (dc) into ch sp, 1 ch, 2 tr (dc) into next ch sp, 5 tr (dc), miss 2 tr (dc), 1 dtr into ch sp, turn.
12th row: 3 ch, miss 2 tr (dc), 5 tr (dc), 1 tr (dc) into ch sp, 7 tr (dc), 3 ch, 2 tr (dc) into next 2 tr (dc), 1 tr (dc) into turning ch, 3 ch, turn.
13th row: 2 tr (dc), 1 lc, 11 tr (dc), miss 2 tr (dc), 1 dtr into sp, 3 ch, turn.
14th row: miss 2 tr (dc), 9 tr (dc), 3 ch, 2 tr (dc) into next 2 tr (dc), 1 tr (dc) into turning ch, 3 ch, turn.
15th row: 2 tr (dc), 1 lc, 7 tr (dc), 1 dtr into sp turn.
16th row: miss 2 tr (dc), 5 tr (dc), 3 ch, 2 tr (dc) into next 2 tr (dc), 1 tr (dc) into turning ch, 3 ch.
17th row: 2 tr (dc), 1 lc, 3 tr (dc), 2 ch, 1 dtr into sp, 5 ch, turn.
Repeat from 2nd row to 17th row until the border is long enough, allowing for a slight gathering. Sew on the border.

Patchwork Frame

THIS PRETTY PATCHWORK FRAME IS IDEAL FOR A CHILD'S PHOTOGRAPH

YOU WILL NEED ■ *Natural sponge* ■ *Blue, yellow and white fabric paints*
■ *70 cm (¾ yd) white cotton fabric* ■ *Iron* ■ *Craft knife* ■ *Ruler* ■ *Thin card*
■ *Mounting board* ■ *Scissors* ■ *Pencil* ■ *Paper* ■ *Pins* ■ *Needle and thread* ■ *Thin
wadding (batting)* ■ *Brown parcel tape* ■ *Strong clear glue*

1 Sponge the fabric using the fabric paints and a natural sponge in pastel shades of blue, yellow and green. Leave to dry before pressing firmly with an iron to fix the dye, following the manufacturer's instructions.

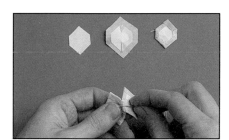

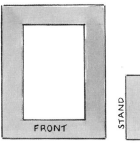

2 Using the template as a guide, cut out all the frame pieces in card and mounting board. Cut out paper hexagonal shapes for the individual patches, being as accurate as possible. Pin the paper shapes to the sponged fabric, with a grain line on one edge.

Cut out the hexagons, leaving a 0.5 cm (³⁄₁₆ in) seam allowance. Turn the edges over and tack (baste). Sew the hexagons together using tiny oversewing stitches until the patchwork fits over the frame. Remove the tacking (basting) and press. Remove the papers.

3 Cut a piece of wadding (batting) slightly larger than the frame, and then sew this and the patchwork to the frame, using herringbone stitch as shown to secure at the back.

4 Make the hinge of the stand with brown parcel tape and cover this and the remaining frame pieces with sponged fabric. Glue the frame together and press it under a heavy weight till dry.

Crocheted Dolls

THESE CHARMING CROCHETED COTTON DOLLS MAKE IDEAL COMPANIONS

YOU WILL NEED ■ *3.5 mm (E) crochet hook* ■ *25 g (1 oz) green double knitting (sport) cotton* ■ *Scissors* ■ *25 g (1 oz) yellow double knitting (sport) cotton* ■ *15 g (¾ oz) pink double knitting (sport) cotton* ■ *2 handfuls of non-toxic, flame retardant polyester filling (batting)* ■ *Tape measure* ■ *15 g (¾ oz) black double knitting (sport) cotton* ■ *Large darning needle* ■ *Oddments of red, dark green and blue double knitting (sport) cotton*

MEASUREMENTS

Crocheted with a 3.5 mm (E) hook, the finished dolls will measure 25 cm (10 in) from head to toe. Using a larger crochet hook will produce a larger doll.

BODY AND HEAD

Starting at the bottom of the body, and using green cotton, work 3 ch, then join into a ring with a ss in first chain.

1st step: 1 ch, 5 dc (sc) into ring. Close with a ss in first dc (sc).
2nd step: 1 ch, now working in a spiral fashion, 2 dc (sc) in each st until you have 24 sts on work.
3rd step: * 1 dc (sc) in each st. Repeat from * 23 more times.
4th step: * 1 dc (sc) in each of next 11 sts, miss 1 st. Repeat from * 1 more time.
5th step: * 1 dc (sc) in each st. Repeat from * 109 more times.

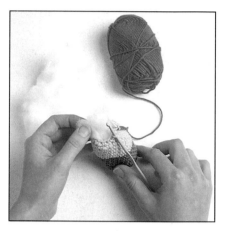

6th step: Cut green cotton and join yellow cotton. Keep short ends inside work. With yellow cotton work upper body as follows:
* 1 dc (sc) in each st. Repeat from * 65 more times.
7th step: 1 dc (sc) in each of the next 5 sts, miss 1 st, 1 dc (sc) in each of next 10 sts, miss 1 st.
8th step: 1 dc (sc) in each of next 54 sts, miss 1 st, 1 dc (sc) in each of next 9 sts, miss 1 st (you now have 18 sts on the work).
9th step: * 1 dc (sc) in first st, miss next st, 1 dc (sc) in following st. Repeat from * 5 more times.
10th step: Cut yellow cotton and join pink cotton. Keep ends inside the work.
  With pink cotton work neck and head as follows:
* 1 dc (sc) in each st. Repeat from * 11 more times.

Take a handful of polyester filling (batting) and stuff the body.
11th step: * 1 dc (sc) in first st, miss next st. Repeat from * 5 more times.
12th step: * 2 dc (sc) in first st, 1 dc (sc) in next st. Repeat from * 5 more times.
13th step: * 1 dc (sc) in each st. Repeat from * 11 more times.
14th step: * 2 dc (sc) in first st, 1 dc (sc) in each of next 2 sts. Repeat from * 7 more times.
15th step: * 1 dc (sc) in each st. Repeat from * 19 more times.
16th step: * 1 dc (sc) in each of next 2 sts, miss 1 st, 1 dc (sc) in next st. Repeat from * 4 more times.
17th step: * 1 dc (sc) in each st. Repeat from * 29 more times.
18th step: Cut pink cotton and join black cotton. Keep short ends inside work. With black cotton work hair as follows:
* 1 dc (sc) in each st. Repeat from * 29 more times.
Take some polyester filling (batting) and stuff the head.
19th step: * miss first st, 1 dc (sc)

in each of next 2 sts. Repeat from * 4 more times.

20th step: * miss first st, 1 dc (sc) in next st. Repeat from * 4 more times. Cast (bind) off last st. Sew end of cotton into the head.

ARMS

1st step: using yellow cotton work 3 ch, approx 60 cm (24 in) from end of cotton. (This will be used later to attach arm to body.) Join into a ring with a ss in first ch.

2nd step: 1 ch, 5 dc (sc) into ring, close with a ss in first dc (sc). Hook the 60 cm (24 in) end of cotton through centre of the ring so it hangs on the right side of work.

3rd step: Working in a spiral fashion, * 2 dc (sc) in first st, 1 dc (sc) in next. Repeat from * 2 more times (you now have 8 sts on the work).

4th step: * 1 dc (sc) in each st. Repeat from * 95 more times.

5th step: Cut yellow cotton and join pink cotton. Keep short ends inside work. With pink cotton work hands as follows:
* 1 dc (sc) in first st, miss next st. Repeat from * 3 more times.

6th step: * 2 dc (sc) in first st, 1 dc (sc) in next st. Repeat from * 3 more times.

7th step: * 1 dc (sc) in each st. Repeat from * 15 more times.

8th step: * miss first st, 1 dc (sc) in each of next 3 sts. Repeat from * 1 more time.
Cast (bind) off last st. Sew end of cotton into hand.
Repeat steps 1–8 for other arm.

LEGS

1st step: using green cotton work the legs by following steps 1–3 as given for the arms.

4th step: * 1 dc (sc) in each of next 3 sts, 2 dc (sc) in following st. Repeat from * 1 more time.

5th step: * 1 dc (sc) in each st. Repeat from * 149 more times.

6th step: Cut green cotton and join pink cotton. Keep short ends inside work. With pink cotton work feet as follows:
* 1 dc (sc) in each st. Repeat from * 9 more times.

7th step: * 1 dc (sc) in each of next 2 sts, miss 1 st. Repeat from * 2 more times.

8th step: * 1 dc (sc) in each st. Repeat from * 8 more times (you now have 7 sts to work).

9th step: 1 dc (sc) in each of next 2 sts, 2 dc (sc) in each of next 4 sts, 1 dc (sc) in next st.

10th step: Cut pink cotton and join black cotton. With black cotton work shoe as follows: 1 dc (sc) in each of next 3 sts, 2 dc (sc) in each of next 6 sts, 1 dc (sc) in each of next 3 sts.

11th step: * 1 dc (sc) in each st. Repeat from * 21 more times.

12th step: Miss first st, 1 dc (sc) in each of next 4 sts, miss 1 st, 1 dc (sc) in each of next 6 sts.

13th step: * ss in each st. Repeat from * 14 more times.
Cast (bind) off last st. Sew end of cotton into shoe.
Repeat steps 1–13 to make the remaining leg.

TO MAKE UP

Attach the arms and legs to the doll's body as follows:

Using 60 cm (24 in) cotton ends, work several slightly loose stitches. Make a shank by twisting the cotton tightly around the stitches. Fasten off.

EARS AND NOSE

Cut a piece of pink cotton measuring approximately 80 cm (32 in) in length. Using it double, embroider as follows:

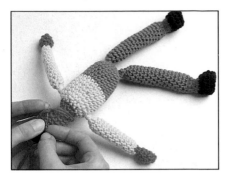

Starting at the bottom of the ear, make a 1 cm (⅜ in) long back stitch, bringing needle out at the starting position (to form a loop). Bind the loop with 3–4 blanket stitches. Repeat on other side of head for remaining ear and in the centre for the nose.

MOUTH

Using a single strand of red cotton, sew mouth in the same way as for the ears.

EYES

Using a single strand of dark green cotton, work several small back stitches in the same place, either side of the nose. Fasten off. Decorate neck edge and cuffs of the doll's body with simple running stitches.

143

Ribbon Motif Frame

BRIGHTEN UP A SIMPLE WOODEN FRAME WITH THIS PRETTY RIBBON DESIGN

YOU WILL NEED ■ *Wooden picture frame* ■ *Masking tape* ■ *Non-toxic acrylic paints* ■ *Small paintbrush* ■ *Pencil* ■ *White paper* ■ *Ruler* ■ *Chalk* ■ *Non-toxic clear acrylic varnish*

1 Undo the frame carefully and stick masking tape around the edges of the glass to keep it clean while you are working. Put the glass back in and paint the frame with your base colour of acrylic paint.

2 Measure the width of the frame and then, using the template as a guide, draw the ribbon design onto the paper. Chalk the opposite side of the design and transfer to the frame by drawing over the outline.

3 Using the small brush, paint in the line of the design with a contrasting colour.

4 Add highlights by painting in touches of a slightly lighter hue and leave to dry. Varnish the frame with a coat of clear acrylic varnish and finally remove the masking tape.

Poppy Hat

THIS FLOWERY HAT IS PERFECT FOR LONG SUMMER DAYS

YOU WILL NEED ■ *Pencil* ■ *White paper* ■ *Scissors* ■ *Ruler* ■ *Pieces of brown, red and green felt*
■ *Absorbent cotton balls* ■ *Needle and thread* ■ *Straw hat*

1 To make the petals, draw a shape 6 × 4 cm (2¼ × 1½ in) at the widest point and cut out of the paper. Using this pattern, cut out 6 petals in the red felt. Cut 2 leaf shapes from green felt. To create the centre of the poppy, cut a 6 cm (2¼ in) square of brown felt and another length of brown felt 2 × 5 cm (¾ × 2 in) with a small fringe cut down one length. Lay a small absorbent cotton ball in the centre of the brown felt square and draw the felt up around it. Stitch neatly in place.

2 Wrap the fringed piece of brown felt around the centre piece, with the fringe side up. Sew in place and carefully cut off any excess.

3 Sew a small tuck in the narrow part of each of the red petals. Lay each petal against the poppy centre and sew in place. Continue round using all the petals, overlapping each one. Repeat the same process to make the second poppy.

4 Finish by sewing the completed poppies onto one side of the hat. Place a leaf shape on either side of the poppies and sew in place.

Party **P**inafore

THIS PRETTY PINAFORE DRESS FITS 1 TO 2-YEAR-OLDS

YOU WILL NEED ■ *Scissors* ■ *Tape measure* ■ *0.5 m (½ yd) of cotton fabric, 115 cm (45 in) wide*
■ *Needle and thread* ■ *Iron* ■ *Pins* ■ *Tailor's chalk*

1 First make the shoulder straps. Cut a 9 cm (3½ in) strip across the width of the fabric. Cut this into 4 equal lengths of 26 cm (10¼ in).

2 Sew the straps together in pairs, with right sides together, leaving 3 cm (1¼ in) open at each end for turning. Press and turn right side out.

3 Cut the remaining fabric in half lengthwise. Mark a 10 cm (4 in) gap in the centre of the top edges of both pieces of fabric. Gather up the fabric evenly on either side of the central section on both the back and front of the pinafore until it fits the shoulder straps exactly. Pin the straps in position and then sew them in place securely. Sew up the side seams and trim to neaten.

4 Turn up the hem to the length required. Pin and stitch all round. Remove the pins and press the pinafore.

Decorated Hair Band

THIS PRETTY HAIR BAND WILL APPEAL TO CHILDREN OF ALL AGES

YOU WILL NEED ■ *Pencil* ■ *Plain coloured hair band* ■ *6 different
coloured yarns* ■ *Scissors* ■ *Large darning needle*

2 To start the embroidery, lay a length of yarn along a pattern line, leaving a long thread at each end. Thread the needle with a contrasting coloured length of yarn and secure the first length of yarn at even intervals with a small stitch into the fabric. Finish by sewing the end into the hair band. Rethread the original yarn and sew each end into the hair band to secure.

1 Using a pencil, draw your design onto the hair band.

3 Following the pattern, use 2 different coloured yarns in the same way, remembering to secure all the ends by sewing them into the hair band. Finish by sewing French knots and small crosses using the last 2 colours.

To sew a French knot, stitch into the fabric at the required position. Hold the thread down with the left thumb and encircle it 2 or 3 times with the threaded needle. Still holding the thread firmly, twist the needle back to the starting point and insert it close to where the original thread emerged. Pull the thread through and secure.

Height Chart

KEEP TRACK OF YOUR CHILD'S GROWTH WITH THIS DECORATIVE CHART

YOU WILL NEED ■ *Metal ruler* ■ *Pencil* ■ *125 × 25 cm (50 × 10 in)*
coloured paper ■ *Craft knife* ■ *Marker pens* ■ *Numerals stencil* ■ *Assorted animal*
pictures ■ *Scissors* ■ *Strong clear glue* ■ *2 rolls iron-on protective laminating film, 4 m × 30 cm*
(5 × 1 ft) ■ *Iron* ■ *60 cm (24 in) wooden dowelling* ■ *Rubber-based glue* ■ *String*

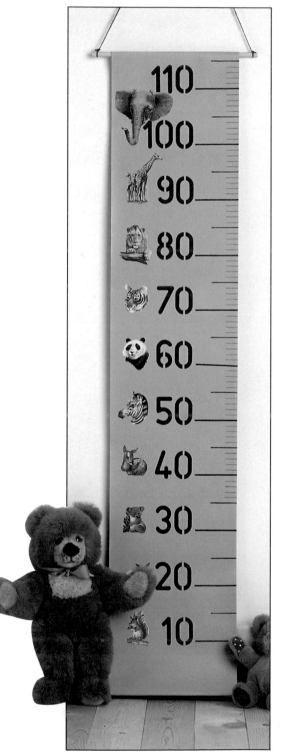

1 Using the metal ruler, mark out two lines 4 and 5 cm (1½ and 2 in) from the top and bottom ends of the paper, and lightly score across them using a craft knife. On the right-hand side of the paper measure from the lower score line and pencil in divisions of 5 and 10 cm or 3 and 6 in, starting at 10 cm or 6 in. Mark single units too after 35 cm or 12 in, making a longer mark for each 5th and 10th unit.

2 Use a thick marker pen to mark out 8 cm (3¼ in) lines at each of the 10 cm or 6 in divisions. Use a medium marker pen to mark out 5 cm (2 in) long lines at the intervening 5 cm or 3 in divisions and finally use a thin pen to mark out the remaining units with 1 cm (⅜ in) long lines.

Using the stencil, number each 10 cm or 6 in division from 10 cm to 110 cm, or each 6 in division from 6 in to 5 ft. Cut out pictures to fit each 10th division, working from the smallest at the first division to the largest at the highest division. Glue in place.

3 Spread the sheet out on an ironing board. Cover the top surface with the iron-on protective laminating film and iron down carefully according to the manufacturer's instructions. Turn the sheet over and repeat the process on the reverse side.

4 Fold the top and bottom of the chart at the score lines. Cut the wooden dowelling in half and glue one length at each end with rubber-based glue. Tie string to each end of the top dowelling and hang the chart so that the base rests on the floor.

Rocking Parrot

GIVE THE PERCH A FEW TWISTS, AND THIS PARROT WILL SWING AROUND UNAIDED

YOU WILL NEED ■ *Pencil* ■ *Paper* ■ *Scissors* ■ *30 × 20 cm (12 × 8 in) plywood, 6 mm (¼ in)*
thick ■ *Fretsaw (scroll saw)* ■ *Scrap wood* ■ *Hand drill* ■ *Sandpaper* ■ *Masking tape* ■ *30 cm (12 in)*
dowelling ■ *Paintbrushes* ■ *Acrylic paints* ■ *Wood glue* ■ *90 cm (36 in) coloured string*

3 Smooth down any rough edges on the parrot shape with sandpaper.

4 Starting from the centre, wind masking tape outwards to each end of the dowelling, leaving uncovered spaces between the tape. Paint the uncovered area and leave to dry before peeling off the tape. Paint the parrot in bright colours, section by section. Drill a 3 mm (⅛ in) hole at each end of the dowelling and slide it into the hole in the parrot. Glue it in the centre, with the 2 holes at the ends facing upwards. Thread the string through the 2 holes, wrap it around the ends and tie securely. Carefully knot a loop at the centre.

1 Scale up the parrot template to the size required and draw the shape onto a sheet of paper. Cut it out and then draw around the outline onto the plywood sheet. Cut out carefully with the fretsaw (scroll saw).

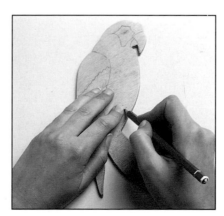

2 Mark the centre of the hole where the dowelling perch is to be inserted. Place the parrot onto a piece of scrap wood and accurately drill a hole to exactly the same diameter as that of the piece of dowelling.

Photo Album

A PLAIN ALBUM CAN EASILY BE MADE INTO A SPECIAL MEMENTO

YOU WILL NEED ■ *Scissors* ■ *Scrap book pictures of ducks* ■ *Photo album with plain cover* ■ *Rubber-based glue* ■ *Pressed flowers such as lady's mantle, French marigold, daisies, verbena and thyme* ■ *Tweezers* ■ *Toothpick* ■ *Iron-on protective laminating film*

1 Cut out a picture of a mother duck and her ducklings, and stick it towards the bottom front of the photo album as shown, using rubber-based glue.

2 Using a selection of the pressed flowers, build up a picture by securing the flowers to the album. The best way to do this is to hold each flower with a pair of tweezers and to apply tiny dots of rubber-based glue with a toothpick. Continue until the ducks appear to be nestling among a profusion of flowers.

3 Cut out a piece of iron-on protective laminating film to the exact size of the front cover. Put a piece of supporting material under the cover and iron on the film, following the manufacturer's instructions.

Train Cake

THIS BIRTHDAY CAKE MAKES AN IMPRESSIVE PARTY PIECE

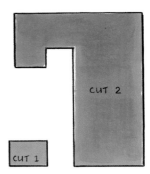

YOU WILL NEED ■ *50 g/2 oz/¹/₂ cup desiccated (shredded) coconut*
■ *Green food colouring* ■ *50 g/2 oz /¹/₃ cup icing (confectioner's) sugar*
■ *Large cake board* ■ *Ruler* ■ *Pen* ■ *Paper* ■ *Scissors* ■ *1 large flat*
chocolate sponge cake ■ *Pastry board* ■ *Sharp knife* ■ *4 cm (1½ in) round pastry*
cutter ■ *175 g/6 oz/³/₄ cup butter* ■ *225 g/8 oz/1½ cups icing (confectioner's) sugar*
■ *50 g/2 oz/¹/₃ cup chocolate powder* ■ *Icing bag and nozzles* ■ *Palette knife*
(spatula) ■ *Chocolate swiss roll* ■ *White chocolate buttons*
■ *Sugar-coated chocolate buttons* ■ *Chocolate flakes*
■ *Cotton wool (absorbent cotton)*

1 Place the desiccated (shredded) coconut in a bag, add 2 drops of green colouring and shake well. Mix the icing (confectioner's) sugar with warm water to make a thin glacé icing. Spread over the cake board and shake over the coloured coconut. Scale up the templates and cut out the pattern pieces. Place the cake on the pastry board, lay the paper patterns on top and use a sharp knife to cut out the cab pieces and engine base.

3 To make the icing, beat together the butter and icing (confectioner's) sugar until light and fluffy, then beat in the chocolate powder. Place half the mixture in the icing bag and chill in the fridge. Place the engine base across the prepared cake board. Use the palette knife (spatula) to spread on a layer of butter icing and then stick down the Swiss roll on its side.

4 Use a generous layer of butter icing to fix and assemble the cab behind the 'engine'. Position the wheels. Pipe around the edges of the cab with the chilled butter icing and decorate the engine with piping and plain and sugar-coated chocolate buttons. Add a chocolate flake for the funnel and a tiny piece of cotton wool (absorbent cotton) for the smoke.

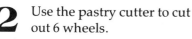

2 Use the pastry cutter to cut out 6 wheels.

Keepsake **P**in **C**ushion

THIS ORNAMENTAL PIN CUSHION MAKES AN ATTRACTIVE MEMENTO

YOU WILL NEED ■ *Needle and thread* ■ *1 m (40 in) lace, 2 cm (¾ in) wide* ■ *Pins* ■ *2 pieces of quilted raw silk fabric, 18 × 13 cm (7 × 5¼ in)* ■ *2 pieces of cotton fabric, 18 × 13 cm (7 × 5¼ in)*
■ *Tape measure* ■ *Decorative motifs* ■ *Bran or sawdust* ■ *Heart-shaped pearl motif* ■ *Funnel*

1 Sew a running stitch along the lace and gather. Pin the lace to the right side of 1 piece of silk, 1.5 cm (⅝ in) from the edge and tack (baste). Lay the other piece of silk on top so that right sides are together. Pin and tack (baste) leaving one short end open. Remove the pins and stitch. Turn through.

2 Pin the 2 pieces of cotton fabric with right sides together, and tack (baste). Remove the pins and stitch all round a 6 cm (2¼ in) opening. Turn the bag through and pour the bran or sawdust through the opening using a funnel until you have a firm, plump cushion. Slip stitch the opening to close.

3 Place the bag inside the silk cover. Hand stitch the opening together behind the lace. Position the motifs and use the pins to hold them in place. You could also include the baby's initials in your design.

Special Celebration Card

A DELICATE EFFECT CAN BE ACHIEVED BY USING COLLAGE TECHNIQUES

YOU WILL NEED ■ *White card, 21 × 14 cm (8½ × 5½ in)* ■ *Stiff card* ■ *Pencil* ■ *Scissors*
■ *Pink tissue paper* ■ *White tissue paper* ■ *Paper glue* ■ *Length of narrow lace* ■ *Length of small fake*
pearls ■ *7 pearlized sequins* ■ *Silver pen* ■ *Length of narrow white ribbon*

1 Fold the white card in half. Draw the template onto a piece of stiff card and cut out 2 hearts. Fold the pink tissue paper to obtain 5 layers. Lay the larger heart template on the tissue paper and draw round it. Carefully tear out the hearts, holding the 5 layers together. It will not matter if you do not tear right on the line. This will only add to the interest of the card. Do the same with the white tissue paper, using the smaller heart template.

2 Arrange the hearts diagonally across the front of the card and glue in place.

3 Position the lace diagonally to create a border on either side of the hearts. Glue the lace in position and trim the ends to neaten. Repeat using the pearls. Stick the sequins at random over the hearts. Add small decorative dots in each of the corners using a silver pen.

4 Cut a piece of tissue paper 21 × 14 cm (8½ × 5½ in). Fold in half and place inside the card. Tie the ribbon to hold the card together and tie in a bow. Use the silver pen to write your message inside, but slip a piece of paper behind the tissue to prevent the ink from seeping through.

Sailing Ship Cabinet

THIS NAUTICAL IDEA WILL BRIGHTEN UP ANY PIECE OF NURSERY FURNITURE

YOU WILL NEED ■ *Sandpaper* ■ *Cabinet or cupboard* ■ *Soft cloth*
■ *Paintbrushes* ■ *Matt white emulsion (flat latex) paint* ■ *Matt blue emulsion (flat latex) paint* ■ *Scissors* ■ *Picture of a ship, photocopied in several sizes* ■ *Rubber-based glue*
■ *Non-toxic acrylic paints* ■ *Non-toxic, clear acrylic varnish* ■ *Oak coloured varnish*

1 Sand your chosen piece of furniture with sandpaper then wipe it with a damp cloth. Paint on a coat of white emulsion (flat latex) paint and allow to dry. Then paint on 2 coats of pale blue emulsion (flat latex), allowing time to dry between coats. Carefully cut out your photocopied images and arrange them on the furniture. Stick them down with rubber-based glue, making sure that they are flat and smooth. Allow to dry for at least 2 hours.

2 Next paint watery washes of acrylic colour onto the photocopied boats to give them depth and make them look realistic. Use plain blue for the sea and yellow ochre for the sails, seams and rigging. Use raw umber for the clouds. Use a mixture of yellow ochre with white for the highlights and raw umber with white for the lowlights, painting in a swirling motion and blending the 2 colours together with your fingers to give added texture.

3 Allow the acrylic paints to dry thoroughly. This will take about 2 hours, although you can speed up the process slightly by placing the piece of furniture in a warm (but not too hot) position. When the paints are completely dry, paint a thin coat of clear acrylic varnish over the whole surface with a fairly large brush. This is an important stage, as this varnish will protect the paper from the final varnishing, which requires some rubbing.

4 When the acrylic varnish is dry, paint on the oak coloured varnish taking a small area at a time, and rub off in a circular motion with a clean cloth. Leave some of the stain in some areas to give the piece an aged look. Finish with another coat of the clear varnish.

Pocketed Quilt

THIS COSY ACTIVITY QUILT HAS POCKETS FOR HIDING SURPRISE GIFTS

YOU WILL NEED ■ *Scissors* ■ *6 pieces of 25 × 25 cm*
(10 × 10 in) fabric for pockets ■ *Pins* ■ *Needle and thread* ■ *Pinking shears*
■ *75 cm (30 in) fringing* ■ *2 pieces of 65 × 120 cm (26 × 47 in) fabric for quilt* ■ *64 × 120 cm*
(25½ × 47 in) light wadding (batting) ■ *3.7 m (4 yd) bias binding*

1 Cut out the pocket pieces. Pin the squares together in pairs and sew round the edges. Trim the edges with pinking shears and turn right side out.

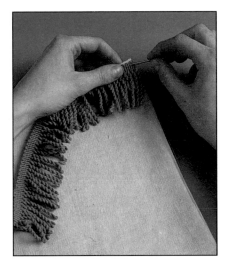

2 Cut 3 lengths of fringing 25 cm (10 in) long and sew one length along the top edges of each of the squares.

3 Sew the 3 pockets in a line down the length of one of the quilt pieces.

4 Sandwich the wadding (batting) between the 2 quilt pieces and sew the bias binding all around the edge.

Teddy Bear Card

THIS TECHNIQUE GIVES A PROFESSIONAL-LOOKING CARD

YOU WILL NEED ■ *Craft knife* ■ *Rectangle of coloured card* ■ *Metal ruler* ■ *Scissors* ■ *Motif cut from wrapping paper* ■ *Drawing paper* ■ *Spray adhesive* ■ *Adhesive foam strips*

1 Score the coloured card across the centre using a craft knife and metal ruler and fold it in half to form the card.

2 Roughly cut out your chosen motif, leaving a margin all around. Stick the motif to drawing paper using spray adhesive, working in a well-ventilated room. Cut out the backed motif carefully.

3 Stick the small strips of adhesive foam to the back of the motif.

4 Peel off the backing papers and carefully stick the picture to the front of the card.

Toy Bag

AN ATTRACTIVE BAG THAT IS PERFECT FOR STORING TOYS

YOU WILL NEED ■ *Scissors* ■ *2 fabric squares 55 × 55 cm (21½ × 21½ in)*
■ *Pins* ■ *Needle and thread* ■ *120 cm (47 in) cord*

1 Cut out the 2 square pieces of fabric. Fold over all the edges and pin down, leaving a slightly larger hem at the top. Sew along the top edge where the cord will pass through.

2 Sew the other 3 sides together, leaving a gap at the top edges to allow the cord to pass through.

3 Thread the cord through and tie a knot at the end.

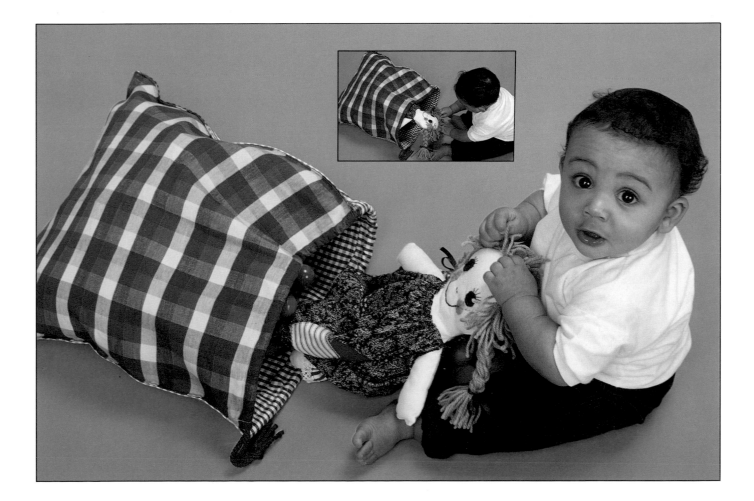

Spiky Fabric Bib

MAKE MEALTIMES MORE FUN WITH THIS UNUSUAL BIB

YOU WILL NEED ■ *White paper* ■ *Pencil* ■ *Ruler* ■ *Scissors*
■ *Pins* ■ *2 pieces of contrasting fabric, 20 × 24 cm (8 × 9½ in)* ■ *Scraps of fabric for spikes*
■ *Needle and thread* ■ *Pinking shears* ■ *48 cm (19 in) ribbon or fabric binding*

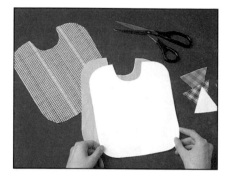

1 Scale up the template onto white paper and cut it out. Pin onto the pieces of contrasting fabric and then cut out 2 bib shapes and 6 spikes.

2 To make the spikes, join the triangular pieces in pairs and sew along 2 edges. Trim the edges with pinking shears and turn right side out.

3 Cut the ribbon in half and sandwich the 2 lengths between the 2 bib pieces along with the 3 spikes, securing them with a pin.

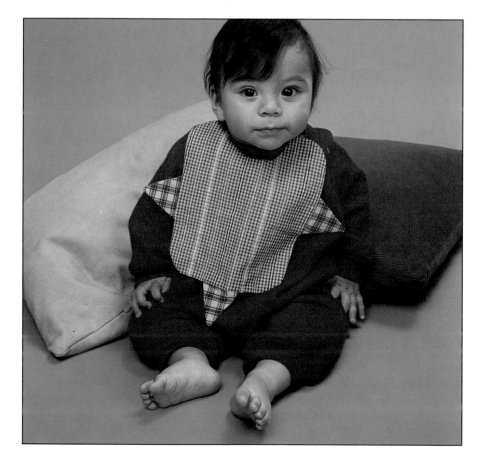

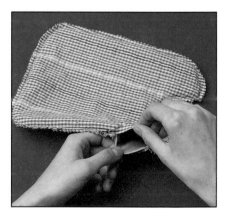

4 Sew around the edge of the bib, leaving a gap in order to turn the whole bib right side out. Once you have done this, sew up the gap and remove all the pins.

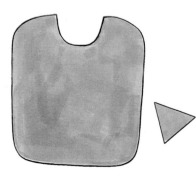

Candy Cushion

LET THE BABY ROLL AROUND THE NURSERY WITH THIS SOFT CUSHION

*YOU WILL NEED ■ Pencil ■ White paper ■ Ruler ■ Scissors ■ Oddments
of fabric for spikes ■ Needle and thread ■ Pinking shears ■ 65 × 92 cm (26 × 37 in) fabric
for the main cushion ■ 65 × 17 cm (26 × 6¾ in) fabric for inner flaps ■ 14 metal eyelets ■ Hammer
■ 92 cm (37 in) bias binding ■ 58 × 47 cm (23 × 18½ in) cushion ■ 120 cm (47 in) cord*

1 Draw a large triangle onto white paper. Cut it out and use it as a template for 16 fabric triangles. Cut out all the triangles and sew them together in pairs, then trim the seams and turn right side out. You should have 4 finished triangles for each end of the cushion.

2 Trim the cushion fabric with pinking shears to make a neat edge. Pin the triangles between the main piece of fabric and the flap, so that they are pointing inwards. Sew along each end to secure.

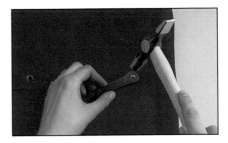

3 Attach 7 metal eyelets to each end of the fabric using a hammer and positioning the fabric over a hard surface.

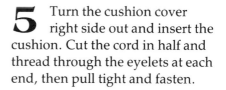

4 Fold the fabric over lengthwise, right sides together, and then sew the bias binding along the seam to give a neat finish.

5 Turn the cushion cover right side out and insert the cushion. Cut the cord in half and thread through the eyelets at each end, then pull tight and fasten.

Pressed Flower Birthday Card

A CHARMING AND DELICATE CARD FOR ANY AGE

YOU WILL NEED ■ *Craft knife* ■ *Metal ruler* ■ *30 × 15 cm (12 × 16 in)*
piece of pink card ■ *30 × 15 cm (12 × 6 in) piece of white card* ■ *Pencil* ■ *Pair of*
compasses ■ *Tweezers* ■ *Pressed flowers: forget-me-not, alyssum, London pride and small leaves*
(or your own alternatives) ■ *Rubber-based glue* ■ *Toothpick* ■ *10 × 12.5 cm*
(4 × 5 in) iron-on protective laminating film ■ *Iron*

3 Pencil the birthday age in the centre of the white card. Using tweezers, lift a forget-me-not and use the toothpick to place a tiny dab of glue onto the reverse side of the flower. Position each flower along the pencil line to form the numeral.

4 Use the remaining flowers to make a border inside the pencilled circle and around the numeral. Cover the design with the iron-on protective laminating film. Remove the backing from the film and iron down following the manufacturer's instructions. Apply glue sparingly all around the edge of the front cover and then carefully stick the white card in position.

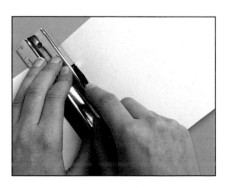

1 Using a craft knife and ruler, score and fold each card in half. Draw a 9 cm (3½ in) diameter circle using a pair of compasses in the centre of the pink card.

2 Cut out the circle from the pink card. Put the white card inside the pink one and draw carefully around the cut-out circle in pencil.

Celebration Tablepiece

THIS MAKES A DELIGHTFUL DECORATION FOR A SUMMER CELEBRATION

YOU WILL NEED ■ *Florist's plastic securing spike* ■ *Large flat bowl*
■ *Adhesive clay tape* ■ *Blunt kitchen knife* ■ *Florist's foam* ■ *Wire mesh* ■ *Strawberry*
leaves ■ *Daisy spray chrysanthemums* ■ *Scissors* ■ *Fresh strawberries* ■ *Small pretty vase*
■ *Euonymus foliage* ■ *Yellow spray carnations* ■ *Yellow tulips*

1 Fix the florist's plastic securing spike to the centre of the bowl with adhesive clay tape. Use a blunt kitchen knife to cut a block of soaked florist's foam into shape and impale on the spike. Place a ring of crumpled wire mesh around the foam at the base of the bowl.

2 Fill the bowl with water. Use the strawberry and chrysanthemum leaves to make a bed of foliage, sticking their stalks around the edges of the foam and leaving the centre free.

3 Cut the stems of the daisy spray chrysanthemums into short lengths and arrange them among the foliage. Scatter the strawberries at random among the flowers.

4 Fill the small vase with soaked foam and wedge in the centre of the foam block on the plate. Make a pretty arrangement of the euonymus, carnations and tulips in the vase to complete the tablepiece. These flowers make a very good combination, but you could of course use any other flowers of your choice.

Smocked Dress

SMOCKING BECOMES SIMPLE WHEN WORKED ON A FRESH COTTON GINGHAM

YOU WILL NEED ■ *Tape measure* ■ *Scissors* ■ *Gingham fabric in a 6 mm (¼ in) check* ■ *Iron*
■ *Needle and thread* ■ *Pins* ■ *Embroidery thread in toning colours*

1 This design can be adapted in order to fit any age or size. Calculating the fabric width you require is best done by working a small, measured practice section and opening it out once you have smocked it. The smocked fabric should cling gently.

Cut out the fabric for the dress, allowing for the smocking, a seam in the back, a generous hem, and a 4 cm (1½ in) allowance at the top. Turn down the top raw edge 4 cm (1½ in) to the wrong side, and press it down along the grain.

2 Starting 4 cm (1½ in) in from the right-hand side and 2 cm (¾ in) down from the folded top, knot a long thread on the upper corner of a light square. Take the needle behind the square and then out at the top left-hand corner.

Continue all the way along until you are 4 cm (1½ in) away from the opposite end. Leave the thread end loose, winding it around a pin to secure it. You will be working through the folded top for a few rows. Work as many rows of gathers as you are going to need for the size of your dress.

3 Draw up the gathers evenly until the tubes of fabric at the front and back are quite firm and lie tightly together. Secure all the thread ends on pins at the left-hand edge, wound in a figure of eight to ensure they cannot come undone.

4 Select your first embroidery colour and use 3 strands of thread. Your first line of smocking should start about 3 squares down and is worked on the front. Working from left to right, start at the top right-hand corner of the first square immediately to the left of the first tube. Knot the end of the thread, and bring the needle through to start working a line of cable stitches. Work a second line, inverting the stitches. Smocking stitches are worked on the surface of and directly behind the tubes.

Use honeycomb stitch for the main depth of the work, using the gingham square as the depth of each stitch, and finish with 2 further close lines of cable stitches. The gingham will make it easy to keep straight lines. Vary the colours of your embroidery threads as you work. Oversew the thread securely at the end of each row. If you run out of thread mid-row, secure the thread end lightly on the inside and re-start with a knot behind the tube at which you finished.

5 Open up the smocking by pulling out all the gathering threads. Sew a seam down the dress back and neaten the raw edges. Make 4 straps allowing extra fabric for bows to be tied at the shoulders and stitch them securely to the tube surfaces of the inside. Hem the dress. Because the smocking expands so effectively, the dress will easily slip over the child's head.

CABLE STITCH

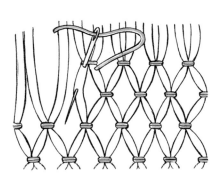

HONEYCOMB STITCH

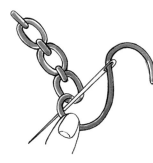

Reversible Dress

CHOOSE CONTRASTING FABRICS TO MAKE TWO DRESSES IN ONE!

YOU WILL NEED ■ *Tape measure* ■ *Pencil* ■ *Paper* ■ *90 × 115 cm (1 yd × 45 in)*
plain fabric ■ *122 × 115 cm (48 × 45 in) patterned fabric* ■ *Scissors* ■ *Iron-on interfacing* ■ *Iron*
■ *Needle and thread* ■ *Pins* ■ *Velcro*

1 Scale up the templates to the size required. Find this by measuring from the base of the child's neck to the desired hemline, and add a small seam allowance. Make paper patterns and cut out the pieces from the plain and patterned fabric, shortening the pattern at the dotted line for the plain dress. Also cut out 2 pieces of patterned fabric measuring 18 × 100 cm (6 × 39 in) to make the ruffle.

Iron the interfacing to the wrong side of the pocket. Doublestitch the straight edge and pin and tack (baste) 1.5 cm (⅝ in) around the edge. Stitch to the plain dress front and trim.

2 With right sides together, adjust and pin the ruffle to the lower edge of the patterned dress and stitch 1.5 cm (⅝ in) from edge, stitch again 6 mm (¼ in) from edge, press towards the top.

3 Double stitch the 2 ruffle pieces together along the side seam, trim, fold over and stitch to the hem. Gather stitch 6 mm (¼ in) from top of ruffle.

4 Pin both garments right sides together. Stitch the back edges. Double stitch the neck edges and armholes. Trim.

5 Trim and nick the edges to ease the curves. Turn right side out and press the garment.

6 With the patterned dress facing, pull through the plain shoulder edges, pin together and double stitch a 1.5 cm (⅝ in) seam. Press open. Fold the patterned front shoulder seam over the back and neatly hand stitch. Press the dress and sew Velcro to the back edges. Adjust and stitch the hems to finish.

PLACE TO FOLD

RUFFLE – CUT 2

Turtle Jigsaw

THIS SIMPLE TO MAKE JIGSAW IS AN ATTRACTIVE TOY FOR 1½ TO 3-YEAR-OLDS

YOU WILL NEED ■ *White paper* ■ *Pencil* ■ *Piece of plywood, 12 mm (½ in)*
thick ■ *Chalk* ■ *Fretsaw (scroll saw)* ■ *Sandpaper* ■ *Matt white emulsion (flat latex) paint*
■ *Small paintbrush* ■ *Non-toxic acrylic paints* ■ *Non-toxic clear acrylic varnish*

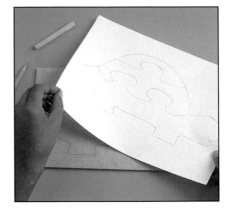

1 Draw the simple tortoise shape onto white paper. Transfer the design onto the piece of plywood by chalking the back of the paper and then drawing over the outline on the front.

2 Cut out the shapes with a fretsaw (scroll saw). Work carefully, especially when cutting the line inside the tortoise. Sand all the edges.

3 Prime each piece with a coat of white emulsion (flat latex) paint. Allow to dry, then paint each section a different colour. Rub down the edges of each piece to ensure a good fit.

4 Finish with a coat of clear acrylic varnish.

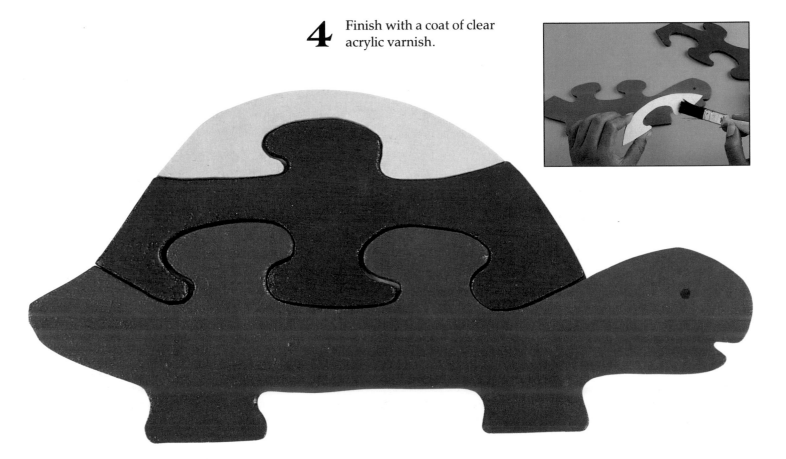

Decorated Baby Shoes

TRANSFORM PLAIN SHOES INTO A PRETTY PARTY PAIR

YOU WILL NEED ■ *Pink embroidery silk* ■ *Scissors* ■ *Needle*
■ *Plain fabric baby shoes* ■ *Pink gingham ribbon*

1 Take a length of the pink embroidery silk and pull out 3 strands with which to work. Thread a needle and sew a small running stitch around the edges of each of the shoes.

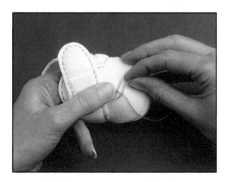

2 Still using 3 strands of the pink embroidery silk, sew 3 small French knots at intervals down the front of each shoe. Finish off the thread neatly on the underside.

3 Make 2 small bows from the gingham ribbon, clipping a 'V' shape into each of the ends as shown. Sew the bows into position on the front of each of the shoes to complete.

Clown Carousel

THIS HAND-OPERATED CAROUSEL WILL PROVIDE ENDLESS AMUSEMENT

YOU WILL NEED ■ *Thin plywood* ■ *Thick plywood* ■ *Pair of compasses* ■ *Pencil*
■ *Fretsaw (scroll saw)* ■ *Hand drill* ■ *Ruler* ■ *Length of wood, 4 cm (1½ in) wide and 2 cm*
(¾ in) thick ■ *Sandpaper* ■ *Non-toxic enamel paints* ■ *Paintbrushes* ■ *Wood glue* ■ *24 cm (9½ in)*
dowelling ■ *Scissors* ■ *Lengths of different coloured ribbons* ■ *Drawing pin (thumb tack)*

1 Using a pair of compasses, draw out the smaller circle onto the thick plywood and the larger one onto the thin plywood. Cut out carefully using a fretsaw (scroll saw). Drill a hole in each circle to fit the dowelling. Enlarge the hole in the larger circle a little with a fretsaw (scroll saw) to allow movement.

2 Transfer the clown shape on the template onto a piece of thick plywood and cut out 3 clown shapes using a fretsaw (scroll saw). Drill a small hole in each of the hats so that ribbon can be threaded through later. To make the knob for the top of the carousel, mark off a line to make a square at the end of the length of

wood. Draw 2 diagonals on the cut square of wood to find the centre of the square. Drill a hole the same diameter as the dowelling in the centre, about 1 cm (⅜ in) deep. Next saw off the square with the hole in the centre from the rest of the length of wood. Sand all the edges of the wooden pieces until smooth with sandpaper.

3 Paint all the pieces of wood with enamel paint in an assortment of bright colours. Paint the main colours first with a fairly large brush, and allow to dry before adding the details with a small brush. When the paint is dry, glue the piece of dowelling into the base (the smaller circle) with wood glue.

Glue the 3 clowns around the platform. Place the platform over the dowelling so that it rests on top of the base. Place a thin piece of plywood or some folded paper between the 2 circles so that there will be a gap between them while you attach the ribbons.

4 Cut 3 lengths of ribbon in different colours and thread through the top of the clowns' hats, securing with a knot at the front. Bring the 3 lengths of ribbon together at the top of the piece of dowelling and secure with wood glue and a drawing pin (thumb tack). Make sure that there is equal tension in the taut ribbon.

Finally, glue the knob onto the top of the dowelling, hiding the pin and the ribbon ends. Leave the glue to dry for at least 2 hours, then remove the thin plywood or paper from between the platforms. Swing the platform in one direction and the ribbons will wind and unwind, moving the clowns backwards and forwards.

Beetle Hat

THIS LOVABLE BEETLE HAT WILL FIT INFANTS AGED 1–2 YEARS

YOU WILL NEED ■ 3.5 mm (E) and 3 mm (D) crochet hooks ■ 40 g (1½ oz) black double knitting (sport) cotton ■ 10 g (½ oz) white double knitting (sport) cotton ■ Scissors ■ 40 g (1½ oz) red double knitting (sport) cotton ■ Large darning needle ■ Tailor's chalk ■ Pins

HEAD AND BODY

Starting with a 3.5 mm (E) hook and using black cotton, work the beetle's head as follows:
3 ch, join with 1 ss in first ch to form a ring.

1st row: 1 ch, 6 dc (sc) into ring, join with 1 ss.

2nd row: 1 ch, 2 dc (sc) in each of next 5 sts, 1 ch, turn.

3rd row: 1 dc (sc) in each of first 3 sts, 2 dc (sc) in next st, 1 dc (sc) in next 2 sts, 2 dc (sc) in next st, 1 dc (sc) in each of last 3 sts, 1 ch, turn.

4th row: 1 dc (sc) in each of first 3 sts, 2 dc (sc) in next st, 1 dc (sc) in next 4 sts, 2 dc (sc) in next st, 1 dc (sc) in last 3 sts, 1 ch, turn.

5th row: 1 dc (sc) in first 2 sts, 2 dc (sc) in next st, 1 dc (sc) in next 2 sts, 2 dc (sc) in next st, 1 dc (sc) in next 2 sts, 2 dc (sc) in next st, 1 dc (sc) in next 2 sts, 2 dc (sc) in next st, 1 dc (sc) in last 2 sts, 1 ch, turn.

6th row: 1 dc (sc) in each of first 3 sts, 2 dc (sc) in next st, 1 dc (sc) in next 2 sts, 2 dc (sc) in next st, 1 dc (sc) in next 4 sts, 2 dc (sc) in next st, 1 dc (sc) in next 2 sts, 2 dc (sc) in next st, 1 dc (sc) in last 3 sts, 1 ch, turn.

7th row: 1 dc (sc) in each of first 6 sts, 2 dc (sc) in next st, 1 dc (sc) in next 2 sts, 2 dc (sc) in next st, 1 dc (sc) in next 2 sts, 2 dc (sc) in next st, 1 dc (sc) in next 2 sts, 2 dc (sc) in next st, 1 dc (sc) in last 6 sts, 1 ch, turn.

8th row: 1 dc (sc) in each of first 7 sts, 2 dc (sc) in next st, 1 dc (sc) in next 10 sts, 2 dc (sc) in next st, 1 dc (sc) in last 7 sts, 1 ch, turn.

9th row: 1 dc (sc) in each of first 11 sts, 2 dc (sc) in next st, 1 dc (sc) in next 4 sts, 2 dc (sc) in next st, 1 dc (sc) in last 11 sts, 1 ch, turn.

10th row: 1 dc (sc) in each of first 3 sts, 2 dc (sc) in next st, 1 dc (sc) in next 22 sts, 2 dc (sc) in next st, 1 dc (sc) in last 3 sts, 1 ch, turn.

11th row: 1 dc (sc) in each of first 13 sts, 2 dc (sc) in next st, 1 dc (sc) in next 4 sts, 2 dc (sc) in next st, 1 dc (sc) in last 13 sts, 1 ch, turn.

12th row: 1 dc (sc) in each of first 3 sts, 2 dc (sc) in next st, 1 dc (sc) in next 26 sts, 2 dc (sc) in next st, 1 dc (sc) in last 3 sts, 1 ch, turn.

13th row: 1 dc (sc) in each of first 15 sts, 2 dc (sc) in next st, 1 dc (sc) in next 4 sts, 2 dc (sc) in next st, 1 dc (sc) in last 15 sts, 1 ch, turn.

14th row: 1 dc (sc) in each of first 13 sts, 2 dc (sc) in next st, 1 dc (sc) in next 10 sts, 2 dc (sc) in next st, 1 dc (sc) in last 13 sts, 1 ch, turn.
Cut black cotton and join red cotton. Work body as follows:

15th row: 1 dc (sc) in each of next 40 sts, 1 ch, turn.

16th row: Repeat 15th row.

17th row: 1 dc (sc) in each of first 15 sts, 2 dc (sc) in next st, 1 dc (sc) in next 8 sts, 2 dc (sc) in next st, 1 dc (sc) in last 15 sts, 1 ch, turn.

18th row: 1 dc (sc) in each of first 16 sts, 2 dc (sc) in next st, 1 dc (sc) in next 8 sts, 2 dc (sc) in next st, 1 dc (sc) in last 16 sts, 1 ch, turn.

19th row: 1 dc (sc) in each of first 6 sts, 1 ht in each of next 4 sts, 1 tr (dc) in each of next 24 sts, 1 ht in each of next 4 sts, 1 dc (sc) in each of last 6 sts, 1 ch, turn.

20th row: 1 dc (sc) in each of first 4 sts, 2 dc (sc) in next st, 1 dc (sc) in next 34 sts, 2 dc (sc) in next st, 1 dc (sc) in last 4 sts, 1 ch, turn.

21st row: 1 dc (sc) in each of first 5 sts, 1 ht in each of next 5 sts, 1 tr (dc) in each of next 26 sts, 1 ht in each of next 5 sts, 1 dc (sc) in each of last 5 sts, 1 ch, turn.

22nd row: 1 dc (sc) in each of first 17 sts, 2 dc (sc) in next st, 1 dc (sc) in next 10 sts, 2 dc (sc) in next st, 1 dc (sc) in last 17 sts, 1 ch, turn.

23rd row: 1 dc (sc) in each of first 5 sts, 1 ht in next 5 sts, 1 tr (dc) in next 28 sts, 1 ht in next 5 sts, 1 dc (sc) in last 5 sts, 1 ch, turn.

24th row: 1 dc (sc) in each of next 48 sts, 1 ch, turn.

25th row: 1 dc (sc) in each of first 5 sts, 1 ht in each of next 5 sts, 1 tr (dc) in each of next 28 sts, 1 ht in each of next 5 sts, 1 dc (sc) in each of last 5 sts, 1 ch, turn.

26th row: start decreasing to form the back of the beetle. 1 dc (sc) in each of first 18 sts, miss 1 st, 1 dc (sc) in next 10 sts, miss 1 st, 1 dc (sc) in last 18 sts, 1 ch, turn.

27th row: 1 dc (sc) in each of first 5 sts, 1 ht in each of next 5 sts, 1 tr (dc) in each of next 26 sts, 1 ht in each of next 5 sts, 1 dc (sc) in each of last 5 sts, 1 ch, turn.

28th row: 1 dc (sc) in each of first 16 sts, miss 1 st, 1 dc (sc) in each of next 12 sts, miss 1 st, 1 dc (sc) in each of last 16 sts, 1 ch, turn.

29th row: 1 dc (sc) in each of first 6 sts, 1 ht in each of next 4 sts, 1 tr (dc) in each of next 24 sts, 1 ht in each of next 4 sts, 1 dc (sc) in each of last 6 sts, 1 ch, turn.

30th row: 1 dc (sc) in each of first 15 sts, miss 1 st, 1 dc (sc) in each of next 12 sts, miss 1 st, 1 dc (sc) in each of last 15 sts, 1 ch, turn.

31st row: 1 dc (sc) in each of first 14 sts, miss 1 st, 1 dc (sc) in each of next 12 sts, miss 1 st, 1 dc (sc) in each of last 14 sts, 1 ch, turn.

32nd row: 1 dc (sc) in each of next 40 sts, 1 ch, turn.

33rd row: 1 dc (sc) in each of first 13 sts, miss 1 st, 1 dc (sc) in each of next 12 sts, miss 1 st, 1 dc (sc) in each of last 13 sts, 1 ch, turn.

34th row: 1 dc (sc) in each of first 12 sts, miss 1 st, 1 dc (sc) in each of next 12 sts, miss 1 st, 1 dc (sc) in each of last 12 sts, 1 ch, turn.

35th row: 1 dc (sc) in each of first 11 sts, miss 1 st, 1 dc (sc) in each of next 12 sts, miss 1 st, 1 dc (sc) in each of last 11 sts, 1 ch, turn.

36th row: 1 dc (sc) in each of first 10 sts, miss 1 st, 1 dc (sc) in each of next 12 sts, miss 1 st, 1 dc (sc) in each of last 10 sts, 1 ch, turn.

37th row: 1 dc (sc) in each of first 9 sts, miss 1 st, 1 dc (sc) in each of next 12 sts, miss 1 st, 1 dc (sc) in each of last 9 sts, 1 ch, turn.

38th row: 1 dc (sc) in each of first 8 sts, miss 1 st, 1 dc (sc) in each of next 12 sts, miss 1 st, 1 dc (sc) in each of last 8 sts, 1 ch, turn.

39th row: 1 dc (sc) in each of first 7 sts, miss 1 st, 1 dc (sc) in each of next 12 sts, miss 1 st, 1 dc (sc) in each of last 7 sts, 1 ch, turn.

40th row: 1 dc (sc) in each of first 6 sts, miss 1 st, 1 dc (sc) in each of next 12 sts. miss 1 st, 1 dc (sc) in each of last 6 sts, 1 ch, turn.

41st row: 1 dc (sc) in each of first 5 sts, miss 1 st, 1 dc (sc) in each of next 12 sts, miss 1 st, 1 dc (sc) in each of last 5 sts, 1 ch, turn.

42nd row: 1 dc (sc) in each of first 4 sts, miss 1 st, 1 dc (sc) in each of next 4 sts, miss 1 st, 1 dc (sc) in each of next 2 sts, miss 1 st, 1 dc (sc) in next 4 sts, miss 1 st, 1 dc (sc) in each of last 4 sts, 1 ch, turn.

43rd row: 1 dc (sc) in each of first 3 sts, miss 1 st, 1 dc (sc) in each of next 3 sts, miss 1 st, 1 dc (sc) in each of next 2 sts, miss 1 st, 1 dc (sc) in each of next 3 sts, miss 1 st, 1 dc (sc) in each of last 3 sts, 1 ch, turn.

44th row: * 1 dc (sc) in each of next 2 sts, miss 1 st. Repeat from * 3 more times, 1 dc (sc) in each of last 2 sts, 1 ch, turn.

45th row: 1 dc (sc) in first st, miss 1 st, 1 dc (sc) in next st, miss 1 st, 1 dc (sc) in next 2 sts, miss 1 st, 1 dc (sc) in next st, miss 1 st, 1 dc (sc) in last st, 1 ch, turn.

46th row: 1 dc (sc) in first st, miss 1 st, 1 dc (sc) in each of next 2 sts, miss 1 st, 1 dc (sc) in last st; turn, work 1 ss into first st. Cast (bind) off last stitch. Sew in all the ends.

Hat band

Change to a 3 mm (D) hook. Using red cotton measure 2 m (6 ft 6 in) from the end of cotton; starting at this point and working with the 2 m (6 ft 6 in) length, work 1 in ss around edge of hat over the red part (approx 60 sts), until you reach the black part. Using black cotton measure 1.5 m (60 in) from end of cotton; starting at this point and working with the 1.5 m (60 in) length, continue with the row of ss until you reach the start.

Change back to red cotton, 3 ch, 1 tr (dc) in each ss until you reach the black, pick up black yarn and continue to work 1 tr (dc) in each ss until you reach the red. Ss in first tr (dc), cast (bind) off last st.

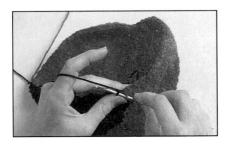

Spots

(Make 6 alike)
Use 3 mm (D) hook and black cotton.

1st step: 3 ch, ss in first chain to make a ring, 1 ch, 6 dc (sc) into ring, join with 1 ss in first st.

2nd step: 2 ch, 2 dc (sc) in each of next 6 sts, ss in first st.

3rd step: 2 ch, * 2 dc (sc) in first st, 1 dc (sc) in next st. Repeat from * 5 more times, ss in 1st st. Cast (bind) off, leaving a 15 cm (6 in) end.

EYES

(Make 2 alike)
Use 3 mm (D) hook and black cotton.

1st step: 3 ch, ss in first chain to make a ring, 1 ch, 6 dc (sc) into ring, join with 1 ss in first st.

2nd step: Cut black cotton and join white cotton. Using white cotton, work 2 ch, 2 dc (sc) in each of next 6 sts, ss in first st.

3rd step: 1 ch, ss in each of next 2 sts, 1 dc (sc) in each of next 2 sts, 2 dc (sc) in each of next 4 sts, 1 dc (sc) in each of next 2 sts, 1 ss in each of last 2 sts.
Cast (bind) off last st, leaving a 15 cm (6 in) end of cotton for attaching eye to hat.

TO MAKE UP

Fold hat in half lengthwise. Mark a line along the centre back of body and chain stitch along line with doubled black cotton.

Now arrange 3 spots equally on each side of the chain-stitched line. Pin in position and sew, using ends attached to spots. Lastly pin eyes onto head and stitch, using white cotton still attached to eyes.

Bow-Tie **T-S**hirt

IT'S EASY TO SMARTEN UP A PLAIN T-SHIRT USING FABRIC PAINTS

YOU WILL NEED ■ *Scissors* ■ *Large piece of card* ■ *Cotton T-shirt* ■ *Tracing paper* ■ *Pencil*
■ *Fine black fabric pen* ■ *Green, orange and pink fabric paints* ■ *Paintbrushes* ■ *Iron*

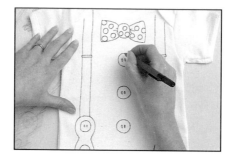

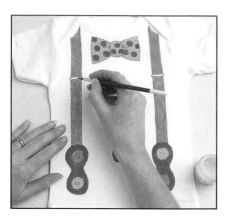

1 Cut a piece of card to the size of the T-shirt and slip it inside in order to give a firm base and to prevent the paint from bleeding through to the back.

2 Using the templates as a guide, lay the tracing paper over the T-shirt and draw on the design to fit the shirt. Transfer the design to the T-shirt by reversing the tracing paper and scribbling over the lines. Draw over the outline in black fabric pen.

3 Fill in the design with the brightly coloured fabric paints. Do not take too much paint onto the brush each time, especially when painting details.

4 Once the paints are dry, turn the T-shirt inside out and press on the inside to fix the paint, as specified in the manufacturer's instructions.

Starry Pinboard

THIS SIMPLE PINBOARD WILL ADD A BRIGHT SPLASH TO THE NURSERY

YOU WILL NEED ■ *Pinboard* ■ *Felt slightly larger than pinboard* ■ *Rubber-based glue or staple gun* ■ *Scissors* ■ *Self-adhesive coloured felt* ■ *2 picture hooks*

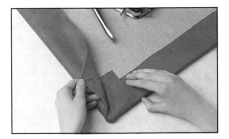

1 Cover the front of the pinboard with the piece of felt and secure it at the back using either a staple gun or glue.

2 Cut out an equal number of star and dot shapes from coloured felt (if you cannot find self-adhesive felt, use rubber-based glue on the reverse of the shapes). Stick the dots in the middle of the star shapes.

3 Arrange the stars over the pinboard and stick down. To secure to the wall attach 2 picture hooks to the back.

Marzipan Animals

USE YOUR IMAGINATION TO MAKE ALL KINDS OF DIFFERENT ANIMALS

YOU WILL NEED ■ *Icing sugar* ■ *Rolling pin and board* ■ *White marzipan* ■ *Pink, yellow and brown food colourings* ■ *Cocoa* ■ *Sharp knife* ■ *Garlic press* ■ *Small paintbrush* ■ *Toothpick*

1 Sprinkle a little icing sugar onto a board. Divide the marzipan into several pieces and roll out each piece.

2 To colour each piece, dot with food colouring and knead until evenly coloured.

3 Knead cocoa into 1 piece of the marzipan to make the brown bear.

4 Mould the marzipan into animal shapes. Press some marzipan through a garlic press to make a fleece for the sheep.

5 Carefully paint on a little extra food colouring with a small paintbrush to pick out special markings.

6 Use a toothpick to mark out eyes, claws and other features. Allow the marzipan to dry thoroughly and pack in an attractive gift box.

Flower Mirror

THIS DELICATE MIRROR WILL DELIGHT SMALL CHILDREN

YOU WILL NEED ■ *Scissors* ■ *Fairy picture* ■ *Strong clear glue*
■ *Small paintbrush* ■ *Mirror on stand* ■ *Glue gun and hot-melt sticks* ■ *Dried
flowers: broom bloom, small helichrysums and small pink rosebuds*

1 Carefully cut out the fairy picture and stick it to the top left side of the mirror using some strong glue applied with a small paintbrush.

2 Using the glue gun secure a few sprays of broom to the base of the mirror, positioning it so that the fairy appears to be flying through the branches. Cover the ends of the broom with a few small helichrysum flowers.

3 Finally, glue a border of roses along the base of the mirror. Be careful to allow the glue gun to cool between each application, so that the hot glue does not damage the mirror.

Fairy Dress and Wand

YOU WILL NEED For dress: ■ *10 silver satin roses* ■ *Frilly vested petticoat*
■ *Pins* ■ *Needle and thread* ■ *75 cm (30 in) silver sequin strip* ■ *12 small bows made*
from silver braid ■ *Rubber-based glue* ■ *Gold and green glitter* ■ *Star sequins in different colours*
■ *Scissors* ■ *1 m (40 in) white and gold ribbon, 2.5 cm (1 in) wide*
For wand: ■ *White card* ■ *Pencil* ■ *Scissors* ■ *Gold spray paint*
■ *Paper glue* ■ *Silver, gold and green glitter mixed together* ■ *Length of silver ribbon*
■ *Green garden cane* ■ *Sticky tape* ■ *Gold metallic strips*

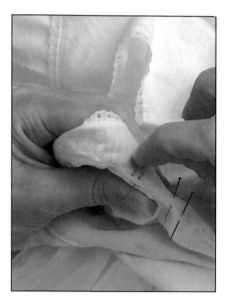

1 Lay the roses around the neck of the dress, spacing them evenly. Pin, and sew on. Remove the pins. Mark the centre front point at the waist with a pin. Lay the sequin strip from the shoulder seam to the pin and pin in place to form a 'V'. Turn the dress wrong side out. Holding the sequin strip tightly against the fabric, slip stitch it in place.

2 Sew a silver braid bow at each end of the sequins and one at the centre of the 'V' at the waistline. Sew the remaining silver bows on the gathered skirt. Using the rubber-based glue, paint a pattern on the sides of the bodice and scatter gold glitter over it. Leave this to dry. Add green glitter dots to the design and a dot between each rose at the neckline using the same technique. Allow to dry thoroughly.

Sew the star sequins in a random fashion in the centre of the bodice. Finally, cut the white and gold ribbon in half and tie each length into a bow, leaving long ends. Decorate the ends by painting down the centre with the glue and sprinkling with the gold glitter. Sew each bow at the waistline on the side seam.

3 To make the wand, use the template to cut 2 star shapes from card. Spray with the gold paint. Leave to dry. Spread glue over the star and sprinkle on the glitter. Start winding the ribbon around the cane, securing the end with sticky tape. When you have covered the cane, cut off any excess; tape in place. Stick the metallic gold strips to the top end.

4 Lay the stick on the wrong side of one star shape and use the sticky tape to secure. Spread paper glue over back of the star. Press the second star shape on top, 'sandwiching' the stick. Make sure the metallic strips do not get caught inside.

Tapestry Cushion

A DECORATIVE AND SIMPLY MADE CUSHION FOR THE NURSERY

YOU WILL NEED ■ *Marker pen* ■ *Square of tapestry canvas*
■ *Tapestry needle* ■ *Tapestry yarns in various bright colours* ■ *Pinking shears* ■ *Square of fabric*
■ *Needle and thread* ■ *Non-toxic, flame retardant polyester filling (batting)*

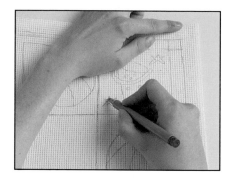

1 Draw out the outlines of your design on the canvas.

2 Using tent stitch and one strand of yarn, begin stitching, using different colours for the different motif sections.

3 When the stitching is complete, cut out a fabric square with pinking shears to fit the canvas. Sew all round the 2 squares, right sides together, leaving a gap for turning.

4 After turning the cover the right way out, stuff the cushion with filling (batting) and sew up the gap to complete.

Gathered Garland

THIS CELEBRATION GARLAND IS PERFECT FOR ANY PARTY

YOU WILL NEED ■ *180 × 90 cm (2 yd × 36 in) white muslin (cheesecloth)* ■ *Tape measure*
■ *1.5 m (60 in) white tape, 12 mm (½ in) wide* ■ *Florist's silver wire* ■ *Dried heather* ■ *Heads of dried hydrangea* ■ *Scissors* ■ *4.5 m (5 yd) wire-edged ribbon, 5 cm (2 in) wide*

1 Lay the muslin (cheesecloth) on a table and bunch together slightly until it measures 25 cm (10 in) across the width. Tie a loop at end of the tape, wrap the tape around one end of the fabric and pull the knot tight, leaving the loop hanging free.

2 Measure 30 cm (12 in) along the muslin (cheesecloth), grip that point in your hand and push the material up until the bunched section measures 23 cm

(9 in). Wrap around the loose end of tape at this point and knot. Repeat 3 more times until you reach the end. Tie a second loop to this end and trim.

3 Turn the garland over. Make 5 flower bunches by wiring several stems of heather to a small head of hydrangea with florist's silver wire.

4 Cut the ribbon into 5 pieces and make 5 bows, each with 3 loops and 2 ends. Wire a bunch of flowers and a bow to each gather and hang up.

Welcome Door Wreath

THIS GLORIOUS WREATH ENTICES YOU INDOORS!

YOU WILL NEED ■ *Silver florist's wire* ■ *Florist's scissors* ■ *36 cm (14 in) diameter florist's foam wreath* ■ *22 × 18 cm (7 in) stub wires* ■ *Cupressus (Leyland cypress) foliage* ■ *Carnations* ■ *Euonymus (wintercreeper) foliage* ■ *Viburnum foliage* ■ *Ivy* ■ *Spray carnations* ■ *Spray chrysanthemums* ■ *Sedum (showy stonecrop) flowers* ■ *2.75 m (3 yd) pearlized cellophane ribbons*

1 Secure a length of florist's wire through the foam wreath to form a hanging loop. Immerse the florist's foam in water and soak thoroughly, preferably overnight or for at least 8 hours. Bend the stub wires in half to make securing pins. Cut the cupressus (Leyland cypress) into 12.5 cm (5 in) lengths and pin them with stub wires to cover the inside and outside of the wreath.

2 Cut a carnation stem to 10 cm (4 in) and push into the centre of the wreath. Position short lengths of mixed foliage to make a crescent shape around the carnation. Cut short stems of spray carnations and position flowers around as an outer ring to the crescent. Intersperse with viburnum and add individual chrysanthemum flowers to highlight the colour.

3 Cut sedum (showy stonecrop) flower heads and push these into the wreath, packing them tightly for about 7.5 cm (3 in) on either side of the spray. Position a carnation surrounded by foliage, then continue positioning the sedum (showy stonecrop) for a further 7.5 cm (3 in). Use the remaining flowers to make a second crescent spray with a central carnation.

4 Use the silver florist's wire to wire the cellophane ribbon into several 12.5 cm (5 in) loops. Bind together tightly with additional wire. Use a stub wire to secure the bow to the bottom of the wreath.

BABY DAYS

A multitude of wonderful toys, bright
clothes and fun accessories for the young child:
a practical wardrobe, cuddly animals
and educational games that are sure to entertain
and amuse the fast-growing tot

Crocheted Bonnet

A COMFORTABLE CROCHETED BONNET FOR CHILLY DAYS OUT

YOU WILL NEED ■ *50 g (2-ounce skein) 4-ply yarn* ■ *3.5 mm (E) crochet hook* ■ *Tape measure*

Make 5 ch, ss into 1st ch to form a ring.

1st row: 3 ch for 1st tr (dc), 11 tr (dc) into ch ring, ss into 3rd ch.

2nd row: 3 ch, tr (dc) into same st, 2 tr (dc) into each tr (dc) to end of row, join with ss.

3rd row: 3 ch, * 2 tr (dc) into next tr (dc), 1 tr (dc). Repeat from * to end of round. Join with ss.

4th row: 3 ch, * 2 tr (dc) into next tr (dc), 2 tr (dc). Repeat from * to end of round. Join with ss.

5th row: 3 ch, * 2 tr (dc) into next tr (dc), 3 ch. Repeat from * to end.

6th row: 3 ch, * 2 tr (dc) into next tr (dc), 4 tr (dc). Repeat from * to end. 1 tr (dc) into 3 ch base, join with ss. 3 ch, * 2 tr (dc) into next tr (dc), 5 ch. Repeat from * to end. 1 tr (dc) into base of 3 tr (dc).

7th row: 3 ch, * 2 tr (dc) into next tr (dc), 5 ch. Repeat from * to end of round. 5 tr (dc) into base of 7 ch.

8th row: 3 ch, * 2 tr (dc) into next tr (dc), 6 tr (dc). Repeat from * to last 3 sts of round, 2 tr (dc) into next tr (dc), 2 tr (dc), 1 tr (dc) into base of

3 ch. Join with ss.

9th row: 3 ch, tr (dc) to last 20 sts, turn with 4 ch.

10th row: * Miss 1 tr (dc), tr (dc) in tr (dc) to end. Turn with 3 ch. Repeat rows 9–10 six times. Fasten off. Join yarn at other end of row. Repeat rows 9–10 three times then row 9 once more.

Work one row crab st (dc (sc) worked from left to right). Turn back 6 rows (inc crab st) to right side for the brim. Join yarn to right side bottom edge. Edge tog 2 ch, 2 dc (sc) into each end st up to crown. (30 dc (sc).)

* 1 dc (sc) into tr (dc), miss 1 tr (dc). Repeat from * 10 times. 2 dc (sc) into each end st to end of row. Turn with 2 ch.

Next row: 1 dc (sc) in each dc (sc) to crown, 1 dc (sc) in alternate dcs (scs) over crown, dc (sc) in each dc (sc) to end of row. Turn with 2 ch.

Next row: 1 dc (sc) in each dc (sc) to end of row, turn with 3 ch.

Next row: 1 tr (dc) in alternate dcs to end of row. Turn with 2 ch.

Next row: * 1 dc (sc) in ch sp, dc (sc) in tr (dc). Repeat from * to end of row. Fasten off.

Braid

2 ch, 1 dc (sc) into 2nd ch, 1 ch, turn. Repeat until 68 cm (27 in) long. Thread through bonnet.

Crocheted Cardigan

A BUTTON-THROUGH CARDIGAN THAT FITS UP TO A 45 CM (18 IN) CHEST

YOU WILL NEED ■ *100 g (4-ounce skein) 4-ply yarn* ■ *3 mm (D) crochet hook*
■ *Tape measure* ■ *Large darning needle* ■ *5 small buttons*

BACK
Make foundation ch of 63 sts.
1 tr (dc) in 4th ch from hook. 1 tr (dc) in each ch to end of row. Turn with one ch.
1st row: 1 dc (sc) into ch sp, * 3 ch, 1 dc (sc) into ch sp. Repeat from * to end. Dc (sc) into turning ch.
2nd row: 3 ch, * 2 tr (dc) into ch loop, 1 ch. Repeat from * to end. 1 tr (dc). Repeat these 2 rows until work measures 16.5 cm (6½ in).
Next row: ss 9 sts. Work pattern to last 9 sts. Turn with 1 tr (dc). Work in pattern over 41 sts until armhole measures 10 cm (4 in). Finish with 2nd row.

RIGHT FRONT
Make 28 ch. 1 tr (dc) into 4th ch from hook, tr (dc) into each ch to end of row, turn with 1 ch.
1 dc (sc) into tr (dc), * 3 ch, miss 2 tr (dc). Repeat from * to end of row. Turn with 3 ch.
Next row: * 2 tr (dc) into ch sp, 1 ch. Repeat from * to end of row. Turn with 1 ch.
Continue in pattern until work measures 16.5 cm (6½ in).

Next row: ss over 9 sts, pattern to end of row, turn with 1 ch.
Next row: 1 tr (dc) into next ch loop, 1 ch, continue in pattern to last 2 sts, 1 ch, 2 dc (sc) into ch sp, turn with 3 ch.
Continue in pattern dec 1 st at neck edge each row until 3 groups left. Continue in pattern until armhole matches back. Fasten off.

LEFT FRONT
Work as right front but reverse shapings.

SLEEVES
Make 37 ch. Tr (dc) into 4th ch from hook. Tr (dc) into each ch to end of row. Pattern as for back increasing 1 st every alternate row until there are 55 sts. Continue until work measures 18 cm (7 in).
Next row: 2 ch, * 2 tr (dc) into ch loop, 1 tr (dc) into dc (sc). Repeat from * to end of row. Fasten off.

Front border
Make 9 ch.
1st row: 1 dc (sc) into 3rd ch from hook, dc (sc) in each ch to end.

Turn with 2 ch.
2nd row: 7 dc (sc), 2 ch.
3rd row: 3 dc (sc), 2 ch, miss 2 ch, 3 dc (sc), turn with 2 ch.
4th row: 2 dc (sc), 2 dc (sc) into ch sp, 3 dc (sc). (1 buttonhole made.) Turn with 2 ch.
Repeat 2nd row 8 times.
13th row: As 3rd row.
Repeat last 10 rows until 5 buttonholes have been made. Continue 8 dc (sc) border until long enough to reach round neck and front. Fasten off.

TO MAKE UP
Join shoulders. Sew in sleeves. Join sleeve and underarm sections. Sew border to cardigan with buttonholes on the right side for a girl or the left side for a boy. Finally, sew on buttons to line up with buttonholes.

Brick Town

THESE FUN HOUSES PROVIDE AN IMAGINATIVE BACKGROUND FOR OTHER TOYS

YOU WILL NEED ■ *Scrap wood* ■ *Pencil* ■ *Ruler* ■ *Saw* ■ *Sandpaper*
■ *Matt white emulsion (flat latex) paint* ■ *Enamel paints* ■ *Paintbrushes*

1 Ask your local wood yard for small pieces of scrap wood which are often free or sold at a cheaper rate. Pieces may already be the right size or you may have to cut them down with a saw. Use a ruler and a pencil to mark off the suitable lengths.

2 Smooth down all the edges and ends of each piece of wood with a sheet of sandpaper wrapped around a wooden block. Be sure to do this carefully, as pieces of scrap wood can be very rough both on the surface and the cut ends.

3 Paint the blocks of wood with a coat of white emulsion (flat latex) paint to seal them, and then paint on the house details and the hedges with enamel paints, following the manufacturer's instructions. Leave to dry thoroughly.

Leg Warmers

THESE COSY LEG WARMERS ARE GIVEN IN TWO SIZES, 0–2 YEARS AND 3–4 YEARS

YOU WILL NEED ■ *Small quantity of double knitting (sport) yarn in each colour:*
Pink – A, Yellow – B, Turquoise – C, Purple – D, Red – E, Natural – F, Orange – G ■ *1 pair of 3.5 mm*
(US 4) knitting needles ■ *1 pair of 4 mm (US 5) knitting needles* ■ *Large darning needle*

Tension (Gauge)

Using 4 mm (US 5) needles, 20 sts
and 26 rows to 10 cm (4 in) (st st).

Using 3.5 mm (US 4) needles and
yarn A, cast on 40 (46) sts. Work
10 (12) rows k 1, p 1, rib. Change
to 4 mm (US 5) needles and yarn
B. Work 2 (4) rows st st.

Stripes

Work 2 rows in yarn C, 2 rows in
yarn D, 2 rows in yarn C, 2 rows in
yarn D.
Change to yarn B and work 2 (4)
rows st st.

Square pattern

K 4 in yarn E, k 4 in yarn F to end
of row.
Next row: p 4 in yarn F, p 4 in yarn
E to end.
Repeat last 2 rows 1 more time.

Stripes

Work 2 rows in yarn A, 2 rows in
yarn G, 2 rows in yarn A.

Square pattern

K 4 in yarn F, k 4 in yarn E to end.
Next row: p 4 in yarn E, p 4 in yarn
F to end.
Repeat last 2 rows 1 more time.
Change to yarn B and work 2 (4)
rows st st.

Stripes

Work 2 rows in yarn C, 2 rows in
yarn D, 2 rows in yarn C, 2 rows in
yarn D.
Change to yarn B and work 2 (4)
rows st st.
Change to 3.5 mm (US 4) needles
and yarn G. Work 10 (12) rows
k 1, p 1, rib.
Cast (bind) off.

TO MAKE UP

With right sides together, sew up
the seams using backstitch. Turn
right side out.

Tugboat

THIS TUG CAN BE USED AS A PUSH ABOUT TOY

YOU WILL NEED ■ *Pen* ■ *Paper* ■ *Scissors* ■ *40 × 7.5 cm (16 × 3 in) wood, 2.5 cm (1 in) thick* ■ *Hand saw* ■ *Sandpaper* ■ *10 × 4.5 cm (4 × 2 in) wood, 12 mm (½ in) thick* ■ *4 × 4 cm (1½ × 1½ in) woodscrews* ■ *Screwdriver* ■ *Plastic wood* ■ *6 × 4.5 cm (2¼ × 2 in) and 4.5 × 4.5 cm (2 × 2 in) wood, all 2 cm (¾ in) thick* ■ *Wood glue* ■ *Panel pins (finishing nails)* ■ *Hammer* ■ *7.5 cm (3 in) dowelling, 3 cm (1¼ in) in diameter* ■ *Hand drill* ■ *Paintbrush* ■ *Non-toxic acrylic paints*

 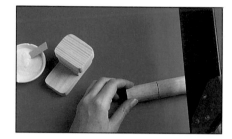 

1 Scale up the hull shape from the template. Cut it out and draw around the outline onto the large piece of wood. Saw round the outline and sand the edges. Use this hull shape to trace out the front 10 cm (4 in) of the bow and the rear 5 cm (2 in) sections on the remaining larger piece of wood.

Cut these 2 pieces at an angle from front to rear to make a slope. Cut out a 'V' from the inside edges. Sand them smooth and screw them onto the hull, through the base, counter-sinking the screws and covering with plastic wood. Sand to match the shape of the bow and stern of the hull.

2 Sand the corners of the other 3 blocks of wood, but leave 2 square corners on the square block. Assemble with the largest piece at the bottom, the square in the middle front and the remaining piece on top.

Attach all pieces using wood glue and panel pins (finishing nails) to make the wheelhouse. Drill a hole in the dowelling to screw to the boat. Sand the base and top of the dowelling so that the funnel stands at a slight angle.

3 Paint all the pieces and leave to dry. Screw the funnel in place, then screw the whole assembly to the hull through the base of the hull, counter-sinking the screws and filling with plastic wood. Paint over the filler.

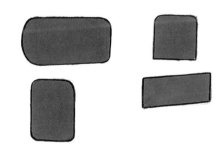

Painted Shoes

TRANSFORM PLAIN SHOES IN MINUTES WITH THESE BRIGHT PAINTS

YOU WILL NEED ■ *Pair of black or white canvas shoes* ■ *Newspaper* ■ *Old fabric*
■ *Puffy fabric paints in 5 colours* ■ *Hairdrier*

1 Stuff the toe of each canvas shoe with newspaper. It is a good idea to test puffy paints on an old piece of fabric before you start. This will reduce the chance of mistakes and also ensure that the paint is flowing freely without any air bubbles.

2 Start by drawing different coloured flowers on the front of the shoes, adding one to the back seam. Then add a different coloured dot to each flower. Leave to dry.

3 Finally, puff up the paint by using a hairdrier, following the manufacturer's instructions. Avoid holding the shoe too close to the heat.

Baseball Cap

THE PERFECT HEAD-GEAR FOR A STAR-STRUCK TODDLER

YOU WILL NEED ■ *Pencil* ■ *Stiff card* ■ *Scissors* ■ *Blue and yellow felt*
■ *Baseball cap* ■ *Pins* ■ *Rubber-based glue*

1 Draw the star shapes onto a piece of card. Cut 2 stars from the card, one large size and one small. Place the small template on the blue felt, draw round with a pencil and cut out 4 stars. In the same way, using the large template, cut out 4 stars from the yellow felt.

2 Arrange the stars across the front of the cap. When you are satisfied with the positions, pin in place. Stick down the stars, ensuring that the glue covers the felt right to the point.

Pig T-Shirt

THIS MOTIF CAN BE SCALED UP TO FIT ANY SIZE OF T-SHIRT

YOU WILL NEED ■ *White paper* ■ *Black felt-tip pen* ■ *White T-shirt* ■ *Pencil* ■ *White card* ■ *Fine black fabric pen* ■ *Pink fabric pen* ■ *Grey yarn* ■ *Scissors* ■ *Large darning needle* ■ *Iron*

1 Scale up the pig template and draw the outline onto white paper using a black pen. Slip the paper inside the T-shirt so the design can be seen through the fabric. Draw the outline onto the T-shirt in pencil. Remove the drawing and replace it with the piece of white card inside the T-shirt beneath the pencil drawing. This will give a firm base when you use the fabric pen and will also prevent the ink from bleeding through to the back.

2 Start drawing with the black fabric pen. Fill in the eyes and colour the snout using the pink fabric pen.

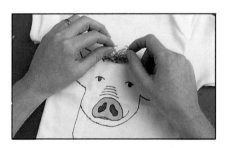

3 Cut some grey yarn into short lengths and use the darning needle to sew them onto the head of the pig. Separate the strands to fluff out the 'hair' and make it look realistic.

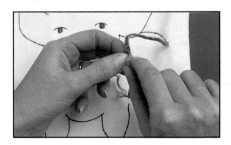

4 Sew 3 long lengths of yarn onto the rear of the pig. Braid the strands, tie into a knot at the end and trim. Press the design on the inside of the T-shirt to fix the fabric colours, according to the manufacturer's instructions.

Reversible Sun Hat

TWO HATS IN ONE FOR BABIES OF 5 TO 12 MONTHS

YOU WILL NEED ■ *Tracing paper* ■ *Pencil* ■ *Ruler*
■ *White paper* ■ *Pins* ■ *Scissors* ■ *23 × 115 cm (9 × 45 in) red striped fabric* ■ *23 × 115 cm*
(9 × 45 in) green striped fabric ■ *Needle and thread* ■ *Iron*

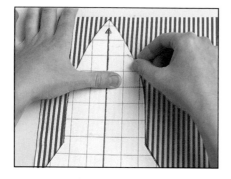

1 Scale up the template onto white paper to the required size and cut out. A 1 cm (⅜ in) seam allowance is included on all template edges. Pin the pattern to the fabric and cut out 6 pieces in each colour.

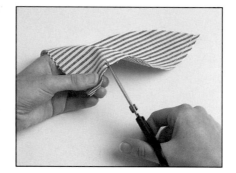

2 Working with one colour at a time, take 2 panels and pin them with right sides together. Sew from the top point along the edge to the brim edge. Snip the seam allowance as marked on the template. Press the seam open.

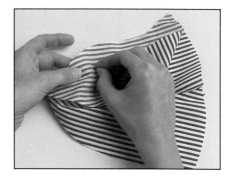

3 Pin on a third panel. Sew from the top point to the brim edge, snip and press seam open. Repeat these stages with the remaining 3 panels so that you have 2 separate 3-panel pieces. Repeat with the other colour.

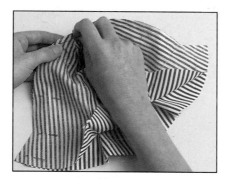

4 Now pin both made-up sections of one colour with right sides together. Match top points and brim edges. Sew from one brim edge, up and over the top points, and down to the other brim edge. Snip as marked and press the seam open. Do the same for the other colour, so that you have 2 separate hats ready to join.

5 Place one hat inside the other with right sides together. Pin in position, carefully matching all the seams. Sew all the way around the outer brim edge, leaving a 7 cm (2¾ in) opening.

Turn the hat by reaching inside the opening, grasping the right side of the hat and pulling it out. Close the opening by turning the 1 cm (⅜ in) seam into the hat and tacking (basting) the edges together. Top stitch right around the outer brim edge. Remove the tacking (basting) threads.

SNIP
HERE

SNIP
HERE

Peg Dolls

MAKE WASHDAY MORE FUN WITH THESE SIMPLE DECORATED PEG DOLLS

YOU WILL NEED ■ *Sandpaper* ■ *Old-fashioned clothes pegs (pins)* ■ *Matt emulsion (flat latex) paint* ■ *Paintbrushes* ■ *Non-toxic acrylic paints* ■ *Non-toxic clear acrylic varnish*

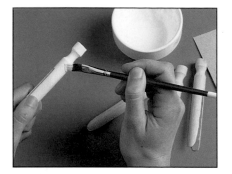

1 Sand down each peg (pin) with sandpaper to smooth any rough edges. Using the white emulsion (flat latex) paint, coat the pegs (pins) evenly.

2 With acrylic paint and a fine brush, paint on the doll's features and clothes: paint the face on the top round piece and the body and legs further down with the shoes at the bottom. Leave to dry thoroughly.

3 Lastly, paint on a protective coat of clear acrylic varnish. Hang all the completed pegs (pins) on the line and have fun hanging out the washing!

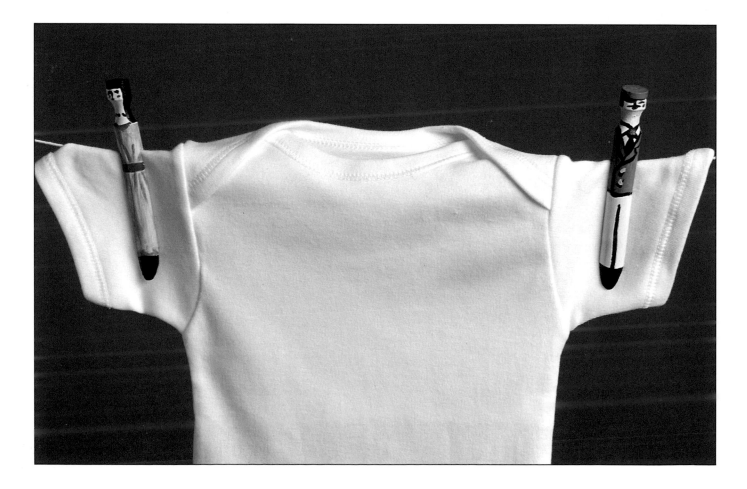

Plastic Bib

A FUN, WIPE-CLEAN BIB FOR MEALTIMES

YOU WILL NEED ■ *Paper* ■ *Pen* ■ *Scissors* ■ *20 × 24 cm*
(8 × 9½ in) fabric ■ *20 × 24 cm (8 × 9½ in) coloured plastic fabric* ■ *20 × 24 cm*
(8 × 9½ in) clear PVC (vinyl) plastic ■ *Oddments of felt* ■ *Rubber-based glue* ■ *Needle and thread*
■ *2 metal eyelets* ■ *Hammer* ■ *50 cm (19½ in) cord*

1 Cut out a bib shape in paper. Draw around the pattern on the different fabrics and cut out 1 fabric and 2 plastic bib pieces. Cut a heart and some spots out of felt.

2 Glue the heart onto the fabric and glue the spots onto the heart.

3 Trap the fabric between the coloured and clear plastic and sew around the edges.

4 Attach 2 metal eyelets to the top edges of the bib with a hammer on a hard surface. Thread a piece of cord through each hole and tie a knot to each end of the cord to secure.

Clapper

THIS TRADITIONAL WOODEN TOY IS SIMPLE TO MAKE BUT VERY EFFECTIVE

YOU WILL NEED ■ *Fretsaw (scroll saw)* ■ *36 × 4.5 cm (14 × 1¾ in) piece of wood, 1 cm (⅜ in) thick* ■ *Ruler* ■ *Pencil* ■ *Masking tape* ■ *Hand drill* ■ *Sandpaper* ■ *Scissors* ■ *Coloured card* ■ *Rubber-based glue* ■ *Length of cord*

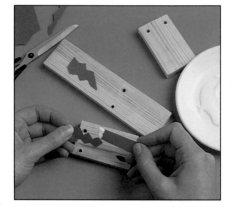

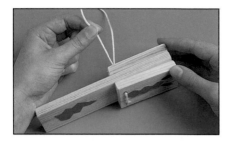

3 Tie all the pieces together with the cord, and knot securely. The cord should be just loose enough to allow the pieces to 'clap' together.

1 Cut 3 lengths of wood, one piece 18 cm (7 in) long and 2 pieces 8 cm (3¼ in) long. Secure the 3 pieces in position on top of each other with masking tape. Lining up one end, and with the longer piece sandwiched in the middle, drill 2 holes 1 cm (⅜ in) in from the inner corners, drilling through all 3 pieces of wood at once. Smooth down all the rough edges of the wood with sandpaper wrapped around a wooden block.

2 Cut out some decorative shapes from coloured card and glue onto the 'handle' and top piece of the clapper.

Snake Mobile

THIS SIMPLE MOBILE SPIRALS ROUND IN A FASCINATING WAY

YOU WILL NEED ■ *Pencil* ■ *Coloured card* ■ *Scissors* ■ *Large darning needle*
■ *Fine cord* ■ *Dowelling, painted white (optional)*

1 Using the template as a guide, draw spiral snake designs onto different pieces of coloured card in a range of different sizes. Cut out the spirals with a sharp pair of scissors, following the lines precisely so that the shapes are accurate.

2 Using a needle threaded with the cord, pierce a hole through the head end of each 'snake'. Pull the thread through to the desired length and secure with a knot at the head end. Either hang the threaded snakes from a length of painted white dowelling or secure them individually from the nursery ceiling.

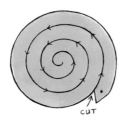

Hooded Jacket

YOU WILL NEED ■ *Paper and pencil if you need to re-scale dimensions*
■ *Tape measure* ■ *Scissors* ■ *Ready-quilted cotton fabric* ■ *Plain fabric in a co-ordinating colour* ■ *Pins* ■ *Needle and thread* ■ *Iron* ■ *2 or 3 toggles*

1 Scale up the templates according to your calculated size, measuring from neck to hem, and cut out the 2 'T' shapes in quilted fabric for the back and front. Cut one of the shapes in half down the centre front. Cut 4 strips of plain fabric for the shoulder stripes to the depth of the sleeve from shoulder to underarm and,

for the size given here, 5 cm (2 in) wide. Turn the long raw edges under 6 mm (¼ in), tack (baste) and press. Pin and tack (baste) them to the sleeves on the 2 front pieces and back so that the raw edge of the side seam and inside edge of the strip form a straight line. Appliqué the 4 strips in place and remove the tacking (basting).

2 Assemble the jacket fronts and back with right sides together. Pin, tack (baste) and stitch each underarm and side seam, rounding off the seam under each arm. Trim the seam allowance to 6 mm (¼ in) and carefully clip the curve under the arm to allow it to turn well. Oversew the raw edges together.

3 With wrong sides together, fold the hood in half along one longer side. Pin and tack (baste) the seam and sew it 6 mm (¼ in) from the edge on the right side. Turn it to the wrong side, press the seam and sew a second line of stitching, 6 mm (¼ in) from the first. Mark the centre bottom of the hood (the edge at the opposite end to the hood seam).

Temporarily position the hood centre to match the centre back and front. Fold the hood sides in so they meet in the centre of the hood. Mark where the folds on the hood sides meet the jacket top with a pin on each side. Pin and tack (baste) the shoulders and sleeves together from the pins outwards. Stitch the seams and neaten the raw edges.

4 Folding the hood as before, match the centre back of the hood with the jacket centre back, with right sides together and the jacket inside out. Pin the hood to the back, then to the fronts when you reach the shoulder stitching, making 2 sets of seams that meet in a 'Y' shape. Stitch the seams. Trim the seams on the jacket fronts only and oversew. Bind the back hood seam.

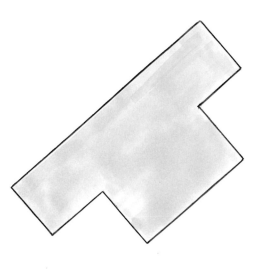

HOOD

5 Cut sufficient bias binding from the plain fabric to go around the entire garment. Make some loops for the toggles, folding and pressing them into shape. Pin, tack (baste) and sew the binding to the jacket edge, right sides together, beginning on the hem. Enclose the toggle loops on the side of one front.

Enclose the binding ends neatly when you return to the beginning. Press the stitching line firmly from the right side to give a crisp edge before you turn the binding to the inside and hem it to the inside of the jacket. Hem the sleeves and sew on the toggles.

Pop-Up Puppet

GIVE CHILDREN HOURS OF FUN WITH THIS DISAPPEARING PUPPET

YOU WILL NEED ■ *White paper* ■ *Pencil* ■ *Card* ■ *Piece of fabric* ■ *Scissors*
■ *Rubber-based glue* ■ *Craft knife* ■ *Large hollow rubber ball* ■ *30 cm (12 in) length of dowelling*
■ *Ribbon* ■ *Needle and thread* ■ *Black felt-tip pen*

1 Scale up the templates shown and cut out a piece of card using the card template. Using the fabric template, cut out the fabric with a sharp pair of scissors.

2 Next fold the piece of card into a cone shape and stick down the edges with glue so that it stays in shape. When the glue is dry, stick the fabric onto the cone leaving a piece of fabric loose at the top end of the cone. At the smaller end snip into the fabric with a pair of scissors so that it can be folded easily into the inside of the cone and glued down.

3 Using a craft knife, cut a small cross into the ball and push the piece of dowelling in through the hole. Secure with a little glue, then place the dowelling through the cone with the ball at the top.

4 Secure the loose fabric to the dowelling with glue and a ribbon tied in a bow just below the ball. To make the bow safe, sew a couple of stitches through it. Draw on the eyes, nose and mouth with a black felt-tip pen. Pull the dowelling up and down through the cone to make the puppet's head pop up and down.

CARD

FABRIC

Circus Toiletries Bag

THIS JOLLY CLOWN MOTIF WILL LIVEN UP BATHTIME

YOU WILL NEED ■ *50.5 × 16 cm (20 × 6¼ in) piece of plasticized fabric*
■ *Tape measure* ■ *Rubber-based glue* ■ *Clothes pegs (pins)* ■ *Scissors* ■ *Oddments of plasticized fabric in red, green, yellow, blue, black and pale yellow or white* ■ *Pencil* ■ *Velcro*

1 Fold the large piece of fabric in half widthways, leaving an 8 cm (3¼ in) overlap. Fold each corner of the overlap over and glue. Use clothes pegs (pins) to hold them while they dry.

3 Cut out an 8 cm (3¼ in) red circle and glue it to the front of the bag, placing it 4 cm (1½ in) from the bottom. Cut out the shapes for the clown's hat, face and features and glue them in place over the red circle.

4 To make the fastening, glue small strips of Velcro to the underside of the red circle and the front of the bag.

2 Cut out 2 blue circles, 4 green circles, 4 yellow circles, all 4 cm (1½ in) in diameter. Spread glue onto the back of each one and start by placing half of one green circle under the back of the bag. Fold the other half over to the front and press. Secure with a peg (pin).

Continue with the yellow circle, then blue, then the green and yellow again. Repeat on the other side. Remove pegs (pins) when dry. Cut out 2 red circles 4 cm (1½ in) in diameter. Glue them together, encasing the point of the flap between the two.

Nightclothes Case

A HAPPY BRIGHT CAT TO CUDDLE AND KEEP NIGHTCLOTHES NEAT AND TIDY

YOU WILL NEED ■ *Pen* ■ *Paper* ■ *Tape measure* ■ *Scissors* ■ *Cotton fabrics in bright reds and blues* ■ *Pins* ■ *Needle and thread* ■ *Iron* ■ *Zip (zipper)* ■ *Gingham fabric* ■ *Wadding (batting)* ■ *Oddments of felt* ■ *Embroidery thread*

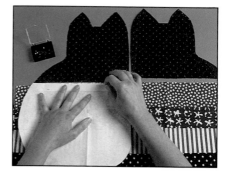

1 The size of this bag can be adjusted as you wish so that larger nightclothes can fit inside. The smallest reasonable size is about 45 cm (18 in) tall. Make a paper pattern of the required size for the cat shape, using the template as a guide, and work out the length and width you will need for the patchwork strips, remembering to add seam allowances of about 1 cm (⅜ in). The strips must be long enough to make both sides of the cat. With the right sides together, join the strips accurately and then press the seams so that they lie flat. Cut 2 opposite cat head shapes and use your pattern to cut 2 opposite bodies from the patchwork strips.

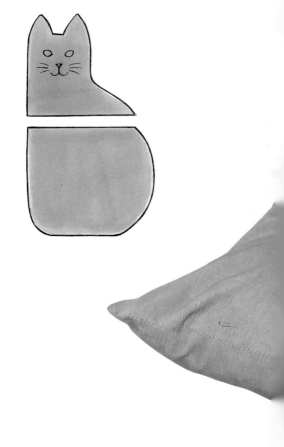

2 With right sides together, join the heads to the bodies and press the seams open. With right sides together, pin the straight edges of the cat together and make a 2 cm (¾ in) long seam at the top (from where the curve of the ear becomes straight) and the same on the straight at the bottom of the seam. Tack (baste) and sew them using a 1 cm (⅜ in) seam allowance. Press back seam allowances of 1 cm (⅜ in) all the way up the fronts which prepares the opening for the zip (zipper). Position the closed zip (zipper) centrally with the cat body opened up flat, and tack (baste) it into place. Stitch the zip (zipper) from the right side. Fold the cat along the zip (zipper) with right sides together and pin, tack (baste) and sew the body together. Turn it to the right side through the open zip (zipper) and press the outside seam flat, picking out the points at the ears if necessary with a pin to make them sharp.

3 Cut 2 complete opposite body shapes from gingham for the bag lining. Cut a piece of wadding (batting) the same size and then trim it down about 1 cm (⅜ in) all the way round. Pin, tack (baste) and sew the lining with right sides together, leaving an opening unstitched. Do not turn to the right side.

Place the wadding (batting) on top. Insert the lining into the cat's body, tucking the wadding (batting) up into the ears and smoothing it flat inside. Remove and re-trim if necessary.

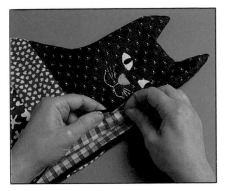

4 Turn the lining opening under and tack (baste) it down round the opening, ensuring that the zip (zipper) runs freely. Cut felt for the eyes and nose and sew them to the head through to the lining which will help keep it in place. Embroider a mouth and whiskers. Backstitches or a few French knots can also be worked on the patchwork strips through to the lining.

Clown Finger Puppets

YOU WILL NEED ■ *Pieces of felt in several colours* ■ *Scissors* ■ *Rubber-based glue*

1 Cut out a rectangle of dark green felt which will fit around your finger for the body. Cut out all the other detail pieces: a face from white felt, two eyes from black felt, a nose, mouth and hat from red felt and two buttons from light green felt.

2 Fold the rectangular piece of felt in half and stick down the side and top edge with glue so that it fits onto your finger. Stick all the detailed features pieces onto this base piece. Leave the completed felt puppet under a heavy book for a couple of hours until the glue is completely dry. You can make other variations using the same methods.

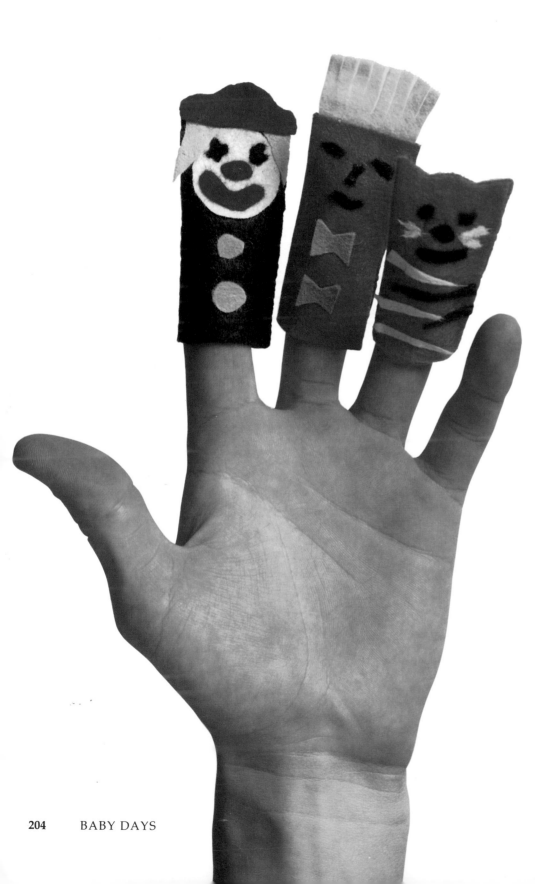

Rotating Clown

NOW HAPPY, NOW SAD, THIS CARD PROVIDES INSTANT REACTIONS

YOU WILL NEED ■ *Pair of compasses* ■ *Pencil* ■ *White card* ■ *Ruler* ■ *Scissors* ■ *Craft knife*
■ *Non-toxic acrylic paints* ■ *Small paintbrush* ■ *Winged paperclip*

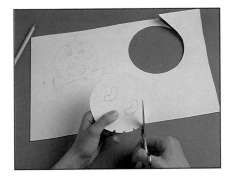

1 Use a pair of compasses to draw two circles, one slightly larger than the other, on a piece of white card. Mark the centres. The larger circle is the under piece which will be moved around. Scale up the templates and draw the two mouth shapes on the larger circle with a pencil.

The smaller circle is for the clown's face, so use the template to draw on the features, hair and bow tie. These must take up a larger area than the circle underneath to hide it, although you must leave a little showing below the bow tie for turning.

Cut out the two circles with scissors and cut triangles into the edge of the larger circle so that it can be easily gripped when being turned. Use a craft knife to cut out a hole for the mouth on the smaller circle.

2 Using a small paintbrush and acrylic paints, paint all the different areas of colour onto the cut out shapes. Leaving the face white, carefully paint the mouth, cheeks and nose red, paint the eyes with black, paint the bow tie blue and the hair orange. The circumference of the circle underneath should be painted in yellow as shown.

3 With the sharp end of a pair of scissors, make a small hole at the centre of each of the two circles marked earlier. Placing the clown's face on top of the piece with the mouths, push the winged paperclip through both holes and open up the clip at the back to secure it. Now move the circle underneath so that the clown has a happy face, then a sad face.

Leaf Counting Book

A BEAUTIFUL AND UNUSUAL CLOTH COUNTING BOOK

YOU WILL NEED ■ *3 sheets of plain paper* ■ *Pencil* ■ *3 pieces of*
33 × 18 cm (13 × 7 in) calico (cotton fabric) ■ *Pressed autumn leaves in different sizes*
■ *Rubber-based glue* ■ *Iron-on protective laminating film* ■ *Iron* ■ *Heat-resistant foam* ■ *Large*
darning needle ■ *Length of fine cord* ■ *Metal ruler* ■ *Craft knife*

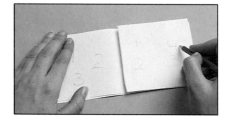

1 To work out how many leaves you will need for each page and how you will arrange them, make up a paper 'dummy' book. Fold each of the sheets of paper in half and put them together to make a 12-page 'book' Turn to the first page and draw a number 1 where you want to stick your first leaf. On the right-hand page draw the numbers 1 and 2. Turn over and draw the numbers 1 to 3 on the left-hand page and 1 to 4 on the right. Continue through the book until the last page is numbered 1 to 10.

2 Using the dummy book as a guide, open it at the centre. Lay out a piece of calico (cotton fabric) and arrange a pattern of 5 leaves on the left-hand side and 6 on the right-hand side, fixing each leaf by using a small piece of card to apply a dot of rubber-based glue on its reverse side. Press each leaf down lightly onto the calico (cotton fabric). It is important that you remember to leave a margin of about 12 mm (½ in) around the edges so that you can trim off the 'pages' neatly when you have finished the book.

3 Cut 6 pieces, about 33 × 19 cm (13 × 7½ in), from the protective laminating film. Carefully smooth one sheet over the leaves on the page so that it adheres lightly. Turn the sheet of calico (cotton fabric) over. Do the same with the centre page of the dummy. Arrange 7 leaves on left, and 4 on right. Cover this side with another sheet of film. Discard the dummy pages. Repeat with the other pieces of calico (cotton fabric), laying out the leaves as shown. Arrange a pretty pattern of leaves on the front cover.

4 Lay each sheet of calico (cotton fabric) on an ironing board and cover with heat resistant foam. Use your iron to seal the laminate. While still warm, fold the calico (cotton fabric) in half, in the same order as the dummy. Pierce 3 holes in the spine of each page and lace with cord. Trim the rough edges of the completed book.

Cat Blackboard

THE ATTRACTIVE SHAPE OF THIS BLACKBOARD WILL ENCOURAGE CHILDREN TO DRAW

YOU WILL NEED ■ *Pencil* ■ *Paper* ■ *Scissors* ■ *20 × 42 cm (8 × 16½ in) plywood,*
1.5 cm (⅝ in) thick ■ *Sticky putty* ■ *Fretsaw (scroll saw)* ■ *Sandpaper* ■ *Matt white emulsion (flat*
latex) paint ■ *Paintbrushes* ■ *Blackboard paint* ■ *Non-toxic white acrylic paint* ■ *Chalk*

1 Draw a cat shape onto a sheet of paper and cut it out.

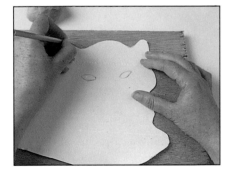

2 Attach the template to the plywood with sticky putty and draw around it in pencil.

3 Cut out the cat shape with a fretsaw (scroll saw) and sand the edges with sandpaper to give a smooth finish.

4 Using white emulsion (flat latex) and then 2 coats of blackboard paint, paint one side and all around the edges. Allow to dry between coats. Mark the eyes on the template and cut them out. Lay the template over the cut shape and paint in the outline of the eyes with white acrylic paint. Lastly paint the whiskers with a fine brush. Supply sticks of chalk for drawing on the board.

Starfish T-Shirt

THIS DETACHABLE STARFISH ACTS AS BOTH MOTIF AND FUN TOY

YOU WILL NEED ■ *Marker pen* ■ *White paper* ■ *Scissors*
■ *Felt in 2 contrasting colours* ■ *Embroidery thread* ■ *Needle and thread* ■ *20 cm (8 in) Velcro*
■ *Wadding (batting)* ■ *Pins* ■ *Pinking shears* ■ *T-shirt*

1 Use the marker pen to draw a starfish shape on a piece of white paper. Cut it out and draw around it on 2 pieces of felt.

2 Cut out some dots in a different coloured felt and attach securely with embroidery thread on one of the stars.

3 Sew 1 piece of Velcro to the middle of the other piece of felt, and another to the front of the T-shirt.

4 Sandwich a piece of wadding (batting) between the 2 felt layers, pin together and sew around the starfish shape.

5 Using pinking shears, cut out the starfish shape just outside the stitching line, and attach to the T-shirt.

Bean Bag Clown

THIS JOLLY CLOWN MAKES A HARDWEARING TOY

YOU WILL NEED ■ *Pencil* ■ *Paper* ■ *Scissors* ■ *20 × 90 cm (8 × 36 in) printed fabric* ■ *Scraps of coloured and white fabric* ■ *Paintbrush* ■ *Fabric paints* ■ *Iron* ■ *Needle and thread* ■ *Polystyrene (styrofoam) ball-bearings or dried peas* ■ *Oddments of felt* ■ *Pinking shears* ■ *Embroidery thread*

1 Scale up the templates onto paper and use as patterns. Cut 2 bodies from printed fabric, 2 hats from coloured fabric and 2 heads from white fabric. Lightly pencil the facial features onto 1 head piece and paint with fabric paints. Leave to dry then press the design carefully, following the manufacturer's instructions.

2 With right sides together, stitch each head to a hat and body, stitching between the dots on the template and leaving a 6 mm (¼ in) seam allowance. Press the seams towards the hat. With right sides together, stitch the clowns together leaving a 6 mm (¼ in) seam allowance and also leaving a 4 cm (1¾ in) gap to turn on one outside leg. Stitch again to reinforce the seam and trim.

3 Turn the clown right side out and fill with polystyrene (styrofoam) ball-bearings or dried peas. Sew up the gap to close.

4 Cut two 2 cm (¾ in) diameter circles from felt using pinking shears. Using embroidery thread, sew each circle to the front of the clown with a cross stitch, for the buttons.

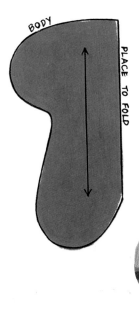

BODY

PLACE TO FOLD

HAT

FOLD

HEAD

FOLD

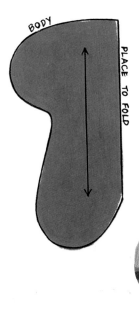

Alphabet Bricks

YOU WILL NEED ■ *5 × 5 cm (2 × 2 in) pine cut into squares* ■ *Sandpaper* ■ *Chalk* ■ *Small paintbrush* ■ *Non-toxic brightly coloured acrylic paints* ■ *Non-toxic clear acrylic varnish*

1 Take your squares of wood and use sandpaper to smooth down any rough edges.

2 Lightly chalk on the outlines of the letters and fill in the colours with a small brush. If you feel confident enough, just paint straight onto the squares.

3 Varnish the bricks with a protective coat of clear acrylic varnish and leave to dry.

Snake Glove Puppet

CREATE HOURS OF FUN FOR 2 TO 3-YEAR-OLDS WITH THIS ENTERTAINING PUPPET

YOU WILL NEED ■ *Squares of green, brown, red, black and yellow felt* ■ *Chalk*
■ *Scissors* ■ *Needle and embroidery thread* ■ *Pins* ■ *Rubber-based glue*

2 Sew the tongue onto the mouth piece using blanket stitch. Sew all along the edge of the puppet, still working in blanket stitch. Pin the brown mouth piece to the green felt and sew the pieces together all around the edges in blanket stitch.

1 Fold the green felt square in half and draw out the shape of the snake in chalk. Cut out the 2 pieces. Fold the brown felt and draw around the top of the green shape on the folded edge to make the inside of the mouth. Cut this shape out. Draw out the shapes of the tongue and the eyes as well as the 'V'-shapes for the back of the snake with a piece of coloured chalk on the red, black and yellow felt and cut out.

3 Finally, glue the eyes and the 'V'-shapes onto the back of the glove puppet.

Jacob's Ladder

THIS TOY WILL FASCINATE CHILDREN AND ADULTS ALIKE

YOU WILL NEED ■ *Fretsaw (scroll saw)* ■ *42 × 4.5 cm (16½ × 1¾ in) wood,
1 cm (⅜ in) thick* ■ *Ruler* ■ *Fine sandpaper* ■ *Scissors* ■ *140 cm (55 in) red ribbon, 6 mm (¼ in) wide*
■ *70 cm (28 in) green ribbon, 6 mm (¼ in) wide* ■ *Rubber-based glue*

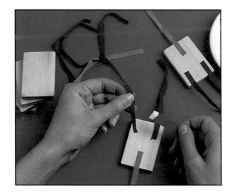

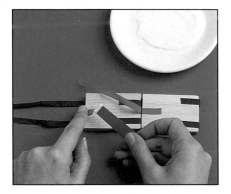

1 Cut the piece of wood into 6 equal sections, each measuring 7 cm (2¾ in) in length. Sand down all the edges until smooth with fine sandpaper, being careful of your hands on the rough surface.

2 Cut the red ribbon into 10 equal pieces, each 14 cm (5½ in) long. Cut the green ribbon into 5 equal pieces, each 14 cm (5½ in) long. Glue the ends of 2 pieces of red ribbon to one end of a piece of wood, 6 mm (¼ in) from the edges, and a length of green ribbon in the centre at the opposite end of the first section. Repeat with 4 more blocks.

3 Lay out all 6 pieces with alternate sides facing upwards. The piece with no ribbons goes at one end. Thread the ribbons under and over to connect all 6 pieces, gluing the ribbon tightly as you go.

Stacking Boxes

THIS EDUCATIONAL TOY IS SUITABLE FOR 2 TO 3-YEAR OLDS

YOU WILL NEED ■ *Wooden stacking boxes* ■ *Matt white emulsion*
(flat latex) paint ■ *Paintbrushes* ■ *Non-toxic acrylic paints in primary colours* ■ *Pencil* ■ *Card*
■ *Ruler* ■ *Scissors* ■ *Rubber-based glue* ■ *Non-toxic clear acrylic varnish*

1 Paint the boxes with matt white emulsion (flat latex) paint to act as a base, leave to dry and then paint over the top in primary colours.

2 Draw out a different shape on the card for each box. Cut out each shape and paint in bright colours.

3 Glue the painted shapes onto the box lids. Make sure that the glue is completely dry, then varnish with a coat of clear acrylic varnish.

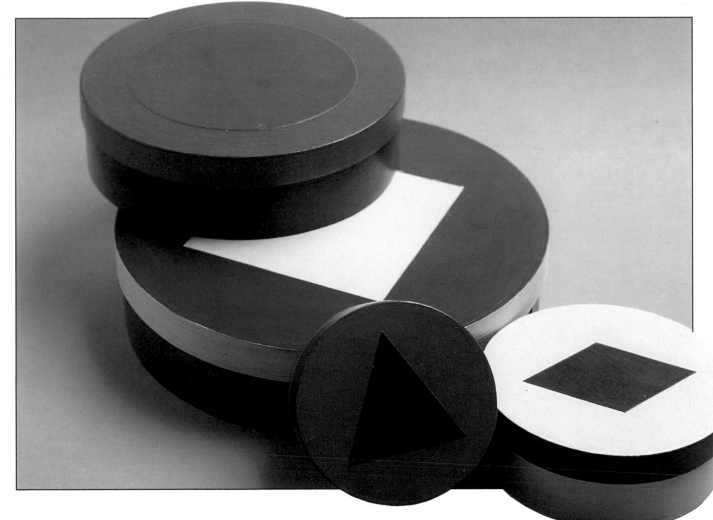

Elephant and Passenger

A CUDDLY ELEPHANT WITH A FUN SECRET PASSENGER

YOU WILL NEED ■ *Pen* ■ *Paper* ■ *Tape measure* ■ *Pins* ■ *Scissors*
■ *Polkadot cotton fabric* ■ *Washable satin fabric* ■ *Iron-on interfacing* ■ *Iron* ■ *Gingham*
■ *Needle and thread* ■ *Oddments of fabric for body and ears* ■ *Non-toxic, flame retardant polyester*
filling (batting) ■ *Length of plain cotton for the saddle strap* ■ *Cotton fabric for*
the rider ■ *Oddments of coloured felt* ■ *Embroidery thread* ■ *Ribbon*

1 Make paper patterns for all the required pieces, using the templates as a guide. Cut 2 opposite shapes in polkadot cotton for the bodies. Cut 2 opposite outer ears from the satin and use an iron-on interfacing on the reverse, being careful not to scorch the satin. Cut 2 opposite ear facings from the gingham.

Place the right sides together and stitch the 2 sets of ears, leaving the straight edges open. Turn them to the right side, press, and tack (baste) the openings closed. Check the position of the ears from the pattern and pin, tack (baste) and sew the ears in place on the opposite bodies.

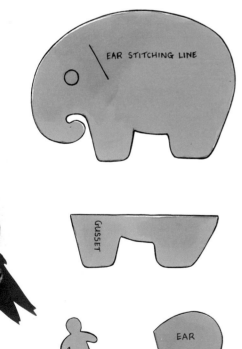

2 Cut the gusset. With wrong sides together, fold the gusset in half matching the legs, and press. Pin, tack (baste) and stitch the gusset to the body and legs with right sides together, starting and finishing your stitch line at the opposite halfway marks folded into the gusset.

Cut 3 strips of cotton and satin fabrics each 12 cm (4¾ in) long and braid them together. Tie a knot just short of one end. Tack (baste) this tail to the body 9 cm (3½ in) above the gusset stitch line.

3 Place the second body on top of the first, right sides together, and tack (baste). To sew, open the gusset out flat to sew the second body side and stitch only the gusset section as before. Break off, fold the gusset back in half, then sew around the upper body, trunk and head. Leave a gap of 10 cm (4 in) for turning. Clip the curves and turn the body to the right side. Stuff firmly, and then oversew the opening.

4 Cut a piece of felt for the saddle about 14 × 10 cm (5½ × 4 in), and a flower shape with an inner circle in a different colour. Appliqué the decorations to the centre of one half of the saddle. Make a 4 cm (1½ in) wide saddle strap about 48 cm (19 in) long from the plain cotton. Sew the strap securely to the back of the saddle, so that you can conceal the overlapping ends behind the folded saddle. Fold the saddle wrong sides together and stitch the edges.

5 Make up the rider from 2 shapes sewn right sides together. Cut a small slit in the figure's back to turn, then stuff and oversew the opening. Embroider loops of hair onto the head and add eyes and mouth. Sew a felt sarong around the waist and a ribbon to the back. For safety, the ribbon should not be longer than about 12 cm (4¾ in). Sew the other end to the inside back of the saddle through to the strap so the rider can be hidden or brought out on the ribbon.

6 Arrange the saddle on the centre of the elephant, wind the strap around and then sew the strap ends together behind the saddle, carefully trimming away any excess to neaten. Hem the saddle to the body all the way round on both edges of the strap so that it cannot slip. Remember that children can be rough with their toys, so strong, secure stitching is essential. Finally, cut felt circles for the eyes and sew them to the head.

Doing Doll

A CUDDLY DOLL WITH LOTS OF FASTENINGS

YOU WILL NEED ■ *Pen* ■ *Paper* ■ *Scissors* ■ *Pre-washed calico (cotton fabric)* ■ *Pins* ■ *Needle and thread* ■ *Non-toxic, flame retardant polyester filling (batting)* ■ *Tape measure* ■ *Card* ■ *Small quantity of yarn* ■ *Denim for the overalls* ■ *Iron* ■ *10 cm (4 in) zip (zipper) in a bright colour* ■ *Patterned cotton for patch, handkerchief and facings* ■ *Striped cotton for shirt and pocket* ■ *Pre-washed striped cotton for straps* ■ *Toggle* ■ *Large button* ■ *Scrap of fabric for toggle loop* ■ *Ribbon* ■ *Embroidery thread* ■ *Felt for eyes* ■ *Velcro*

1 Cut the paper patterns for all the pieces shown on the templates. Cut out 2 body shapes from calico (cotton fabric). Noting the position from the pattern, cut a slit in the body back. Pin, tack (baste) and stitch the body shapes right sides together. Clip the curves and turn the body right side out. Stuff firmly, pushing the filling well into the ends of the hands and feet.

2 Cut a length of card 8 cm (3¼ in) wide and at least 20 cm (8 in) long. Wind the yarn around the whole length and cut through to form 16 cm (6¼ in) lengths. If you have a sewing machine, feed the yarn through the machine joining them together along the centre. You will need a length about 50 cm (19½ in) long.

3 If you have no machine, sew the centre of each strand individually onto the head. If using the machined strip, fold it along the centre stitching, and beginning at the crown, sew the end to the head catching in the central stitching. Work in a spiral fashion around the scalp to give the doll a ragged look.

4 Cut 2 opposites for each overalls shape, front and back, from the denim. Sew the first 3 cm (1¼ in) of the seam at the crotch of the overalls front. Press the seam flat and press the seam allowances back, making a crisp fold all the way up the front pieces of fabric.

Set the zip (zipper) behind the turned-back edges, pinning and tacking (basting) it neatly into place. Cut out a patch shape from patterned cotton and tack (baste) it to the left front. Cut a pocket flap and neaten it so that it measures about 6 × 3 cm (2¼ × 1¼ in). Cut and neaten a pocket to fit below the flap. Pin and tack (baste) the flap and pocket to the right front of the overalls.

5 Sew the zip (zipper), patch and pocket to the overalls. Make up the overalls back by joining the back seam. Trim the raw edges to 6 mm (¼ in) and oversew to neaten them. Turn the back waist edge down 1 cm (⅜ in), turn it under and stitch a hem.

6 Matching leg hems and inner leg seams, pin and tack (baste) the side seams. The overalls front will be a little higher than the back at the waist. Stitch the side seams. Sew the inner leg seams. Trim all the raw edges to 6 mm (¼ in) and oversew to neaten them. Turn the overalls so that they are right side out.

Cut 2 opposite shapes from the selected fabric for the facings. Turn up a narrow hem. Matching the underarm curve and side seam, pin and tack (baste) the front facings to the overalls front, right sides together. The centre front edges will overlap the zip (zipper) opening by 1 cm (⅜ in). Stitch the top and underarm curves only, using a 1 cm (⅜ in) seam allowance. Clip the curves,

and then carefully trim the seam allowance to 6 mm (¼ in).

Turn the facings to the inside, turn them under at the side seams and zip (zipper) opening and hem them to the seam allowance. Make up 2 straps to cross over at the back. Sew on the toggle and button securely. Insert a small loop into the end of one strap to fasten the toggle and work a buttonhole in the other.

Cut out the shirt pieces, sew the side and shoulder seams and neaten all raw edges, leaving the back open. Sew ribbons to the top back. Embroider the doll's features, adding felt circles for the eyes. Make a handkerchief to put in the pocket and use Velcro on the pocket and flap so that it can be opened and closed.

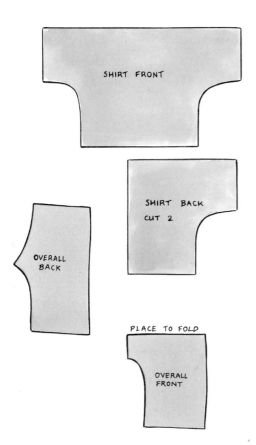

SHIRT FRONT

SHIRT BACK
CUT 2

OVERALL
BACK

PLACE TO FOLD

OVERALL
FRONT

Pompon Decorations

POMPONS CAN BE USED TO LIVEN UP ALMOST ANYTHING!

YOU WILL NEED ■ *Pencil* ■ *Something circular to draw round, e.g. spice jar, small glass*
■ *Stiff card* ■ *Scissors* ■ *Oddments of yarn* ■ *Ruler* ■ *Large darning needle*

1 Draw around your circular object onto the stiff card. The circle will define the final size of the pompon. Cut out 2 identical circles, then cut a slightly smaller circle out of the centre of each so that you are left with 2 rings. Place them on top of each other. Wind a long piece of yarn into a ball, small enough to go through the hole in the middle. Start winding the yarn around the 2 rings, threading it through the middle. Keep winding until the hole has been completely filled.

2 Carefully push one blade of the scissors between the 2 pieces of card and cut the yarn all the way around the outer edge of the ring.

3 Once this is done, carefully separate the two cards, tie some yarn tightly around the middle of the pompon and knot. Remove the card.

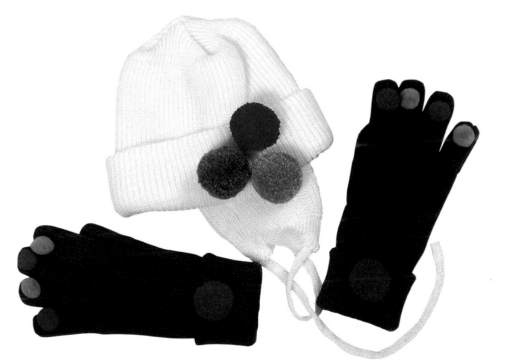

4 To decorate the hat, cut 6 rings of card 4 cm (1½ in) in diameter. Following the instructions given above, make 3 pompons in different colours. When tying the middle of each pompon, leave one long end of the yarn. Use this to sew into the hat. Position the pompons on the side of the hat and sew into place.

5 To decorate the gloves, cut 20 rounds of card 1.5 cm (⅝ in) in diameter. Following the instructions above, make 5 pompons in one colour and 5 in a contrasting colour. Sew each pompon onto the end of each finger, alternating the colours. It is helpful to push something into the fingers of the gloves to help prevent sewing into the back. Make 2 further pompons using a 3 cm (1¼ in) diameter card. Sew onto the cuff of each glove.

Sunshine T-Shirt

BRIGHTEN UP A PLAIN WHITE T-SHIRT WITH THIS SMILING SUN

YOU WILL NEED ■ *Pencil* ■ *Card* ■ *Scissors* ■ *T-shirt* ■ *Iron* ■ *Paintbrushes*
■ *Yellow, red and gold fabric paints* ■ *Black fabric pen*

1 Scale up the template onto a piece of card and cut it out. Press the T-shirt, then lay it out on a flat surface and place some card inside to protect the back from paint. Position the template on the front side of the T-shirt and draw around the edge in pencil to transfer the design.

2 Using a small paintbrush and yellow fabric paint, colour in the sun shape.

3 Mix a little red paint with some yellow and blend into the rays. Add some gold around the edges and enhance the circle around the face. When dry, use the black fabric pen to draw on the eyes, nose and mouth and outline the whole sun to give a bolder effect. Iron the shirt carefully to fix the paint according to the manufacturer's instructions, and wash before use.

Acrobatic Clown

THIS TRADITIONAL MOVING CLOWN MAKES A FASCINATING TOY

YOU WILL NEED ■ *Ruler* ■ *Pencil* ■ *Paper* ■ *Scissors* ■ *2 sheets of 20 × 15 cm (8 × 6 in)*
plywood, 6 mm (¼ in) thick ■ *Clamp* ■ *Hand drill* ■ *Fretsaw (scroll saw)* ■ *Length of dowelling, 5 mm (³⁄₁₆ in)*
in diameter ■ *Fine sandpaper* ■ *Non-toxic acrylic paints* ■ *Paintbrushes* ■ *Wood glue* ■ *Coloured string*

1 Scale up the clown templates onto paper and cut out. Draw around the body, leg and arm pieces onto one of the sheets of plywood. Clamp the 2 sheets together firmly, and then drill out the 4 × 5 mm (³⁄₁₆ in) holes in the body and 6 mm (¼ in) holes in the arms and legs. Cut and push two 2 cm (¾ in) lengths of dowelling into 2 of the body holes to help hold the sheets together before cutting out all the shapes.

2 Sand down the 2 arms, 2 legs and the bodies held together with dowelling with fine sandpaper. Remove the pieces of dowelling. Carefully paint the backs and fronts of the legs and arms, and paint a face on the front body and a back on the back body piece. Allow to dry.

3 Ensure that the holes in the arms and legs allow them to move freely on the dowelling and then drill a small hole in the top of each as indicated, and glue one end of a 20 cm (8 in) length of string in each.

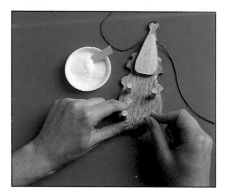

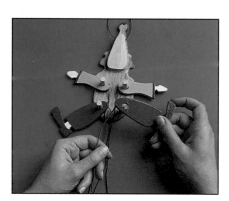

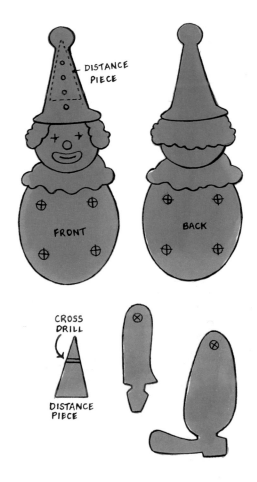

4 Place the front body piece face down. Cut out a triangular distance piece from the waste plywood, cross-drill a hole at the top and thread through the hanging string. Glue into position near the top of the 'hat'. Glue the 4 cut lengths of dowelling into the front body piece.

5 Attach the arms and legs onto the dowelling and draw all the strings down between the legs as shown. Put a little glue on the distance piece and in each of the holes in the back piece, and carefully press in position over the dowelling, making sure that the arms and legs move freely. When the glue has dried completely, smooth down the dowelling with a piece of sandpaper and cover the ends with a little paint.

Shape **M**atcher

YOU WILL NEED ■ *Scissors* ■ *1 m (1 yd) white cotton fabric,*
115 cm (45 in) wide, washed and pressed ■ *Ruler* ■ *Needle and thread* ■ *Pencil*
■ *Card* ■ *Red, yellow and blue fabric paints* ■ *Natural sponge* ■ *Iron* ■ *0.5 m (½ yd)*
lightweight iron-on interfacing ■ *Pins* ■ *Wadding (batting)*

1 Cut out the pattern pieces from the fabric. Fold the 6 pocket pieces in half, with right sides together, and sew round 6 mm (¼ in) from the edge, leaving a small gap for turning. Trim the seams and clip the corners before turning out to the right side. Make the 6 ties in the same way and press all pieces.

2 Cut out 6 templates in card, drawing a different shape on each. Using a new colour for each shape, use the templates like stencils and print the pockets with a sponge and fabric paints. Print the shapes all over the main body piece and twice each on spare fabric for the soft shapes. Fix the dye by ironing.

3 Cut a piece of interfacing to the size of the printed main body and iron it on carefully, following the manufacturer's instructions. Pin the ties in position between the two main body pieces and sew all round. Turn through to the right way out and edge stitch. Position the pockets and stitch into place.

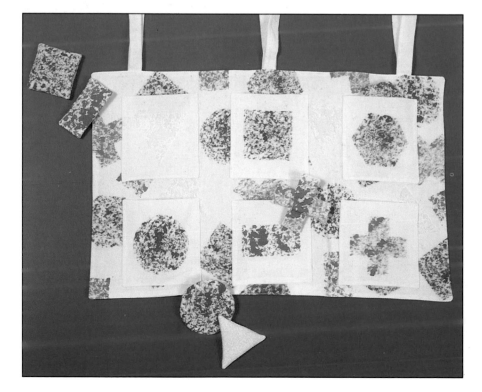

4 Cut out the printed shapes leaving a 6 mm (¼ in) seam (12 pieces). Pin them together in matching pairs, with right sides together, and tack (baste) wadding (batting) into place. Sew through all the layers, leaving a gap for turning. Trim all the edges and clip the corners. Turn through and oversew the gap securely.

Scented Mobile

YOU WILL NEED ■ *Pencil* ■ *Paper* ■ *Pinking shears* ■ *Wadding (batting)* ■ *Scraps of plain and patterned fabrics* ■ *Pins* ■ *Needle and thread* ■ *Pot pourri* ■ *Dowelling (optional)*

1 Scale up the template and transfer onto paper. Use this to cut out several butterflies from wadding (batting). Place a piece of patterned fabric onto plain fabric and pin on the pattern. Cut out the butterfly shape using pinking shears. Repeat with different combinations of fabric.

2 Sandwich the wadding (batting) between each pair of fabric butterfly pieces, pin in position and tack (baste) around the edge, taking a 6 mm (¼ in) seam allowance and leaving a 5 cm (2 in) gap in the upper wing. Spoon the pot pourri into the gap and shake well.

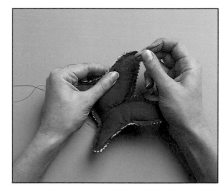

3 Top stitch neatly around the edge of each butterfly, taking a 6 mm (¼ in) seam. Fold each butterfly in half, and then use a double thread to stitch through the centre of each as shown, to keep the folded shape. Attach a single thread to each wing 2.5 cm (1 in) from the tip and knot securely. Hang the butterflies directly from the ceiling or from a piece of wooden dowelling.

Rag Doll

THIS OLD-FASHIONED RAG DOLL IS SURE TO BECOME A TRUE FRIEND

YOU WILL NEED ■ *Pen* ■ *Paper* ■ *Tape measure* ■ *Scissors* ■ *Pre-washed calico (cotton fabric)* ■ *Pins* ■ *Needle and thread* ■ *Non-toxic, fire retardant polyester filling (batting)* ■ *Striped fabric for bloomers* ■ *Pretty cotton fabric for the dress* ■ *Contrasting fabric for patches* ■ *Elastic* ■ *Lace trimming* ■ *Card* ■ *Yarn* ■ *Ribbon* ■ *Oddments of felt* ■ *Embroidery thread* ■ *Velcro*

1 Cut out a paper pattern, using the template as a guide. Cut out 2 body shapes from the calico (cotton fabric). Cut a small slit in the body back. Pin, tack (baste) and stitch the body shapes together, clip the curves and turn the body right side out. Stuff the body firmly, pushing the filling well into the ends of the hands and feet.

2 Cut out 2 pieces of striped fabric for the bloomers. Pin them right sides together and sew the curved seam with a 6 mm (¼ in) allowance. Oversew the raw edges. Cut a piece of fabric for the dress 85 × 26 cm (34 × 10¼ in) and several squares for patches.

Pin and appliqué these at random to the dress front. Make a back seam in the dress by joining the 2 shorter edges, leaving a small opening at the neck. Neaten the seam. Make 1 cm (⅜ in) hems at the top and bottom and mark the centre front with a pin.

3 Turn the bloomers so that the curved crotch seam is in the centre position with right sides together. Stitch and neaten the side seams. Make a narrow casing at the waist and insert a piece of elastic to fit round the doll's waist. Make a narrow casing at the leg bottoms and insert elastic to fit. Trim with lace.

4 Cut 2 lengths of card 4 cm (1½ in) and 10 cm (4 in) wide. Use the narrower width to make the fringe. Wind yarn around both cards and then cut through to form short lengths of yarn. Make enough for a fringe about 2.5 cm (1 in) long when the strands are laid side to side. You will need about 16 cm (6¼ in) for the hair. If you have a sewing machine, feed the fringe lengths through the machine, joining them together along the centre. Do the same with the hair lengths.

5 Put the doll in the dress with her arms out at the top. Catch the dress up at the sides from under the arms and make armholes by oversewing the back to the front at the shoulders. Gather the front and the back sections with a double thread to fit the doll, and stitch a line through the gathers to hold them securely.

6 If you have no machine, attach the hair by sewing each strand firmly in place. If using a machined strip, place it centrally down the back of the head with the stitching line as a 'parting'. Stitch, catching in the machined stitches as you go.

Fold the fringe strip along the centre stitching and sew it round the front of the head. Make 2 braids, secure and tie with 2 narrow ribbon bows. Sew the braids to the head. Cut felt for the eyes and cheeks and embroider the other features. Stitch a Velcro fastening to the sides of the dress back at the neck.

T-Bar Shoes

THESE COMFORTABLE SHOES FIT BABIES UP TO 6 MONTHS

YOU WILL NEED ■ *1 pair 3 mm (US 3) knitting needles* ■ *Oddments of double knitting (sport) yarn in red, yellow, pink and turquoise* ■ *2 buttons (or suitable beads)* ■ *Large darning needle*

Tension (Gauge)
Using 3 mm (US 3) needles, 21 sts and 30 rows to 10 cm (4 in) (st st).

Sole
Using red yarn, cast on 37 sts.
Work 2 rows garter st.
1st row: inc 1, k 35 sts, inc 1.
2nd row: k to end.
3rd row: inc 1, k 37 sts, inc 1.
4th row: k to end.
5th row: inc 1, k 39 sts, inc 1.
6th row: k to end.
7th row: inc 1, k 41 sts, inc 1.
8th row: k to end.
Break yarn, change to pink.
9th row: inc 1, k 43 sts, inc 1.
10th row: p to end (47 sts).

To shape top
11th row: k 16, sl 1, k 1, psso, k 11, k 2 tog, k 16.
12th row: p to end.
13th row: k 16, sl 1, k 1, psso, k 9, k 2 tog, k 16.

14th row: p to end.
15th row: k 16, sl 1, k 1, psso, k 7, k 2 tog, k 16.
16th row: p to end.
17th row: k 16, sl 1, k 1, psso, k 5, k 2 tog, k 16.
18th row: p to end.

To shape strap
K 7, cast (bind) off 10 sts, k 5 (including st on needle after cast (bind) off). Cast (bind) off 10 sts, k 7 sts, work 4 rows st st on these 7 sts. Cast (bind) off. Return to centre 5 sts (for bar). Starting with a p row and yellow yarn, work 7 rows st st.
Next row: k 2 tog, k 1, k 2 tog.
Work a further 5 rows st st.
Next row: k 3 tog, fasten off.
Return to remaining 7 sts and using turquoise yarn cast on 15 sts (onto same needle as 7 sts), p across these sts then p across the group of 7 sts.

Next row: k 18, ynfwd, k 2 tog (for buttonhole).
Work 2 rows st st. Cast (bind) off.

SECOND SHOE
Make the same as the first shoe reversing the shaping of strap.

TO MAKE UP
Join sole and back seams.
Fold yellow T-bar over turquoise strap and sew to inside.
Attach button to side of shoe.

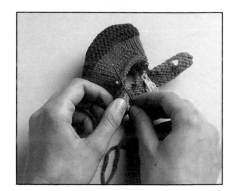

Earflap Hat

THIS STRIPY HAT WITH ITS BRIGHT TASSELS FITS 1 TO 3-YEAR-OLDS

YOU WILL NEED ■ *Small quantity of double knitting (sport) yarn in each of the following colours: Yellow – A; Cerise – B; Orange – C; Turquoise – D; Lime – E; Pink – F; Red – G; Blue – H; Purple – I* ■ *1 pair of 4 mm (US 5) knitting needles* ■ *Tape measure* ■ *Scissors* ■ *Brush*

Tension (Gauge)
Using 4 mm (US 5) needles, 20 sts and 26 rows to 10 cm (4 in) (st st).

HAT
Cast on 72 sts using yarn A. Work 6 rows garter st (every row k). Continue in st st (1 row k, 1 row p) for 46 rows in the following colour sequence: (4 rows B, 6 rows C, 8 rows D, 4 rows E, 8 rows F, 6 rows G, 4 rows A, 6 rows H).
Inc row: *k 7, k into front and back of next st. Repeat from * to end.
Next row and every even numbered row: p to end.
Inc row: * k 8, k into front and back of next st. Repeat from * to end of row.
Continue in this way, increasing 9 sts every alternate row until *k 13, k into front and back of next st. Repeat from * to end (135 sts). Work 4 rows without shaping.
Dec row: *k 13, k 2 tog. Repeat from * to end.
Next row and every even numbered row: p to end.
Dec row: *k 12, k 2 tog. Repeat from * to end.
Continue decreasing in this way on every odd numbered row until 9 sts remain.
Break yarn, thread end through sts, draw up and sew seam.

EARFLAPS
(Make 1 in yarn E and 1 in yarn I)
With right side facing, pick up 18 sts (7 sts from back of head seam) along cast-on edge of hat. Work 4 rows garter stitch (every row k).
5th row: k 2 tog, k 14, k 2 tog.
Next 3 rows: k to end.
9th row: k 2 tog, k 12, k 2 tog.
Next 3 rows: k to end.

13th row: k 2 tog, k 10, k 2 tog.
Next 2 rows: k to end.
16th row: k 2 tog, k 8, k 2 tog.
17th row: k to end.
18th row: k 2 tog, k 6, k 2 tog (8 sts).
Cast (bind) off.

Toggle
Using yarn C, cast on 7 sts.
Next row: cast (bind) off 7 sts.
Attach toggle to centre of hat.

Braided cords
Cut 3 strands of different coloured yarn 58 cm (23 in) long. Thread the strands through centre of cast-off (bound-off) edge on earflaps. Braid the 6 strands, keeping like colours together, and knot the end leaving 6 cm (2¼ in) of spare yarn with which to make the tassel.

Tassel
Cut several different coloured strands of yarn, 12 cm (4¾ in) long. Tie a length of yarn tightly around the centre of the strands. Place the knot of the braid in the centre of the strands and tie firmly into place. Brush the tassel to separate the strands and trim the ends neatly.

Bright Sweater

THIS EYE-CATCHING SWEATER IS GIVEN IN 2 SIZES – 6–12 MONTHS AND 2–3 YEARS

YOU WILL NEED ■ *Double knitting (sport) cotton in the quantities given below*
for each colour: 50 g (2-ounce skein) yellow – A; 50 g (2-ounce skein) lime – B; 100 g (4-ounce
skein) red – C; 50 g (2-ounce skein) orange – D; 100 g (4-ounce skein) pink – E; 50 g (2-ounce skein)
turquoise – F; 50 g (2-ounce skein) purple – G ■ *1 pair size 4 mm (US 5) knitting needles* ■ *1 pair*
size 3.5 mm (US 4) knitting needles ■ *Iron* ■ *Large darning needle* ■ *Tape measure*

Tension (Gauge)
Using 4 mm (US 5) needles, 20 sts
and 26 rows to 10 cm (4 in) (st st).

FRONT
Begin at the front neck edge.
Using 4 mm (US 5) needles and
yarn A, cast on 60(68) sts. Work
8 rows st st (1 row k, 1 row p).

Picot
K 17(19), (ynfwd, k 2 tog) to last
17(19) sts, k 17(19). Beginning with
a p row, work 3 rows st st. Join in
yarn B and continue with the
pattern as follows:
1st row: (k 2 in B, k 2 in A) to end
of row.
2nd row: (p 2 in A, p 2 in B) to end.
3rd row: (k 2 in A, k 2 in B) to end.
4th row: (p 2 in B, p 2 in A) to end.
Using yarn A work 2 rows st st.
Break cotton. Join in cotton C and
work 36(48) rows st st.

To shape sides
Inc 1 st at each end of next and
every following 8th row 3(4)
times more (68(78) sts).
Next row: p to end.

Ruffle
Inc row: using yarn A inc in every
st (k into front and back of each st)
(136(158) sts). Beginning with a p
row, work 9(11) rows st st. For the
picot, k 1 (ynfwd, k 2 tog) to last
st, k 1. Beginning with a p row
work 5 rows st st. Cast (bind) off.

BACK
Work same as the front, changing
the colours as follows.

Use D in place of A, A in place of
B, E in place of C.

SLEEVES
Using 4 mm (US 5) needles and
yarn F (G for second sleeve) cast
on 34(36) sts. To shape the sides,
inc 1 st at each end of 5th and
every following 5th row until
56(62) sts and 55(65) rows are
completed. Work 2 rows st st
without shaping. Cast (bind) off.

Wrist ruffles
(Knit 2 alike)
With the right side facing and
using 4 mm (US 5) needles and
yarn G, pick up 34(36) sts from the
cast-on edge of the sleeve.
Dec row: (k 1, k 2 tog) to end
(23(24) sts).
Next row: p to end.
Inc row: double sts (k into front
and back of each st) (46(48) sts).
Beginning with a p row work 5(7)
rows st st.

Picot
K 1, (ynfwd, k 2 tog) to last st, k 1.
Work 3 rows st st and then cast
(bind) off.

Bobbles
For flowers: make 4 in yarn E and
1 in yarn B.
For buttons: make 2 in yarn A.

Using 3.5 mm (US 4) needles,
cast on 3 sts.
Inc row: k into front and back of
each st (6 sts). Beginning with a
p row, work 5 rows st st.
Dec row: (k 2 tog) 3 times (3 sts).

Dec row: p 3 tog. Break yarn, thread end through remaining st. Run a gathering thread around edge, draw up to form bobble and secure.

TO MAKE UP

Press all pieces on the wrong side under a damp cloth. Fold under neck edge on picot and hem cast-on edge to wrong side of row. Fold under ruffle edge on picot and hem cast-off (bound-off) edge to inside of work. Join shoulder seams up to picot.

Place a marker 15(16) cm (6(6½) in) below shoulder seam on back and front for sleeve position. Sew the top of the sleeve between the markers using backstitch. Fold under the ruffle edge at the cuff on the picot and hem cast-off (bound-off) edge to wrong side of work. Join sleeve and side seams.

To make the buttonhole loops, use yarn D to make a small loop each side of the shoulder seam. Blanket stitch around the edge of the loop. Secure into place. Sew the bobbles to the front of the work to correspond with the loops. For the flower, sew the green bobble to centre front (10 rows above the ruffle). Sew on the pink bobbles to form the petals.

Tickle Mitts

JAZZ UP A SIMPLE PAIR OF BABY MITTS BY ADDING A BRIGHT FRINGE

YOU WILL NEED ■ *1 pair of 3.5 mm (US 4) knitting needles*
■ *25 g (1-ounce skein) blue 4-ply yarn* ■ *Tape measure* ■ *Large darning needle* ■ *Scissors*
■ *Small amount of bright pink double knitting (sport) yarn*

Tension (Gauge)
Using 3.5 mm (US 4) needles,
22 sts and 28 rows to 10 cm (4 in)
(st st).

MITTS
(Knit 2 alike)
Using 3.5 mm (US 4) needles, cast
on 32 sts and work 12 rows in k 1,
p 1 rib.
Next row (lace hole row): (k 2,
ynfwd, k 2 tog) 8 times.
Work straight in st st, starting with
a p row, until mitt measures 10 cm
(4 in), ending with a p row.

Shape top as follows
1st row: (k 1, k 2 tog through back
of loop, k 10, k 2 tog, k 1) twice.
2nd and 4th rows: p to end.
3rd row: (k 1, k 2 tog through back
of loops, k 8, k 2 tog, k 1) twice.
5th row: (k 1, k 2 tog through back

of loops, k 6, k 2 tog, k 1) twice.
Cast (bind) off on a knit row.

TO MAKE UP
Fold mitt in half (right sides
together) and sew up side seam
leaving end of mitt open. Cut 10
lengths of the bright pink yarn and
taking 2 strands at a time, knot
along end of mitt (joining open
end of mitt at the same time) to
form a fringe. Trim fringe to the
length required. Repeat this with
the other mitt. Finally, using 3
strands of bright pink yarn, make
2 braids, each 32 cm (12½ in) long,
and thread them through the lace
holes on each mitt.

Imp Hat

THIS COSY LITTLE HELMET WILL LOOK CUTE ON ANY BABY

YOU WILL NEED ■ *50 g (2-ounce skein) red 4-ply baby yarn* ■ *Pairs of 3 mm (US 3) and 3.5 mm (US 4) knitting needles* ■ *Stitch holder* ■ *Tape measure* ■ *Large darning needle* ■ *Scissors* ■ *Non-toxic, flame retardant polyester filling (batting)*

Tension (Gauge)
Using 3.5 mm (US 4) needles, 22 sts and 28 rows to 10 cm (4 in) (st st).

EAR PIECES
(Knit 2 alike)
Using 3 mm (US 3) needles, cast on 2 sts.
1st row: inc in 1st st, k 1.
2nd row: k 1, p 1, k 1.
3rd row: inc in first st, p 1, inc in last st.
4th row: *p 1, k 1. Repeat from * to last st, p 1.
5th row: inc in first st, k 1, p 1, k 1, inc in last st.
6th row: k 1, *p 1, k 1. Repeat from * to end.
7th row: inc in first st, *p 1, k 1. Repeat from * to last 2 sts, p 1, inc in last st.
8th row: p 1, *k 1, p 1. Repeat from * to end.
9th row: inc in first st, *k 1, p 1. Repeat from * to last 2 sts, k 1, inc in last st.
Repeat rows 6–9 twice (19 sts).
Leave sts on a stitch holder.

Main part
Using 3 mm (US 3) needles, cast on 9 sts. With wrong side facing, work across 19 sts from first ear piece as follows:
(k 1, p 1) 9 times, k 1; cast on 31 sts, work across 19 sts from second ear piece as for first ear piece, cast on 9 sts (87 sts).
Continue in moss stitch as follows:
Next row: p 1, *k 1, p 1. Repeat from * to end. Repeat last row until main part measures 4 cm (1½ in), ending with right side facing for next row and inc 1 st at centre of last row (88 sts).
Change to 3.5 mm (US 4) needles and st st, starting with a knit row and work until main part measures 10 cm (4 in), ending with a p row. Shape crown as follows:
1st row: (k 6, k 2 tog) 11 times (77 sts).
2nd row and every alternate row: p.
3rd row: (k 5, k 2 tog) 11 times (66 sts).
5th row: (k 4, k 2 tog) 11 times (55 sts).
7th row: (k 3, k 2 tog) 11 times (44 sts).
9th row: (k 2, k 2 tog) 11 times (33 sts).
11th row: (k 1, k 2 tog) 11 times (22 sts).
13th row: (k 2 tog) 11 times (11 sts).
Break yarn, thread through remaining 11 sts, draw up tightly and fasten off.

Border
Using 3 mm (US 3) needles and with right side facing, start at centre back and work as follows:
Knit up 9 sts from cast-on sts, 15 sts along first side of ear piece and 15 sts up other side, k up 31 sts from cast-on sts, 15 sts along first side of second ear piece and 15 sts up other side, then k up 9 sts from cast-on sts (109 sts).
K 2 rows. Cast (bind) off.

HORNS
(Knit 2 alike)
Knit as for ear pieces. Cast (bind) off the 19 sts.

TO MAKE UP
Sew up the back seam. Fold each horn shape in half and oversew the seams leaving the bottom edge open. Stuff and sew to the hat. Using 5 strands of yarn, make 2 twisted cords 35 cm (13½ in) long. To do this, knot the 5 strands to a hook or drawer knob. Stretch them out and knot at the other end. Place a pencil in the loop and twist in one direction to make a firm cord. Knot both ends, and sew to the border at the bottom of each ear piece.

Train Jigsaw

THIS EASILY MADE PUZZLE WILL PLEASE ANY 1 TO 3-YEAR-OLD

YOU WILL NEED ■ *Pencil* ■ *Paper* ■ *Ruler* ■ *Coloured card* ■ *Craft knife*
■ *Scissors* ■ *Coloured paper* ■ *Paper glue*

 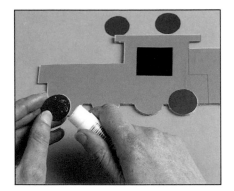 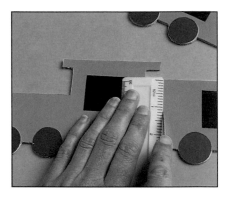

1 Scale up the train template onto paper to the required size and transfer this onto your coloured card. Cut out the whole shape of the train either with scissors or with a craft knife. Cut out square shapes for the windows and circles for the wheels and draw in the dividing lines between each carriage.

2 Glue down the shapes for the train's windows and wheels with paper glue.

3 Cut down the dividing lines using a craft knife and ruler to make the jigsaw pieces.

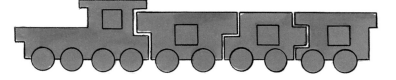

Bear Crayon Holder

A DECORATIVE LITTLE HOLDER FOR CRAYONS OR PENS

YOU WILL NEED ■ *Scissors* ■ *Brown, orange, red and yellow gummed paper* ■ *Cardboard tube from a toilet paper roll* ■ *Soft cloth* ■ *White card* ■ *Pencil* ■ *Black felt-tip pen*

2 Cut out 2 oval shapes for the feet and a bear's head from the card. Place the card onto orange and brown gummed paper and draw around the card shape with a pencil. Cut out the gummed paper and stick it on to the relevant card shapes, using orange for the bear's feet and brown for the head.

1 Cut a piece of brown gummed paper to fit exactly around the cardboard tube, allowing for a small overlap at the join. Stick the paper down onto the tube using a damp cloth to moisten the gummed side.

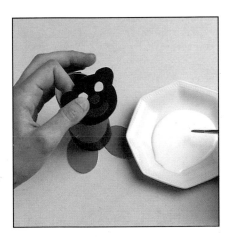

3 Add an orange belly and a red nose and mouth plus two yellow eyes, all cut out from gummed paper and stuck to the card as before by moistening the gum with a damp cloth. Glue the feet to the bottom edge and stick the head and belly onto the front of the body. Finally, draw on the eyes and claws with black felt-tip pen. Leave the crayon holder to dry thoroughly before use.

Toddler's Overall

THESE DIMENSIONS ARE FOR A 15-MONTH CHILD, BUT CAN EASILY BE ADJUSTED

YOU WILL NEED ■ *Paper and pencil if you need to re-scale dimensions* ■ *Tape measure*
■ *Strong cotton fabric in a plain colour* ■ *Scissors* ■ *Striped cotton fabric which will be cut on the bias* ■ *Pins* ■ *Needle and thread* ■ *Iron* ■ *Scrap of fabric to co-ordinate with striped fabric*

1 Using the plain cotton fabric, cut 1 front piece 30 × 42 cm (12 × 16½ in), 2 back pieces 30 × 21 cm (12 × 8½ in) and a yoke section 22 × 74 cm (8¾ × 29½ in). Cut 4 undersleeves from striped fabric, each 10 × 21 cm (4 × 8½ in), ensuring that the bias-cut stripes run the correct way.

Pin, tack (baste) and sew the 2 undersleeves to the top front of the overall, right sides together. Trim the seam allowance along the 10 cm (4 in) seam edge to 6 mm (¼ in) and oversew. Press the seam towards the sleeve end.

2 Turn back 5 cm (2 in) on one long edge of each back section and stitch down the raw edges. Placing right sides together, join the neatened edges in a seam, leaving a 9 cm (3½ in) opening. Press flat.

Join the 2 other undersleeve sections to the back section as before. With a pin, mark the centre of the front. Run a gathering thread along the top edge, starting 8 cm (3¼ in) from the undersleeve seams. Gather the back on each side, to 2 cm (¾ in) from the opening.

3 Fold the yoke section across its narrow, vertical width and mark the centre front. Also mark the centre of the yoke running horizontally. Cut an opening vertically in the centre front as far as the horizontal centre. Cut a neck opening 8 cm (3¼ in) in each direction from the centre and 16 cm (6½ in) long, to form a 'T' shape.

Lay all the pieces flat, wrong sides up and with the yoke central, matching the vertical opening on the yoke to the back opening seam and the centre front of the yoke to the centre of the front section. Pin the 4 sleeve ends to the yoke, right sides together.

4 Pulling the gathering threads on the front and back, draw up the sections to fit the yoke. Adjust the gathers evenly and secure. Pin, tack (baste) and stitch the 3 seams. Press the seams flat towards the top, trim the raw edges and oversew them together.

Fold the garment into a 'T' shape, right sides together, and pin and tack (baste) each side and underarm seam in one. Stitch both sides, working a curve at the corner. Check that the undersleeve seam is completely concealed from the outside, then trim the seam and oversew the edges together. Press firmly.

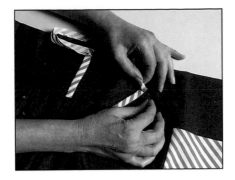

5 Prepare 60 cm (24 in) of 3 cm (1¼ in) wide bias binding from the striped fabric. Enclosing all raw edges, bind the back openings on the yoke by sewing the binding to the yoke right sides together and turning to the inside to hem. Bind the neck in the same way, enclosing the back opening binding ends as you start and finish. Take care not to pucker the yoke at the outer corners of the neck opening. Press firmly.

6 Make a small neatened square from the scrap of co-ordinating fabric for a pocket, and appliqué a striped heart to match the undersleeves and bindings. Stitch it to the overall front. Make some ties from striped fabric to tie the neck opening at the back.

Toy Carrier

THIS STURDY BOX IS IDEAL FOR CARRYING AND STORING TOYS

YOU WILL NEED ■ *2 pieces of 22 × 16 cm (8¾ × 6¼ in) plywood, 10 mm (⅜ in) thick* ■ *Metal ruler* ■ *Pencil* ■ *Hand saw* ■ *Sandpaper* ■ *2 pieces of 35 × 12 cm (13½ × 4¾ in) plywood, 10 mm (⅜ in) thick* ■ *33.5 × 14.5 cm (13 × 5¾ in) plywood, 10 mm (⅜ in) thick* ■ *Wood glue* ■ *2.5 cm (1 in) panel pins (finishing nails)* ■ *Hammer* ■ *13.5 × 2.5 cm (5¼ × 1 in) square softwood batten* ■ *Hand drill* ■ *2 × 4.5 cm (1¾ in) screws* ■ *Plastic wood* ■ *Matt white emulsion (flat latex) paint* ■ *Paintbrushes* ■ *Non-toxic enamel paints*

2 Smooth down the softwood handle piece with sandpaper and position at the top of the end pieces. Drill in each end to accept the screws. Fix together using glue and screws, countersinking and filling the heads with plastic wood.

1 Take the 22 × 16 cm (8¾ × 6¼ in) pieces (the box ends) and make marks at 7 cm (2¾ in) and 9 cm (3½ in) on 1 shorter side. Mark 12.5 cm (5 in) on both longer sides. Rule diagonals to join the marks and saw off the triangles. Sand the tops into smooth corners. Join together an end piece, a 35 × 12 cm (13½ × 4¾ in) side piece and the base piece using wood glue and panel pins (finishing nails). Note that the sides and ends overlap the base. Repeat the same process with the other side and end.

3 Give the carrier a final sanding and paint on a coat of matt white emulsion (flat latex) paint. Allow to dry then finish with 2 coats of enamel paint in bright colours. Use a light colour for the inside so that small toys can be seen more easily.

SIDE PIECE — CUT 2

END PIECE CUT 2

BASE — CUT 1

Play Dough

STORE PLAY DOUGH IN A PLASTIC CONTAINER WITH AN AIRTIGHT LID

YOU WILL NEED ■ *225 g/8 oz/2 cups plain (all-purpose) flour* ■ *115 g/4 oz/1 cup salt*
■ *2 tsp cream of tartar* ■ *Mixing bowl* ■ *Spoon* ■ *Thick-bottomed saucepan* ■ *2 tbsp oil* ■ *10 fl oz/*
½ pt/2 cups water ■ *Food colouring* ■ *Vanilla essence (extract) for fragrance* ■ *Pastry board*

1 Measure out the dry ingredients into a large mixing bowl and then stir them together thoroughly.

2 Put the dry ingredients in the saucepan with the oil, water, colouring and vanilla essence (extract) and stir continuously over a low heat until a dough forms.

3 Turn the dough out onto a lightly floured pastry board and knead while the mixture cools. Continue to knead for 5–10 minutes. If the mixture is too dry, occasionally dampen your hands while kneading, and if it is too sticky, dust with a little extra flour.

Shoe Lacer

A SIMPLE AID TO HELP CHILDREN LEARN TO TIE THEIR OWN SHOELACES

YOU WILL NEED ■ *Pencil* ■ *Tracing paper* ■ *10 × 20 cm (4 × 8 in) plywood, 8 mm (⁵⁄₁₆ in) thick* ■ *Fretsaw (scroll saw)* ■ *Hand drill* ■ *Sandpaper* ■ *Matt white emulsion (flat latex) paint* ■ *Paintbrush* ■ *Non-toxic acrylic paints* ■ *58 cm (23 in) decorated shoelace*

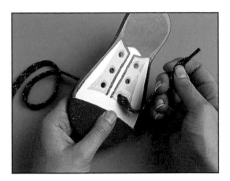

1 Scale up the shoe template and trace onto the plywood. Cut out carefully with the fretsaw (scroll saw). Place the shoe shape on a piece of scrap material and drill out the lace holes with a 6 mm (¼ in) bit. Sand out the top and bottom of the holes, and smooth the whole piece to get rid of any rough edges.

2 Paint the shoe shape all over with a coat of matt white emulsion (flat latex) paint. When dry, paint with 2 coats of different coloured acrylic paints, sanding lightly between each of the coats.

3 When the paint has dried completely, lace up the 'shoe' with a decorative, brightly coloured shoelace.

Noah's Ark Bag

A FUN NEW WAY TO TELL AN OLD STORY

YOU WILL NEED ■ *Assorted blue and white fabrics* ■ *Tape measure* ■ *Scissors* ■ *Pins* ■ *Needle and thread* ■ *Iron* ■ *Paper* ■ *Pencil* ■ *Iron-on interfacing* ■ *White felt* ■ *Green embroidery thread* ■ *Ribbon* ■ *Safety pin* ■ *Non-toxic, flame retardant polyester filling (batting)*

1 Choose 2 different fabrics for the bag front to represent sea and sky. Cut the sky 36 × 36 cm (14 × 14 in) and the sea 36 × 19 cm (14 × 7½ in). With right sides together, join the 2 fabrics along one long edge as shown. Press the seam to one side and oversew the raw edges together.

2 Cut paper templates for the design on the bag front. Cut out different fabric shapes for the ark using an iron-on interfacing on all the shapes to strengthen them. Cut the dove from white felt.

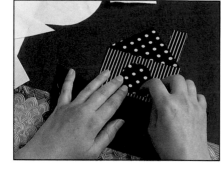

3 Assemble the cut shapes for the Ark on the bag front so that the boat appears to be floating on the sea. Pin them all in place, then tack (baste) and appliqué them to the bag. Sew the dove to the bag with tiny blanket stitches, and embroider the olive leaf with green thread.

4 Cut a bag back to the same size as the assembled front. Stitch all round the bag back and front, right sides together, leaving the top edge open for turning. Trim the seam allowances and oversew the raw edges.

5 Turn the bag right side out. Fold down a casing at the top for the drawstring, wide enough to take your ribbon. Carefully unpick one side seam stitching inside where the casing turns over, to allow you to thread the ribbon through the drawstring using a safety pin at one end. Sew up the seam and tie the ends of the drawstring in a knot, neatening any ends. For reasons of safety, do not make the drawstring any longer than is necessary to open and shut the bag.

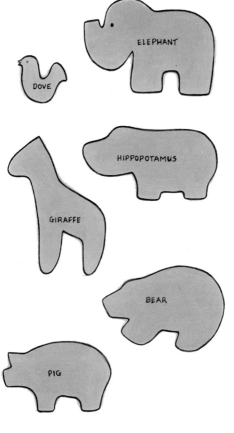

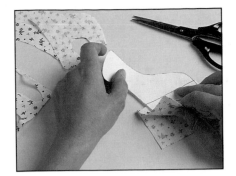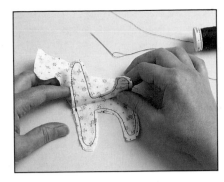

6 Make paper patterns for all the animals following the templates. All the animals are made from 3 pieces and are sewn the same way. For each animal, cut 2 opposite shapes for the body and 1 for a gusset. The gusset shape is cut using the lower part of the animal pattern from the straight line downwards. If you place the folded fabric along the line and cut the lower body and legs double, it will open out into the full shape you need.

7 For each animal, match up one body half to the gusset, right sides together. Tack (baste) round the legs, joining the gusset to half of the body from gusset fold line at the back to the gusset fold line at the front. Stitch about 6 mm (¼ in) from the edge.

Join the second body side to the other half of the gusset with both sets of stitching meeting at the gusset fold line. Fold the stitched gusset with the right and left legs matching flat, so that you can stitch around the head and body, leaving a short length on the animal's back to turn it.

8 Turn the animal right side out and stuff it firmly, pushing the filling into the legs with a knitting needle or pencil. Oversew the opening to close it.

9 Make a paper pattern for Mr and Mrs Noah following the template. Cut 2 pieces of fabric for each figure, and join them by sewing around the outside edges with right sides together. With the points of the scissors, carefully make a small vertical slit in the back of each assembled figure and turn it to the right side. Stuff the figures firmly and oversew the openings. Make clothes by finishing squares and strips of fabric and sewing them in place.

THE NOAHS

ARK HULL

241

French Knot Smock

AN ADAPTABLE DRESS WHICH SUITS ALL SHAPES AND SIZES

YOU WILL NEED ■ *Tape measure* ■ *Pen* ■ *Paper* ■ *Scissors* ■ *Washable cotton velvet* ■ *Wadding (batting)* ■ *Pins* ■ *Needle and thread* ■ *Iron* ■ *Bias binding or patterned fabric* ■ *Zip (zipper)* ■ *Embroidery thread* ■ *Hook and eye fastening*

1 This design can be adapted to fit any age or size. Scale up the template according to the size you require and make a paper pattern for the bodice. The skirt width must be calculated to include gathering and will vary according to your fabric, but looks prettiest when it is quite full. Cut out 2 opposite bodice backs and a front from the velvet and the wadding (batting). Tack (baste) the wadding (batting) to the wrong side of the velvet.

2 Pin, tack (baste) and sew the bodice sections right sides together at the shoulder seams. Press the seams open with a cool iron. Tack (baste) the back opening edges down 1 cm (⅜ in) and press flat.

3 Cut the bodice linings from patterned fabric. Join the shoulders right sides together and press the seams open.

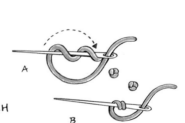

FRENCH KNOT

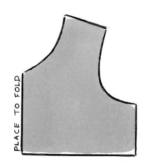

PLACE TO FOLD

4 Cut the skirt in 1 piece and tack (baste) the back seam closed leaving sufficient open at the top end for the zip (zipper). Stitch the seam and neaten the raw edges. Gather the skirt around the waist, draw up the gathers and pin to the bodice right sides together, adjusting the gathers evenly to fit.

Tack (baste) the bodice to the skirt, taking a 1 cm (⅜ in) seam allowance, lining up the tacked-(basted-)down bodice opening and the neatened back seam of the skirt. Stitch the skirt to the bodice, trim and oversew the raw edges. Turn right side out and pin, tack (baste) and sew the zip (zipper) into the back opening.

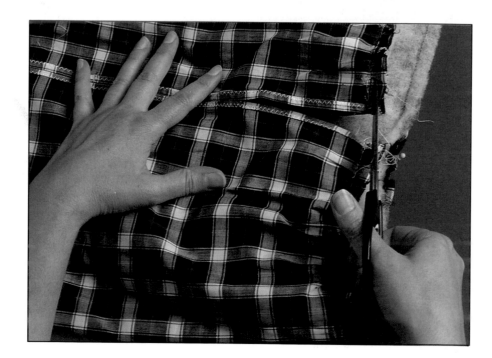

5 Matching shoulder seams, pin the bodice lining to the dress, wrong sides together. Turn the back lining openings under and tack (baste) them to the back seam allowance. Tack (baste) the lining to the bodice around the neck and armholes. Hem the lining to the back openings.

Concealing all the raw edges at the top back opening, pin, tack (baste) and sew bias binding or strips of patterned fabric right sides together around the neck about 1 cm (⅜ in) from the edge. Turn to the wrong side and hem the binding neatly under, catching it to the lining. Work the armholes in the same way. Hem the bottom of the lining to the dress/bodice seam allowance.

6 Using 3 strands of embroidery thread, decorate the bodice by stitching French knots to join the lining to the bodice through the wadding (batting). Use the patterned lining to guide you in placing your knots evenly. Backstitch the thread on the inside to secure it, take the needle to the outside and sew the knot before returning the needle through to the lining at exactly the same point. Secure the thread and cut. Continue to complete the bodice backs and fronts. Sew a hook and eye to the bodice opening, and hem the skirt.

Cuddly **P**lane

AN UNUSUAL SOFT TOY THAT IS SUITABLE FOR A SMALL BABY

YOU WILL NEED ■ Pen ■ Paper ■ Scissors ■ Pins ■ *2 patterned cotton fabrics in contrasting colours* ■ *Wadding (batting)* ■ *Needle and thread* ■ *Iron* ■ *Non-toxic, flame retardant polyester filling (batting)* ■ *Oddments of black and white felt* ■ *Embroidery thread*

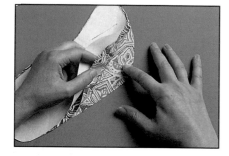

1 Make a paper pattern for the plane body, wings and tail fins using the template as a guide. Cut 2 opposite shapes for the body from 1 fabric and 4 each of the wing and fin shapes from the contrasting fabric. Cut 4 pieces of wadding (batting), 2 for the wings and 2 for the fins.

2 Place 2 wing shapes right sides together and lay a piece of wadding (batting) on the top. Stitch together, 6 mm (¼ in) from the edge, leaving the straight edge open. Make the second wing and 2 fins in the same way. Turn all shapes right side out and press carefully. Check the width of your wing and cut a slit in the plane body to exactly the same width, noting the position of the slit on the pattern. Fold the plane body along the slit with the right sides

together and insert the open wing end from the outside through to the inside of the slit. Pin and tack (baste). Start sewing from the folded edge about 4 mm (⅛ in) before the slit. Curve the seam out gently and sew through all layers so that at the centre of wing the stitches are about 4 mm (⅛ in) from the raw edge of the slit. Curve in again for the second half of the seam. Secure all threads firmly. Repeat this process for the second wing and the tail fins.

3 Place the plane bodies right sides together, and, tucking in the wings and fins, pin and tack (baste) them. Stitch the seam 1 cm (⅜ in) from the edge, leaving a short length on the underside for turning. Turn the body right side out. Stuff the plane firmly with filling and oversew the opening to close. Sew on felt circles for the eyes and embroider the mouth.

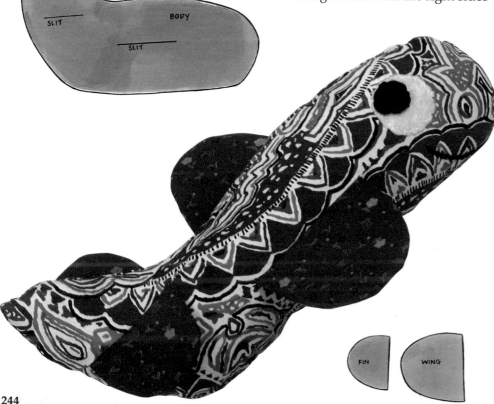

244

Crocheted Mittens

A PRETTY AND PRACTICAL PAIR OF MITTENS FOR BABIES UP TO 3 MONTHS OLD

YOU WILL NEED ■ *50 g (2-ounce skein) 4-ply yarn* ■ *2.5 mm (C) crochet hook*

Make 33 ch.
1 dc (sc) in 4th ch from hook, 1 dc (sc) in each ch to end of row. Turn with 3 ch. (29 dc (sc).)
1st row: 3 tr (dc) in alternate dcs (scs) to end of row. Turn with 3 ch. (15 3tr (dc) groups.)
2nd row: 3 tr (dc) in each space to end of row. Turn with 3 ch.
3rd row: repeat row 2 twice more. Turn with 2 ch on row 4.
5th row: 1 dc (sc) in each tr (dc) to end of row. Turn with 2 ch.
6th row: To make picot: * 3 dc (sc) over next 3 dc (sc), 3 ch, ss into first of 3 ch. Repeat from * to end. Fasten off. Rejoin yarn to one end of beginning ch.
Next row: 4 ch (miss 1 ch, 1 ch, 2 tr (dc)), to end of row. Turn with 3 ch. (Row in which to insert the draw threads.)
2nd row: 1 tr (dc) into tr (dc), (tr (dc) into space, 2 tr (dc)), to end of row. Turn with 3 ch.
3rd row: tr (dc) into each tr (dc). (29 trs (dcs).) Turn with 3 ch. Repeat 3rd row 5 times.
8th row: 1 tr (dc), dec 1 in next 2 tr (dc), 8 tr (dc), dec 1 in next 2 tr (dc), 1 tr (dc), dec 1 in next 2 tr (dc), 8 tr (dc), dec 1 in next 2 tr (dc), 2 tr (dc), turn with 3 ch.
9th row: 1 tr (dc) in each tr (dc), to end. Turn with 3 ch.
10th row: 1 tr (dc), dec 1 in next 2 tr (dc), 6 tr (dc), dec 1 in next 2 tr (dc), 1 tr (dc), dec 1 in next 2 tr (dc), 6 tr (dc), dec 1 in next 2 tr (dc), 2 tr (dc), turn with 3 ch.
11th row: 20 tr (dc). Fasten off.

Draw threads
(Make 2 alike)
5 ch, ss into first ch, 105 ch, ss into 5th ch from hook. Fasten off. Sew sides and top of mitten. Thread drawstring through eyelet holes and tie in a bow. Repeat for second mitten.

Matinée Jacket

THIS COSY JACKET WILL FIT UP TO A 50 CM (20 IN) CHEST

YOU WILL NEED ■ 400 g (2 × 8 ounce skeins) 4 ply yarn ■ 3.5 (E) crochet hook
■ Tape measure ■ Large darning needle ■ 3 small buttons

BACK
Make 62 ch.
3 tr (dc) into 4th ch from hook.
*Miss 2 ch, 3 tr (dc) into next st.
Repeat from * to last 2 sts, 1 tr (dc)
in last st, turn with 3 ch.
2nd row: 1 tr (dc) into 1st sp, 3 tr
(dc) into each sp to end of row,
turn with 3 ch.
3rd row: 3 tr (dc) in each sp, 1 tr
(dc) into end st, turn with 3 ch.
Work for 5 rows. Turn with 3 ch.
9th row: *1 tr (dc) in sp. 1 tr (dc)
over each tr (dc) to end of row.
(58 tr (dc).) Turn with 3 ch.
Work in trs (dcs) on these 58 sts for
16.5 cm (6½ in).

Next row: ss over 7 sts, tr (dc) to
last 7 sts, turn with 3 ch. Work on
these remaining sts until armhole
measures 7.5 cm (3 in). Fasten off.

RIGHT FRONT
Make 32 ch.
Tr (dc) into 4th ch from hook, 2 tr
(dc) into same st. *Miss 2 ch, 3 tr
(dc) into next st. Repeat from * to
end of ch, turn with 3 ch.
Next row: 3 tr (dc) into each sp to
end of row, 1 tr (dc), turn with
3 ch.
Continue for 6 more rows.
9th row: 3 tr (dc) in 1st sp, 3 trs
(dcs) in each of next 3 sps, 1 tr (dc)

in each tr (dc). Tr (dc) to end of
row. (19 trs (dcs).) Turn with 3 ch.
Next row: 18 tr (dc), 3 groups of tr
(dc) in sps, 2 tr (dc) in last 2 trs
(dcs). Return with 3 ch.
Continue in pattern and tr (dc)
until work matches back to
armhole.
Next row: ss over 6 tr (dc) at
armhole edge.
Continue on remaining sts until
work is 3 rows less than back.
Next row: ss over 8 sts at neck
edge, complete row.
Next rows: dec 1 st at neck edge on
next 2 rows. Fasten off.

LEFT FRONT
As above; reverse shapings.

SLEEVES
Make 33 ch. Work in tr (dc) group
pattern for 3 rows.
4th row: tr (dc) into each tr (dc).
(29 tr (dc).)
Repeat this row until sleeve
measures 20 cm (8 in).

TO MAKE UP
Sew shoulder seams and sleeves.
Sew sleeve and side seams. 5 ch,
miss 1 st, 1 dc (sc) into next st, and
repeat round neck to next edge.
Sew on buttons. Use sps in pattern
as buttonholes.

Crocheted Bootees

THESE WARM BOOTEES MATCH THE MATINÉE JACKET

YOU WILL NEED ■ *50 g (2-ounce skein) 4-ply yarn* ■ *3.5 mm (E) crochet hook*
Scissors ■ *Large darning needle*

Make 30 ch. 1 dc (sc) into 3rd ch from hook. 1 dc (sc) into each ch to end of row. Turn with 3 ch.
1st row: 2 tr (dc). *miss 1 dc (sc), 1 ch, 3 tr (dc) into next 3 dc (sc). Repeat from * to end of row. Turn with 3 ch.
2nd row: 3 tr (dc) into each space (7 groups).
Turn with 3 ch.
Repeat 2nd row 3 times turning with 3 ch on 5th row.
6th row: *Miss 1 tr (dc), 2 tr (dc), 1 ch. Repeat from * to end of row. Turn with 2 ch.
7th row: 1 dc (sc) into next tr (dc), *1 dc (sc) in space, 2 dc (sc) in next 2 tr (dc). Repeat from * to end of row. Turn with 2 ch.
8th row: dc (sc) in each dc (sc) to end of row. (26 dc (sc).). Turn with 2 ch. Repeat twice more.

11th row: dec over next 2 dc (sc). 8 dc (sc), dec once in next 2 dc (sc), 2 ch, turn.
(Mark 7th st in remaining sts for centre of heel.)
12th row: dc (sc) into each dc (sc) to end of row, turn with 2 ch. Repeat 12th row 3 times.
16th row: dec 1 st each end of next and following 4th row then each end of next row.
21st row: dc (sc) in each st to end of row. Fasten off. Rejoin yarn to first dec row on edge furthest away from 13 unworked sts. 2 ch. 1 dc (sc) into same row end, 1 dc (sc) into each following row end, 6 dc (sc) across toe, 1 dc (sc) into each row end, 1 dc (sc) into each of 13 unworked sts.
Work 4 rows of dc (sc) on these sts, turning with 2 ch. Fasten off.

Make second bootee, reversing instructions after eyelet hole row.

Draw threads
5 ch, ss into 1st ch, 105 ch, ss into 4th ch from hook.

TO MAKE UP
Sew sides of cuff and foot seam. Thread through draw threads.

FABRICS, SEWING, QUILTING AND HABERDASHERY SUPPLIES

The Cotton Club
Coxeter House
21–27 Ock Street
Abingdon
OX14 5AJ
UK
(0235) 550067

The Cotton Club
1 Rosemary Lane
Bampton
Oxon
OX8 2JJ
UK
(0993) 851234
(*Natural dress fabrics*)

DMC Creative World
Pullman Road
Wigston
Leicester
LE18 2DY
UK
(*Threads and cottons*)

Magpie Patchworks
Department G
37 Palfrey Road
Northbourne
Bournemouth
Dorset
BH10 6DN
UK

Mulberry Silks
2 Old Rectory Cottage
Easton Grey
Malmesbury
Wiltshire
SN16 0PE
UK
(0666) 840881

Patchworks and Quilts
9 West Place
Wimbledon
London
SW19 4UH
UK
(*Quilts and Fabrics*)

Quilt Basics
2 Meades Lane
Chesham
Bucks
HP5 1ND
UK

The Quilt Room
20 West Street
Dorking
Surrey
RH4 1BL
UK

Silken Strands
33 Linksway
Gatley
Cheadle
Cheshire
SK8 4LA
UK
(*Embroidery requisites*)

Strawberry Fayre
Chagford
Devon
TQ13 8EN
UK
(*Mail order fabrics*)

Threadbear Supplies
11 Northway
Deanshanger
Milton Keynes
MK19 6NF
UK
(*Waddings/battings*)

George Weil & Sons Ltd
The Warehouse
Reading Arch Road
Redhill
Surrey
RH1 1HG
UK
(0737) 778868
(*Fabric paints and equipment. Shop, mail order and export*)

DMC Corporation
Port Kearney
Building 10
South Kearney
New Jersey 07032–4688
USA
(*Threads and cottons*)

P & B Fabrics
898 Mahler Road
Burlingame
California 94010
USA

DMC Needlecraft Ltd
PO Box 317
Earlswood
NSW 2206
Australia

Auckland Folk Art Centre
591 Remuera Road
Remuera
Auckland
New Zealand
(09) 524 0936

Quilt Connection Ltd
214 Nights Road
Lower Hutt
New Zealand
(04) 569 3427

Faysons Art Needlework Centre
135a Greenway
Box 84036
Greenside
Johannesburg
South Africa
(11) 646 0642

KNITTING AND CROCHET YARN SUPPLIES

Arnotts
Argyle Street
Glasgow
UK
(041) 248 2951

Rowan Yarns
Green Lane Mill
Holmfirth
West Yorkshire
UK
(0484) 681881

Christa's Ball & Skein
971 Lexington Avenue No.1A
New York
New York 10021
USA
(212) 772 6960

Greenwich Yarns
2073 Greenwich Street
San Francisco 94123
USA
(415) 567 2535

Hook 'N' Needle
1869 Post Road East
Westport
Connecticut 06880
USA
(203) 259 5119

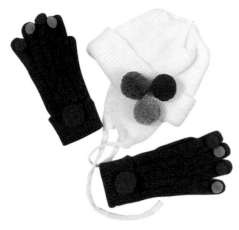

The London Knitting Company
2531 Rocky Ridge Road No.101
Birmingham
Alabama 35243
USA
(205) 822 5855

Westminster Trading Corporation
5 Northern Boulevard
Amherst
New Hampshire 03031
USA
(803) 886 5041
(Yarn by mail order)

A Knit Above
2427 Granville Street
Vancouver
V6H 3G5
Canada
(604) 734 0975

Imagiknit
2586 Yonge Street
Toronto
M4P 2J3
Canada
(416) 482 5287

Indigo Inc
155 Rue St Paul
Quebec City
G1K 3W2
Canada
(418) 694 1419

Greta's Handcrafts Centre
25 Lindfield Avenue
Lindfield
NSW 2070
Australia
(02) 416 2488

Mateira
250 Park Street
Victoria 3205
Australia
(03) 690 7651

Pots 'N' Stitches
113 London Circuit
ACT 2600
Australia
(062) 487 563

Randburg Needlework
19 Centre Point
Hill Street
Randburg
South Africa
(11) 787 3307

ART SUPPLIES AND SPECIALIST PAPERS

Daler-Rowney Ltd
PO Box 10
Bracknell
Berkshire
RG12 8ST
UK
(0344) 424621
(Paint specialists)

One Four Nine Paper Supplies
PO Box A13
Huddersfield
West Yorkshire
HD3 4LW
UK
(Mail order specialist)

Paperchase
213 Tottenham Court
Road London
W1A 4US
(071) 580 8496

Kate's Paperie
8 West 13th Street
New York
New York 10001
USA

Papersource Inc
730 N Franklin Suite 111
Chicago
Illinois 60610
USA

ACT Papers Pty Ltd
10 McGlone Street
Micham
Victoria 3132
Australia

**Karori Art, Craft and
Wallpaper Centre**
264 Karon Road
Karori
New Zealand
(04) 476 8426

Littlejohns
170 Victoria Street
Wellington
New Zealand
(04) 385 2099

Academy of Crafts
28 Goldman Street
Florida
South Africa
(11) 472 4884

Arts and Crafts Depot
40 Harrison Street
Johannesburg
South Africa
(11) 838 2286

DÉCOUPAGE AND BOX SUPPLIES

The Dover Bookshop
18 Earlham Street
London
WC2H 9LN
UK
(071) 836 2111

Mamelok Press Ltd
Northern Way
Bury St Edmunds
Suffolk
IP32 6NJ
UK
(0284) 762291
(*Specialist scrap printers*)

Panduro Hobby Ltd
West Way House
Transport Avenue
Brentford
Middlesex
TW8 9HE
UK
(081) 847 6161
(*Hatboxes by mail order*)

Dover Publications Inc
180 Varick Street
New York 11501
USA
(212) 255 3755

Paper E Clips
401 Richmond Street W.
Suite 140
Toronto
Ontario M5W 1X3
Canada
(416) 595 5997

Rosenhain, Lipman & Peers Pty
147 Burnley Street
Richmond
Melbourne
Victoria 3121
Australia
(03) 428 1485

The Partners
St Martins Stationery
5 Austin-Kirk Lane
Christchurch 2
New Zealand

PRESSED AND DRIED FLOWER SUPPLIES

Swancraft Gallery
Ashfield
Stowmarket
IP14 6LU
UK
(0728) 685703
(*Pressed and dried flowers and
pot-pourri supplies by mail order*)

Crafte Supplies
33 Oldridge Road
London
SW12 8PN
UK
(081) 673 6370

Flowers Forever
Queensgate
Knights Road
Lower Hutt
New Zealand
(04) 566 5830

SPECIALIST TOY SUPPLIERS

Hamleys Ltd
188 Regent Street
London
W1R 5DF
UK
(071) 734 3161

Tridias
25 Bute Street
London
SW7 3EY
UK
(071) 584 2330

Tridias
6 Lichfield Terrace
Sheen Road
Richmond
TW9 1AF
UK
(081) 948 3459

Tridias
The Cider Press Centre
Dartington
Devon
TQ9 6JB
UK
(0803) 863957

Tridias
6 Bennet Street
Bath
BA1 2QP
UK
(0225) 314 730

Childcraft
P.O. Box 29149
Mission
KS 66201-9149
USA
(800) 367 3255

The Great Kids Company
P.O. Box 609
Lewisville
NC 27023-0609
USA
(800) 533 2166

FAO Schwartz

767 Fifth Avenue
New York
NY 10022
USA
(212) 644 9400

Index

A

Acrobatic clown, 220
Alphabet bricks, 210
Apple tree hooks, 113
Appliqué
 sleepsuit, 8
 toys, 58
Apron
 bathtime, 12
 practical, 20
Asleep/awake bear, 118–119

B

Baby announcement card, 36
Baby changing bag, 92
Baby's gift box, 139
Bags
 baby changing, 92
 balloons toy bag, 95
 changing bag, 40–41
 cylindrical bag, 39
 Noah's Ark, 240–241
 toy bag, 157
 waist hold-all, 45
 washbag, 37
Balloons toy bag, 95
Baseball cap, 190

Bathroom pockets, 38
Bathtime apron, 12
Batik quilt, 66, 67
Beaker mat, 84
Bean bag clown, 209
Bear crayon holder, 233
Bears
 asleep/awake, 118–119
 denim, 57
 family of, 75
Bedroom tidy, 60
Bedtime friends, 24, 25
Beetle drawer freshener, 52
Beetle hat, 170–171
Bibs
 plastic, 195
 spiky fabric, 158
Bird on a stick, 81
Blackboard, cat, 207
Blanket, crocheted, 140
Bonnets
 crocheted, 184
 knitted, 133
Book, fabric, 103
Book-ends, cat, 120
Bootees
 crocheted, 247
 cutie, 18
 fringed, 59
 knitted cuff bootees, 49
 quilted, 9
 sweetheart shoes, 44
 tall bootees, 51
Bow-tie T-shirt, 172
Bowl, papier mâché, 96
Braided mat, 116
Brick town, 186
Bright-finned fish, 32–33
Bright hangers, 109
Bright sweater, 228–229
Bumper, reversible, 34
Busy bee slippers, 46–47
Butterfly and daisy lampshade, 76

C

Cake, train, 151
Candy cushion, 159
Cardigan, crocheted, 185

Cards
 baby announcement, 36
 pop-up card, 42
 pop-up cloud card, 53
 pressed flower birthday card,
  160
 quilted, 9
 rocking cradle, 138
 rotating clown, 205
 special celebration, 153
 teddy bear, 156
Carousel, clown, 168–169
Cat blackboard, 207
Cat book-ends, 120
Celebration tablepiece, 161
Chairs
 painted, 89
 two-height, 73
Changing bag, 40–41
Cherub place cards, 134
Cherubic tablepiece, 135
Chest of drawers, marine, 69
Child's jacket, 136–137
Christening robe, 130–131
Christening shoes, 129
Clapper, 196
Clock, découpage, 80
Clown carousel, 168–169
Clown finger puppets, 204
Clutch ball, 112
Coathangers
 bright hangers, 109
 scented, 79
Collar, knitted, 132
Counting book, leaf, 206
Crayon holder, bear, 233

Contributors

Dorothy Wood trained in embroidery and textiles. She contributes regularly to craft magazines and books, working particularly in the areas of embroidery, salt dough and papercrafts.

Petra Boase trained in embroidery and textiles. Her distinctive mixture of bright patterns and colours can be seen widely in books, magazine articles and commercial gift wrap illustration.

Mary Lawrence is a specialist in flowercrafts and edible and scented gifts, and runs a flourishing pressed flower and craft gallery in the county of Suffolk.

Jean Renwick is an accomplished needlewoman, specializing in crochet and knitting, transforming traditional and intricate patterns into modern adaptations.

Christine Clarke works mainly with handpainting and batik dyeing techniques. She produces a variety of designs for furnishing fabrics, textile paintings and soft toys in imaginative colour combinations.

Josephine Whitfield is a specialist in decorated furniture and restoration. She employs her training in fine art to transform everyday objects into pieces of distinctive beauty.

Freddie Robins teaches textiles in colleges of art and design in Great Britain, and specializes in millinery, felting and knitwear.

Rachel Howard trained as a pattern cutter and stylist. She now specializes in crochet and fashion design, while also making clothes to commission.

Catherine Whitfield is a versatile craftswoman with many areas of expertise, including papier mâché, embroidery and toy making, through which she adapts traditional designs for the modern nursery.

Isabella Whitworth trained as an illustrator and later specialized in pre-school toys for a major US games manufacturer. She now concentrates on her beautifully detailed silk paintings.

Jan Bridge is a talented seamstress; she fashions *objets d'art* from fabric and natural materials. She contributes to many craft magazines and books on handicrafts.

Cheryl Owen is a well-known crafts artist with varied and wide-ranging skills. Her designs in needlework, papier mâché, papercrafts and salt dough can be seen in a large number of books and magazines.

Philippa Madden is an expert in dyeing techniques. She runs dyeing workshops and teaches batik, tie-dye and freehand painting, using her own vibrant designs as a basis for the classes.

Emma Whitfield specializes in the art of decoupage, particularly the decorating of hat boxes. Trained in fine art, she exhibits at prestigious craft fairs around Great Britain.

Julie Johnson trained in fine art and later moved into knitting design. Her popular designs are made mainly to commission and are exhibited at leading craft fairs.

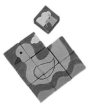